ORGANIZING PEACE

IN THE NUCLEAR AGE

Organizing Peace
in the
Nuclear Age

Commission to Study the Organization of Peace
ARTHUR N. HOLCOMBE, *Chairman*

REPORT OF THE COMMISSION
INIS L. CLAUDE, JR., *Chairman, Drafting Committee*

SUPPLEMENTARY PAPERS BY

QUINCY WRIGHT
ARTHUR N. HOLCOMBE
JOHN G. STOESSINGER

NEW YORK UNIVERSITY PRESS · 1959

COMMISSION TO STUDY

THE ORGANIZATION OF PEACE

Research Affiliate of the

AMERICAN ASSOCIATION FOR THE UNITED NATIONS

FOREWORD

This Eleventh Report of the Commission to Study the Organization of Peace is the third in a series dealing with the general problem of strengthening the United Nations. A few years ago it seemed likely that the General Assembly would at its tenth session utilize its special opportunity under the Charter to call a Charter Review Conference. In 1955 the General Assembly did authorize such a conference, but on account of the unfavorable political situation—the cold war was threatening to rage more furiously—no date was fixed for a meeting of the conference. Nor has a date been fixed in the succeeding years. The cold war has raged more furiously, and it would be futile and might even be dangerous to venture upon a general revision of the Charter before the nuclear powers are ready to make peace.

Our program of studies in preparation for a revision of the Charter has gradually evolved into a program of studies for making the most of the Organization under the Charter pending an end of the cold war. Our Ninth Report (published by the Commission in 1955) was entitled *Charter Review Conference* and dealt with various problems which then seemed likely to come before an eventual conference. Our Tenth Report (Harper, 1957) was entitled *Strengthening the United Nations* and dealt with certain problems which, we believed, could be solved by the General Assembly and the member states without the aid of a special Charter Review Conference. Now we have reached the point where the question arises whether the United Nations can be made much stronger and more effective without at the same time ending the cold war. The two projects seem to be inextricably involved with one another.

More than five years ago (January, 1954) Secretary of State John Foster Dulles, testifying before a subcommittee of the Senate Foreign Relations Committee, posed a series of questions which, he declared, should be studied by the American people in preparation for an eventual Charter Review Conference. The last two of these questions are also two of the principal questions which call for answers in the search for an end of the cold war. One is: "Shall the Organization have power to deal more positively with the problem created by the development of terrible new weapons with vast possibilities of mass destruction?" The other is the more general question: "In view of the importance of the rule of law as a standard of international conduct, are the provisions of the Charter relating to the lawmaking processes adequate for achieving the purposes of the United Nations?" This Eleventh Report is devoted to the search for acceptable answers to these two questions.

We do not profess to be able to predict the course of events in the nuclear age. What seems least likely is that the cold war will continue to rage more and more furiously without any end. It is of course possible that the end will be the use of the new weapons in a hot war of universal and ruinous destructiveness. Up to now nearly every arms race between great powers has ended in hot war. It is also possible, however, that the cold war will be ended by a durable peace between the nuclear powers. There seems to be an ample supply of professional planners in the General Staffs of all the nuclear powers for dealing with the technical problems of war, hot or cold. We prefer to turn our thoughts to the planning of peace.

If there is to be peace in the nuclear age, at least among the nuclear powers, then the development of policy in the United Nations becomes predictable. There will be a massive diversion of public expenditures from preparation for war, and for intimidation by measures short of war, to the exploitation of natural resources throughout the world for the benefit of all mankind. If only 10 per cent of the present expenditures by the nuclear powers on preparations for international intimidation and violence were diverted to internal improvements, particularly in the underdeveloped regions of the earth, the sums annually available would exceed ten billions of dollars. Such sums are probably several times as great as could be wisely spent on such improvements at the present time. But the further expansion of the United Nations expanded program of technical assistance and the prospective returns from the new Special Fund program, authorized by the Thirteenth General Assembly (October, 1958), will rapidly develop the practical capacity of the United Nations to direct the productive employment of capital funds.

As more thinking people turn their thoughts to the problems of the nuclear age, the opportunities for peace-loving men and women everywhere, particularly in agencies operating within the framework of the United Nations, will become greater and more attractive. Above all, service in the UN Security Council and General Assembly will appeal ever more strongly to ambitious and realistic politicians in all countries. One of the most urgent and in the long run most useful tasks in pacific planning for the nuclear age is to strengthen the United Nations so that the ablest statesmen will find adequate scope for their talents in the management of United Nations affairs. The latest fruits of our own thinking along these lines will be found in the main text of this Eleventh Report. Some of the reasoning behind this cold-war peace planning will be found in the supporting papers. The authors of these supporting papers take personal responsibility for their contents respectively, the Commission being responsible only for their publication.

The two parts of our Eleventh Report are closely related. Part I treats of the general theory of international legislation; the second part, of its practical application in a particular case. International regulation and control of nuclear power raise many problems in the development of an adequate process of international lawmaking. Experience in this field of legislation, opened by President Eisenhower's atoms-for-peace proposal to the United Nations General Assembly six years ago, lights up the way toward better legislative methods in other fields of international interest. It is too soon to know how successful the International Atomic Energy Agency may be in the development of nuclear power for peaceful purposes, to say nothing of its helping to protect mankind against the disaster of atomic bombing in war, but it is already clear that we have in this instance the most striking example in recent years of a creative act of international legislation.

There is good ground for the belief that in the nuclear age the improvement of the international legislative process may become as important as the limitation of armaments. Indeed, if the methods and scope of international lawmaking can be rationally developed, the reduction of armaments will not be as serious a problem as it is

now. If peoples can get acceptable settlements of international conflicts by political methods, it will be difficult to persuade them to
maintain armaments as costly as those which have given a name to
the nuclear age. The rule of law in international affairs may seem remote in a period of frightening cold war. Yet even modest improvements in the international lawmaking process, by reducing tension,
may contribute to the ending of the cold war and thus help prepare
the way for an international reign of law that could make the nuclear
age one of unprecedented improvement in man's mode of life.

Organizing peace in the nuclear age means improving the existing
arrangements for protecting and promoting the common interests of
mankind. The nuclear age is already upon us, and the new weapons
have greatly diminished both the importance of the physical boundaries between so-called sovereign states and the usefulness of the
classical doctrine of state sovereignty. Only a state with a permanent seat in the United Nations Security Council can assert a clear
title to a status of unimpaired sovereignty in the contemporary world,
since any other state may find itself at any time in the position of
objecting to a proposed amendment to the United Nations Charter
without power to prevent its adoption except with the support of
at least one of the privileged powers or of more than a third of the
other unprivileged member states. Thus the process of amending the
United Nations Charter has become a kind of international legislative process with unpredictable possibilities for changing the law
of nations and affecting the national interests of a member state contrary to its wishes. Thus also the doctrine of state sovereignty, like
the boundaries between states, which are incapable of producing the
new weapons out of their own resources, tends to lose its historical
significance for the national defense.

The nuclear age is indeed something essentially different from
what we used to call modern times. It is not only new weapons that
have unsettled the old state system which flourished before the first,
if not before the second, of the world wars. There are also the concomitant new ideas that prevent any fresh settlement of the relations between nations until these relations can be adjusted to the
changing needs of the new age. The ordinary unprivileged states can
share in the use of the new weapons only through participation in
the control of an international police force. To share in the benefits
of the new ideas it is necessary in the interest of all states, unprivi-

leged and privileged alike, to perfect the system of international
service agencies which together with the United Nations Organization constitute the United Nations family.

It is in this connection that the study of the International Atomic
Energy Agency is most timely and significant. Of all the agencies
this is the one which illustrates best both the problems and the possibilities inherent in the effective coordination of the various service
organizations now seeking to function in the public interest of the
civilized world. The particular relationship between the International
Atomic Energy Agency and the United Nations is not necessarily the
best that might be established within the family. There is more
thinking to be done before this problem will be satisfactorily solved.
But the further improvement of the relationships between members
of the family, as well as the further development of the family itself,
is in this new age of unparalleled opportunity the most imperative
challenge to the rapidly developing international lawmaking process.

To those who take a realistic view of the course of human events
an important fact about the nuclear age is the unbalanced development of the art of war. The introduction of nuclear weapons has
brought an unprecedented ascendancy of the offense over the defense. The multiplication of methods of delivering the most modern
weapons on their targets—manned supersonic-speed bombers, guided
intercontinental missiles with atomic warheads, offshore bombardment from atomic-powered submarines—finds the methods of protection for peace-loving peoples against an aggressor armed with these
weapons terrifyingly inferior. No modern military establishment can
provide adequate security against ruinous surprise attacks. Better political arrangements, including measures to enforce agreements to
disarm, must be devised to redress the balance between a potential
aggressor and his intended victim.

Happily the nuclear age is also an electronic age. The improvements in the means of communication facilitate the development of
stronger peace-keeping institutions without excessive risk of their
getting out of effective control. Radio and television bring the proceedings of international organizations within the view of all peoples
everywhere. International politicians with a sense of responsibility to
mankind may become even more familiar to those whom they wish
to serve than the strictly national politicians were able to be in the
bygone age of steam locomotion and the electric telegraph. The ma-

terial foundations are rapidly being laid for better management of the common affairs of mankind.

Opinions differ concerning the development of the legal foundations for a better world order. The defects of the present system of international organization are so clear, and the dangers inherent in its imperfections are so imminent, that radical improvements in the organization of peace are manifestly urgent. Yet measures for strengthening the United Nations, as we have remarked before, must be adapted to the spirit of the times and the temper of the nations. We believe that the recommendations in this Report are practical proposals in the existing state of world tension. A broad interpretation of the Charter, the creation of new international service agencies within the framework of the United Nations, and an expanding role for the Secretary-General as well as for the International Court of Justice in the settlement of international disputes—these are important steps toward better international organization which are both timely and capable of reducing present tensions. As in our preceding Tenth Report, we emphasize those changes which seem to be most feasible in the immediate future and most capable of guiding the further development of the United Nations in the way it should go. We continue confident that their adoption will help clear the road for more far-reaching improvements in the organization of peace which may be expected to follow without undue delay.

This Eleventh Report of the Commission is a genuine product of collective thinking on the part of its members. The text was produced by a Drafting Committee of three, who were aided at all stages of its production by the Executive Committee, serving as a policy committee. Additional members of the Commission took part in the meetings which planned the project and approved the final text for publication. Others contributed good advice without actual attendance at meetings. Eighty-one members have signed the Report.

We have substantial debts to acknowledge. A generous grant by the General Service Foundation of St. Paul, Minnesota, covered the expenses of Committee and Commission meetings, without which the Report could not have been written, as well as the costs of publication. For this indispensable aid, as for the similar aid in producing our Tenth Report, we are deeply grateful to the members of this useful Foundation. The Fontenay Corporation of New York gave us the means of sending a skilled investigator to Europe in the summer of 1958 to collect material for our study of the International Atomic Energy Agency, thereby adding greatly to the value of this Report. For this aid, too, we are deeply grateful. One of our own members, who has preferred to remain anonymous, has given generously toward the cost of maintaining our Commission in good working order. We continue, as always, to profit greatly from our affiliation with the American Association for the United Nations by sharing in its office facilities and staff services and by the steadfast encouragement received from its officers. To all we give thanks, reserving however to ourselves full responsibility for our findings and recommendations.

ARTHUR N. HOLCOMBE, *Chairman*
Commission to Study the Organization of Peace

TABLE OF CONTENTS

ELEVENTH

REPORT OF THE COMMISSION

PART I:

LAW AND POLITICS

Testifying before a subcommittee of the Senate Committee on Foreign Relations on 18 January 1954, Secretary of State Dulles outlined six major questions which might be brought before a Charter Review Conference of the United Nations. Four of these questions, primarily concerned with membership in the Organization, powers of the Security Council, and voting arrangements in both the Security Council and the General Assembly, were discussed by the Commission to Study the Organization of Peace in its Ninth and Tenth Reports.

In its continuing effort to develop intelligent public opinion about the vital international issues of our time and the constructive role of the United Nations, the Commission is devoting its Eleventh Report to the two remaining questions posed by Mr. Dulles for the attention of a Charter Review Conference, namely:

> In view of the importance of the rule of law as a standard of international conduct, are the provisions of the Charter relating to law-making processes adequate for achieving the purposes of the United Nations?

> Shall the Organization have power to deal more positively with the problem created by the development of terrible new weapons with vast possibilities of mass destruction?

Part I of the Commission's Report, therefore, indicates the pressing need for a universal juridical community in which the organs of the United Nations, properly weighted to reflect political forces, may further develop international law and condition international behavior. Part II of the Report addresses itself to the problem of invest-

3

ing the United Nations with more power to deal with the hopes and fears raised by the use of atomic energy.

While it may require boldness to speak of "international legislation," international lawmaking is essential to the creation of world order. The United Nations not only provides facilities for ordinary international lawmaking, but also serves as a kind of continuous constitutional convention. Multilateral international instruments are increasing in number; more apparatus for the formulation of international agreements, judgments, and rules are available to the community of nations than ever before in history. But the possibility of widening the dimension of international law provides no guarantee that the nations of the world will adjust their policies to an international consensus. Only a conviction that the individual state is best served in the long run through world order, founded upon pacific adjustment through political processes, will nudge governments to utilize the several instruments of international legislation and administration now at hand.

1. We adhere to the ideal of a world system in which law and politics effectively combine their respective contributions to the development and maintenance of order, security, justice, and progress for the entire human family.

The ideal version of human society is an objective which must be approached through improved international processes of both law and politics. While the Commission shares the hopes for the world which are commonly expressed in the phrase "the rule of law," it stresses the reality that a good society is never produced at any level by law alone but requires a suitable combination and fruitful interaction of law *and* politics. International politics is not an evil to be eliminated, but an essential process which is in need of improvement. International law has the largely unrealized potentiality of serving as a stabilizing framework within which the dynamic processes of politics may be contained. The creation of law is a political process; the moderation and control of political action is the function of a legal system. The vital requirements of world order make unprecedented demands upon both politicians and lawyers, upon both statesmen and judges.

Lawmaking at the international level, as at the national level, is in large part a process of political adjustment rather than merely the registration of authoritative decrees. Hence the improvement of the international legislative process is a task involving the alteration of political attitudes as well as the development of lawmaking procedures.

2. We believe that every independent state should be a member of the United Nations and that every government actually in power within such a state should be permitted and encouraged to take part in the work of the Organization, thereby clearly acknowledging the obligation to respect the provisions of the Charter.

The Charter contains the most advanced statement of the principles of civilized international relations to which states have thus far bound themselves by agreement. Universal acceptance of the obligations incorporated in the Charter is the necessary foundation for progress toward world order. Thus membership in the United Nations should not be considered simply as a privilege, but as a solemn responsibility.

Such an entity as the government of the People's Republic of China, which rules mainland China, should be clearly subjected to the obligations stated in the Charter. The American urge to have that government respect the renunciation of the aggressive use of force in the Charter may or may not be realized by having its representatives take part in the work of the Organization. Doubts, however, concerning the Communist government's prospective obedience to the obligations of United Nations membership strengthen rather than weaken the case for participation; lawbreakers are the last persons to whom one should grant even the semblance of exemption from the law. Under Article 2, paragraph 6, of the Charter even a nonmember state is warned to act in accordance with the Principles of the Charter. If the Central People's Government is the government of China, as it claims to be, it certainly is bound by the Charter. Nevertheless, refusal to recognize the government of the People's Republic of China as the agency responsible for the participation of mainland China in the United Nations weakens the case for regarding that regime as bound by the Charter. It is difficult to reconcile the two propositions: (a) that the Chinese Communist regime does not have the legal status of a government and (b) that it does have the legal obligations of a government.

The timing of the action to seat the government of the People's Republic of China is important. Moreover, it should be clearly understood that the government of the Republic of China, which is in effective control of Formosa and the related islands, should also be appropriately represented in the United Nations. The political complexity of the Chinese situation should not be permitted to obscure the fact that it is desirable to have the existing governments of both China and Formosa clearly committed to observe the standards of international behavior which are set forth in the Charter.

3. We urge full acceptance of the central role of the General Assembly in directing and coordinating the creation of new and improved international institutions. We welcome the growing tendency to recognize the Secretary-General's wide discretion in the development of useful international instruments and to use Assembly resolutions as authority for the formation of new agencies. We recommend that use be made of the technique of Charter amendment as well as of the multilateral treaty as devices for the establishment of major additions to the machinery of international organization. While we value such initiative as the United States exercised in the creation of the International Atomic Energy Agency, we recognize the propriety of the Assembly's insistence that the negotiation of its Statute should be so arranged as to indicate clearly that the new Agency was to be a product of United Nations sponsorship and not merely an American-sponsored institution.

In an important sense the organs of the United Nations serve as a continuous constitutional convention. They provide a focal point for the consideration and implementation of such plans for the enlargement and improvement of the world's organizational structure as states may be willing to undertake. There is an expanding role for the General Assembly as the major forum for the presentation of new institutional projects and for the creative leadership of the Secretary-General as spokesman for the world community.

There is great merit in entrusting to the United Nations the responsibility for the establishment of new international bodies. Negotiating groups of reasonable size and carefully balanced composition, chosen by the Assembly, and advisory groups combining expertness and the international viewpoint, provided by the Secretary-General, have the greatest utility. Hence, any tendency for states to bypass the United Nations in designing new elements of the international organizational system is to be deplored.

The various methods available to the United Nations for the formal creation of new agencies provide splendid opportunities for improving the world's machinery for common action. In recent years the creation of such notable instruments as the United Nations Emergency Force, the United Nations Observation Group in Lebanon, the United Nations Presence in the Middle Eastern area, the International Finance Corporation, the International Atomic Energy Agency, and the Special Fund for technical assistance indicates the significance of the United Nations as an international laboratory and workshop. It is vitally important to have, use, and strengthen for future use the United Nations as an international facility for designing essential additions to the world's institutional structure.

4. We note with satisfaction the progress that has been achieved, particularly in some of the specialized agencies, in developing what might be called quasi legislation: procedures for the establishment of rules which bind member states, or create some limited type of obligation for them, even without their expressed consent or ratification. This kind of arrangement derives from the consent of states, expressed in their adherence to the constitutions of international agencies. We urge states to support its increasing use and expanded application, in order to achieve a more adequate body of international law.

"The international legislative process" refers to the procedures by which rules recognized as having legal force for states are created. Traditionally the sole method for the deliberate enactment of new international law, as distinguished from the crystallization of customary law, has been the treaty technique, whereby rights and duties are established only for those states which express consent through ratification or acceptance of a given treaty.

The need for a more satisfactory method of adapting international law to the requirements of an interdependent world has long been evident, and it is encouraging that states have been willing, in regard to some subjects of minor political sensitivity, to forego the sovereignty-inspired requirement of ratification and to recognize the legal validity of regulations made by majority action in international bodies. For instance, the Assembly of the World Health Organization adopts regulations concerning such matters as international sanitary codes and the potency and purity of drugs moving in international commerce, which bind all members of the Organization except those which expressly claim exemption. The Assembly of the International Civil Aviation Organization adopts a similar procedure with respect to rules of the air and air traffic control practices and the transport of radioactive materials in international commerce.

This innovation does not presage the wholesale conversion of the international legislative process into legislation-by-parliamentary-majority. Given the reality of states as the fundamentally important units of international affairs, there is inescapable logic in the proposition that most international legislation should involve the acquiescence or consent of states. But it is clear that statesmen whose eyes are fixed less on the dogma of sovereignty than upon the need for promoting the interests of their peoples in an interdependent world can and should identify many areas where the quasi-legislative method may be used to advantage.

5. We urge acceptance of a broad construction of the Charter of the United Nations. The Organization should assume control over such zones as the polar regions, the high seas, the air above them and the bed below, and outer space. We urge that this competence be asserted and exercised through the legislative capacity inherent in the Organization.

The traditional international legal concept of *res communis* was an artificial construct so long as there was no organized international community with agencies capable of exercising dominion over the zones which belong to the community as a whole rather than to its constituent states. Now there is such a global organization, with appropriate agencies, and it is vitally important that *res communis* should not, through default, be left for appropriation by states.

The Commission believes, as it emphasized in its Tenth Report,[1] that the United Nations has authority to internationalize those zones which have not been recognized as falling within the domain of states, and implied power to take the necessary legislative action for their effective administration. This authority derives from the status of the United Nations as the agency of the general community of nations and its mandate to create the conditions of order in that community. While that agency is distinctly limited by the established rights of states, it encounters no such limitations in the zones to which we refer and can address its efforts to the task of promoting the general interests of mankind and of harmonizing such conflicting national interests as may develop.

The control and administration of the zones outside the spheres of states should be exercised by mechanisms especially designed for that purpose, operating under the General Assembly or the Security Council as appropriate.

6. Recognizing that decisions relating to the raising and spending of money constitute one of the most important areas of modern legislation, and that the conduct of constructive programs, even when they require substantial expenditures, is potentially one of the most valuable functions of the United Nations, we make the following recommendations:

(a) United Nations programs falling outside the realm of normal administrative operations should be placed in separate budgets, to be supported by assessment upon member states, by independent sources of revenue, or by voluntary contributions as may be appropriate.

[1] *Strengthening the United Nations (Tenth Report of the Commission to Study the Organization of Peace)*, 1957, Pt. 1, pp. 6–7, 40–41; Pt. 2, ch. 9 (pp. 207–223).

(b) A foundation for a massive enlargement of the funds to be made available to the United Nations for certain programs should be laid by the adoption of a system of weighted voting. This would permit the states contributing most heavily to those programs to have increased power in the managing boards.

Legislative control of the finances which support governmental services rivals legislative direction of citizens' behavior as the major component of the legislative process within national states. Analogously, the legislative competence of international organizations involves the significant question of authority over financial arrangements.

The most challenging opportunities of the United Nations to be of service to mankind are, in large part, opportunities which require the availability of substantially larger funds than are likely to be supplied under the present system. Dependence upon voluntary contributions of states for support of all activities except normal administrative functions is the decisive limiting factor in the growth of the United Nations program.

While there is a sound logical case for the total abolition of the one-state-one-vote rule in the General Assembly, realism requires the recognition that the equality of all states in that body is largely a matter of form. The proposition that the United States, for example, with only one vote out of eighty-two, actually has only a correspondingly minute share of political influence over the activities of the Assembly is untenable. In fact the major powers have at least as much influence in that body as their significance entitles them to exercise. In these terms, the urgency of developing a general scheme for weighted voting in the Assembly is not great.

However, in the sphere which has to do with the raising and spending of substantial sums of money the practical case for giving the major states a formal increase in voting power is impressive. Useful precedents exist in the constitutional procedures of the World Bank and the International Monetary Fund, and in the arrangements for the administration of the United Nations Special Fund. It is equitable as well as politically realistic to grant the primary contributors a share in the legislative control of program budgets sufficient to meet their claims for protection against undue demands upon their resources and for a leading voice in the determination of the uses to which their contributions are put.[2]

Given such arrangements as the Commission recommends, the prospects for the progressive strengthening of the United Nations as a working institution would be greatly enhanced.

7. We recommend that strenuous effort be made to revitalize the Security Council as an organ for promoting political accommodation within the framework of law provided by the Charter. To this end we propose that the Council be enlarged and effective provision made for assuring a more realistic and equitable distribution of its seats among the significant political groupings.

No other organ of the United Nations is fully capable of discharging the responsibilities originally entrusted to the Security Council. The decline in significance of that body is attributable only in part to the frustrations caused by the veto power; hence it is conceivable that the Council may achieve a role of real importance, even though it may not be feasible to alter the veto rule. An appropriate modification of the composition of the Council, with a view to securing a better political balance in its membership and particularly to opening up the possibilities of leadership by the middle powers, would be a promising development. The Security Council, thus reconstituted, might become the focal point for the practice of international political negotiation at the highest level. In this situation the veto power might function less as an impediment to action than as a potent reminder that accommodation and adjustment, rather than parliamentary victories and propaganda triumphs, are the essential products of political bargaining. Such an effective political process would be a vital contribution to the rule of law in international affairs.[3]

[2] Such a program budget, with weighted voting, was also strongly urged in the Tenth Report; there was an extended analysis and discussion of weighted voting in the General Assembly on its own merits, with reference to other questions as well. *Ibid.*, Pt. 1, pp. 10, 50–52; Pt. 2, pp. 256–259, and ch. 10 (pp. 224–237).

[3] See recommendation and discussion in Tenth Report. *Ibid.*, Pt. 1, pp. 4, 32–33; Pt. 2, pp. 238–239, 243–247.

8. We welcome the development of international machinery, in the United Nations and the specialized agencies, for stimulating and facilitating the most effective use of the multilateral treaty device for the creation of new legal rules in the many areas of international relations where the law is inadequately developed. We urge the United States government to participate more fully in the realization of the opportunities afforded by this system for developing international law.

The introduction of the improved methods of creating international law noted above does not detract from the importance of continuing and accelerating the refinement of the international treaty as an instrument of international legislation. The contemporary system of international organization does not purport to abolish or replace multilateral treaty making as the primary device of the international legislative process. On the contrary, it provides opportunities and facilities for making that device serve more adequately in the development of international law to meet the needs of our time: expert groups to identify the problems which are ripe for legislative action; forums in which legislative initiative may be exercised; administrative services and expert assistance to promote the negotiation and drafting of treaties; and methods to stimulate the ratification of treaties by the states concerned. The world is now equipped to realize the maximum potentialities of the treaty-making device for the creation of new legal regulations.

In this situation it is unfortunate that the United States has tended to abstain from active participation in the development of new segments of international law through the multilateral treaty process. This tendency, attributable in part to the bias against lawmaking treaties exhibited by the advocates of the so-called Bricker Amendment, has seriously slowed progress toward the elaboration of a more adequate body of international law. The formulation of multilateral treaties should not be regarded as an automatic solution of all international problems. However, the United States should take less account of the objections to and fears of the treaty-making process which characterize certain elements in the domestic political arena and should recognize that progress in creating a good society on a global scale may be advanced by American participation in that process in selected areas of international relations. Legislation must be appropriate to the expressed needs of a society: some needs call for local ordinances; others require national action; still others may be met by international agreements.

> 9. We urge that steps be taken to enhance the effectiveness of the International Law Commission in promoting the development and codification of international law. To this end we recommend that the financial resources of the Commission be increased so as to permit its members to serve on a full-time basis and that it be strengthened by the development of a staff of experts in comparative law, comparative civilizations, and other relevant fields.

The International Law Commission, properly constituted and supported, could function as an expert body to provide the impetus for a significant campaign to remedy the deficiencies of international law. Under present conditions that Commission is performing highly useful work, but a vigorous effort should be made to enlarge its capacity and increase its suitability for the task of international legislative leadership. Such a change would not alter the fact that states, through their constitutional processes of ratification, maintain ultimate control over the application of international law, but the International Law Commission could stimulate progress by elaborating and clarifying the norms which should guide the international action of states.

> 10. We urge the United States to exercise positive leadership in promoting the rule of law by using the International Court of Justice in all appropriate cases and by encouraging wider acceptance of the compulsory jurisdiction of the Court under the optional clause of Article 36 of the Statute. To this end the United States should withdraw its reservation of unilateral competence to determine

which matters fall within the domestic jurisdiction of the United States. Moreover, we reiterate the proposal, made in our Tenth Report,[4] that organs of the United Nations resort more frequently to the Court for advisory opinions.

There is widespread recognition, reflected in President Eisenhower's 1959 State of the Union message, that the United States has set a bad example for other states in qualifying its ratification of the optional clause so severely as to make that ratification virtually meaningless. No amount of exhortation by American leaders in favor of promoting the rule of law in international affairs would be so effective as the simple act of transforming United States ratification of the optional clause into a genuine acceptance of the Court's compulsory jurisdiction in legal disputes. Such an act might stimulate widespread alteration of attitudes toward the International Court of Justice and pave the way for the full realization of the Court's potential as an instrument for the settlement of disputes and the clarification and development of international law. The Court has a limited but vitally important role to play in the evolution of world order, and it is essential that its opportunities for service through both decisions and advisory opinions be expanded.

[4] *Ibid.*, pp. 4, 6, 35, 39.

PART II:

THE ATOM

Part II of the Commission's Report addresses itself to the problem, raised for Charter Review by Mr. Dulles, of investing the United Nations with more power to deal with the hopes and fears raised by the use of atomic energy. In a larger sense, however, this part of the Report points the way by which international machinery could be utilized to promote, harmonize, and regulate international interests, thereby strengthening the legal fabric of world order. Atomic energy presents a fourfold challenge: development of the new science for peaceful purposes; control of the peaceful development process; international control of the testing of nuclear weapons; and finally, the control of the production of nuclear weapons.

The International Atomic Energy Agency was designed by the nations of the world, under the leadership of the United States, to exploit the marvelous potentialities of atomic energy for the improvement of health, communications, industry, and other peaceful purposes. Properly buttressed, the Agency could provide outstanding services for mankind by channeling international atomic resources into technical assistance, aiding the research and training of scientists, and strengthening safeguards against dangerous accidents or deliberate diversion of nuclear materials from projects designed for peaceful purposes. In addition, it could ultimately be utilized in controlling the production and testing of nuclear weapons. The key to the development of the International Atomic Energy Agency is the willingness of the nations to use this multilateral agency and to increase its effectiveness.

Neither the vast power for good inherent in atomic energy nor the threat of annihilation can be a monopoly of any one nation.

15

The uncoordinated exploitation of atomic energy for peaceful purposes will not permit the most economical use of the resources of the world; the uncontrolled production and testing of atomic weapons put mankind in a noose of tension and fear.

The United Nations and the specialized agencies, with the newly created International Atomic Energy Agency, have laid down a structure for the kinds of international regulation that can lead toward a law-abiding community of states. The support of public opinion for this process toward world order—in labor, health, agriculture, aviation, finance, and so forth—is important; in the field of atomic energy it is essential.

11. We welcome the creation and entry into active operation of the International Atomic Energy Agency, representing, in the words of its Preparatory Commission, "the first attempt on a world-wide basis to face the challenge and opportunity of the peaceful uses of atomic energy."

The Agency represents the grasping of the opportunity, rare in the history of mankind, to impose a pattern of international purpose and policy upon a process of basic change at the very beginning of its operation. Atomic energy is a fundamental new force in the world, full of both peril and promise for the future of mankind. It adds new dimensions to the problems of warfare and welfare at the global level. The International Atomic Energy Agency is a vital institutional framework designed to promote and coordinate efforts to realize the constructive potential of atomic science and technology, and to provide safeguards against the perversion of those efforts to military purposes. In this beginning of international action in the atomic field there is the promise of a contribution to the solution of the difficulties which have impeded agreement on a workable system of disarmament.

12. We strongly urge the United States to make the International Atomic Energy Agency the focal point and major instrumentality of its activity in support of the development of the peaceful uses of atomic energy in other countries. In specific terms, the United States should give priority to the Agency rather than to bilateral or regional arrangements. Such a policy, however, should not be allowed to discourage peaceful cooperative efforts on a regional basis, such as Euratom.

The establishment of the Agency was largely a product of American initiative. Insistence upon the vital importance of exploiting the constructive potentialities of atomic energy through international action was explicit in the original American proposal relating to the atomic problem, the Acheson-Lilienthal-Baruch plan, which was presented to the United Nations in 1946. President Eisenhower reiterated this point and provided the immediate initiative for the creation of a special organization in this field in his famous "Atoms for Peace" speech to the General Assembly in December, 1953. It is ironic indeed that the United States, having taken the lead in the creation of the Agency, has tended to neglect it and relegate it to the periphery of the American program for assisting other states in the atoms-for-peace field. Yet this is what has been done, and the Commission is concerned that American preference for bilateral arrangements may prevent the effective development of the Agency. The importance of the creation of an orderly system of international cooperation in this field indicates the desirability of giving the Agency a major role in atoms-for-peace programs.

13. We recommend that the Agency's program of technical assistance in the field of atomic energy be rapidly and vigorously developed, with careful attention to the coordination of its work with that of the United Nations and the specialized agencies. We recommend further that the Agency be enabled to establish, as quickly as possible, its own laboratories for the conduct of research and the training of specialists in the peaceful application of atomic energy.

The most significant contributions which can be made immediately by the Agency lie in the area of technical assistance. Given international laboratory facilities and adequate financial resources the Agency will be in a position to promote the research, planning, and training programs which are essential preliminaries to the actual exploitation of atomic energy on a large scale to meet the economic and other needs of underdeveloped countries.

While numerous other international organizations are legitimately engaged in activities which involve the peaceful uses of atomic energy, the central responsibility for international development in this field should clearly be assigned to the Agency and appropriate measures should be taken to assure its role in the coordination of related activities undertaken by other organizations.

14. We emphasize the importance of the Agency's maintaining a bank of fissionable material and of launching, at the earliest possible time, its program of assistance in the establishment and operation of atomic reactors for peaceful purposes in member states which desire such facilities. The United States and other major contributing members should offer essential equipment and materials to the Agency on such favorable terms as to enable it to establish itself as the major sponsor of atomic energy projects in countries requiring outside assistance.

Technical assistance is but a preliminary means to the end of equipping underdeveloped countries to exploit the beneficent possibilities of atomic energy. The transition from the preparatory stage to the actual construction of reactors for production of electrical power and other nonmilitary uses should be reached as soon as possible, if the Agency is to justify the hopes which have been vested in it. It should be stressed that the success of the Agency in realizing its purposes is dependent upon the willingness of the atomically advanced states, particularly the United States, to give the Agency preferential treatment in supplying necessary equipment and material. The United States should make the necessary legislative and policy changes to meet this requirement. Otherwise the Agency may not be able to compete with bilateral and regional programs. It is incumbent upon the United States, as the major sponsor of the Agency, to avoid the anomaly of sponsoring competing programs which may stifle the development of the Agency by offering aid on more attractive terms.

15. *We favor making the Agency the authoritative legislator and responsible administrator of uniform minimum standards of safety against radiation hazards, accidental explosions, and perversion to military purposes in all projects for the peaceful exploitation of atomic energy, under whatever sponsorship they may be established and operated. To this end, we recommend that all member states of the Agency take steps to authorize the application of the Agency's safeguards and inspection system first to bilateral and regional atomic projects of a nonmilitary nature and ultimately to their national programs as well.*

The developmental function of the Agency is matched in importance by its task of preventing the peaceful exploitation of atomic energy from creating hazards to health and safety, including the hazard of diversion to military purposes. So long as no international agreement on a system of enforceable prohibition of atomic weapons has been reached, activities in the military atomic field are legitimate and necessary. However, it would represent considerable progress toward the ideal of eliminating the atomic threat to human survival if a universally applicable system of controls could be established over atomic facilities which are devoted to nonmilitary purposes.

Under the Statute of the Agency its control system is automatically applicable only to projects developed under the sponsorship of the Agency. However, the Agency is authorized to extend the system to facilities developed under national, bilateral, or regional auspices, upon request of the states concerned. The Commission urges that member states exercise this option, contributing to the development of a universal system of safeguards over nonmilitary atomic facilities. While it is clear that this objective is unlikely to be fully realized in the short run, it would be advantageous for those states which are willing to utilize the Agency in this manner to go ahead, as the United States and Japan have recently done in their bilateral arrangement, without being deterred by the present refusal of other states to follow suit. In particular, the United States should do so, regardless of the prospects for similar Soviet action. Such a policy might be a useful bargaining counter in negotiations with the People's Republic of China; it would be desirable to admit that regime to the Agency, on condition that it also accept the Agency's controls over its atomic facilities of nonmilitary character.

Whatever progress toward the creation of a universal system of standards and controls can be made in the early stages of the world's development of atomic facilities for peaceful uses will be sheer gain for international order and welfare.

16. As the Agency develops a substantial body of experience in the administration of international standards and safeguards relating to the operation of atomic facilities for peaceful purposes, we urge that constant effort be made to translate the lessons of that experience into terms applicable to the development of an international control system over the military uses of atomic energy.

The Agency was created for the specific purpose of promoting, with adequate safeguards, the maximum development of the peaceful uses of atomic energy for the enhancement of human welfare. The Commission applauds this purpose and hopes that the Agency will be energetically devoted to its realization. But the constructive and destructive potentialities of atomic energy are inextricably related to each other, and the Agency may contribute, directly or indirectly, to solution of the problems in the military field. In the words of Secretary of State Dulles, "The Agency can help in moving toward control of nuclear weapons . . . We hope that it will demonstrate the feasibility of controls in a way that will have an impact on negotiations for the regulation and reduction of armaments."

Aside from providing a demonstration of international controls in operation, the Agency may enhance the feasibility of a disarmament system by promoting the free flow of scientific information relating to atomic energy, training a staff of international specialists in the inspection and supervision of atomic facilities, and undertaking studies of the dangers as well as the potential benefits of atomic energy in all fields.

17. We urge the United Nations Disarmament Commission and other negotiating groups attempting to produce agreement regarding a system for the effective restriction or prohibition of the testing and production of nuclear weapons to utilize the Agency's resources in achieving their objectives.

The existence of the Agency as an international organization authorized and equipped to implement the principle of inspection in atomic matters provides the world with an invaluable asset.

Without sacrificing its role in the promotion of the beneficent exploitation of atomic energy, the Agency should stand ready to carry out any appropriate functions which might be assigned to it under agreements designed to achieve full or partial elimination of atomic activity in the military field. Every state should recognize its stake in the growth of the Agency as an effective international organization, capable of contributing to world order by operating in the atoms-for-peace field and by influencing—directly or indirectly— the solution of the security problems posed by the destructive potential of nuclear energy.

18. The United Nations does not at this time need further authority under the Charter to deal more positively with the problem created by the development of terrible new weapons with vast possibilities of mass destruction. The achievement of disarmament is ultimately dependent upon the agreement of the states which are significant military powers. Whether there be a comprehensive scheme for limiting and controlling military resources or a more modest objective, such as the prohibition of the testing of nuclear weapons, there is no substitute for agreement among the principal member states. If such agreements can be reached, they should be kept within the framework of the United Nations and should utilize its machinery for carrying out their provisions. We emphasize not the power of the United Nations to impose its will upon the major military states but its power to assist them in eliminating the obstacles to agreed solutions of the problems of the nuclear arms race.

The most useful approach to the problem created by the development of nuclear weapons is to recognize that the United Nations has no power to impose decisions in this field. But this recognition should not obscure the fact that the United Nations has the practical capacity to assist states in reaching agreement—by promoting negotiation, by providing facilities, and by creating mechanisms for the effective operation of such control systems as states may agree to establish. The power to be useful is no less important than the power to be authoritative.

The vital problem of disarmament should be approached with full awareness of the rich and varied institutional resources of the United Nations family. These constitute a priceless possession of the nascent world community.

The following members of the Commission have signed this Report. Signature means approval of the general principles outlined in the Report, but not necessarily of all the details. Specific reservations in a few cases are noted below.

> James T. Shotwell, *Honorary Chairman*
> Arthur N. Holcombe, *Chairman*
> Inis L. Claude, Jr., *Chairman, Drafting Committee*

Dana Converse Backus
Harding F. Bancroft
G. Hinman Barrett
Cyril J. Bath
Clarence A. Berdahl
Donald C. Blaisdell
Roy Blough
Charles G. Bolté
Frank G. Boudreau
Harry J. Carman (See 1, below)
David F. Cavers
Waldo Chamberlin (See 2, below)

Daniel S. Cheever
Ben M. Cherrington
John L. Childs
Benjamin V. Cohen
J. B. Condliffe
Norman Cousins
Royden Dangerfield
Malcolm W. Davis (See 1, below)
Oscar A. de Lima
Albert I. Edelman
Clark M. Eichelberger
Rupert Emerson
Charles G. Fenwick

Lawrence S. Finkelstein
Edgar J. Fisher
Denna F. Fleming
Richard N. Gardner
Arthur J. Goldsmith (See 1, below)
Leland M. Goodrich
Frank P. Graham
J. Eugene Harley (See 3, below)
Donald Harrington
H. Field Haviland, Jr.
Walter D. Head
Melvin D. Hildreth
Willard N. Hogan
Erling M. Hunt
Samuel Guy Inman
Elmore Jackson
Philip E. Jacob
Joseph E. Johnson
Peter Kihss (See 1, below)
John I. Knudson
Hans Kohn
Walter H. C. Laves
Lance N. Lazo
Gerard J. Mangone
Boyd A. Martin
Charles E. Martin

Herbert L. May
Hugh Moore
Laura Puffer Morgan
Forrest D. Murden, Jr.
Ernest Minor Patterson
Josephine Pomerance
James P. Pope
Charles C. Price
George L. Ridgeway
J. William Robinson
Eleanor Roosevelt
Irving Salomon
Stephen M. Schwebel
Paul E. Smith
Louis B. Sohn
Eugene Staley
C. M. Stanley
John G. Stoessinger
Arthur Sweetser
Amos E. Taylor
Willard L. Thorp
Edgar Turlington
Amry Vandenbosch
James P. Warburg
Harris Wofford, Jr.
Richard R. Wood
Quincy Wright

RESERVATIONS

1. The undersigned are in general agreement with the Eleventh Report of the Commission to Study the Organization of Peace. We note that it states that the timing of the action to seat the government of the People's Republic of China is important and we emphasize our opposition to seating that regime under present conditions. The Charter of the United Nations states that membership is open to "peace-loving states which accept the obligations contained in the present Charter." A resolution of the General Assembly on February 1, 1951, declared that the People's Republic of China had "engaged in

aggression in Korea," from which charge it has never cleared itself. The recent violent intervention of the People's Republic of China in Tibet is further evidence of its lack of qualification for being seated in the United Nations. We therefore believe that it would be inconsistent with the Charter to admit representatives of the People's Republic of China until it is evident that it is in fact "peace-loving" and willing to accept the duties and obligations of United Nations membership.

Harry J. Carman
Malcolm W. Davis
Arthur J. Goldsmith
Peter Kihss

2. The validity of the statement on page 11 that enlargement of the Security Council will assure "a more realistic and equitable distribution" of seats needs further examination.

Waldo Chamberlin

3. In view of the more recent developments in the policies and program of the People's Republic of China—such as the extension of communes on the mainland of China and the use of force to overthrow the government of Tibet (March, 1959) and the consequent implications of these developments in curtailing fundamental human rights—more time is needed for the government of the People's Republic of China to clarify its peaceful intentions and to demonstrate a harmonization of its conduct with the protection of fundamental human rights.

J. Eugene Harley

SUPPORTING PAPERS

THE ROLE OF LAW

IN THE ORGANIZATION OF PEACE

by Quincy Wright

THE LIMITATIONS OF INTERNATIONAL LAW

The opinion is generally accepted that peace is a product of society and that society cannot exist without law. *Ubi societas ibi jus est.* Consequently, if there is to be peace among nations there must be a universal law. This was the opinion of the publicists of the sixteenth and seventeenth centuries who initiated the discipline of international law. They did not, however, succeed in creating a law sustaining a universal society capable of maintaining peace. Consequently, since the World Wars of the twentieth century many have said there must be a more comprehensive law to which not only states but also individuals are subject. And this law must both establish and be sustained by a world government equipped with adequate material force to assure that the writ of its courts will run in every state of the world.

The concepts of an international criminal law, exemplified in the Nuremberg, Tokyo, and other war crimes trials, and of a universal civil law maintaining the human rights declared in the United Nations Charter and the Universal Declaration of Human Rights have been steps toward such a law, but the world still lacks legally binding codes of international criminal law and international tribunals or other procedures for punishing international crimes and maintaining human rights in so far as these have been established by custom, although the United Nations has made continuous efforts in these directions.

Many jurists believe that the diversity of national cultures, the powerful resistance of the sentiment of nationalism, and the general assumption of sovereignty by independent states render impracticable and perhaps undesirable effective universal law penetrating to the individual within the state. The difficulty faced by the central government of federal states, such as the United States, in enforcing national standards within the states raises doubts as to the feasibility of enforcing universal standards within the much more diverse, independent, and sovereign states of the world community.

Nevertheless, the need for such a development has induced scholarly consideration of it in a number of law schools engaged in research and teaching on "international legal studies" or "transnational law." These terms embrace much more than public international law of which states are the only subjects and private international law or conflict of laws determining the selection of the rules of national law to be applied in litigations between individuals involving transnational elements. These terms include also world constitutional law dealing with the purposes, principles, powers, and procedures of the United Nations and other international organizations and the general principles of law accepted by civilized nations. The latter subject looks toward the development of a universal law for individuals through the comparison of national legal systems and abstraction from this comparison of common elements or through the development of rules of law defining universally accepted human rights and international crimes. Through such scholarly studies, presenting rational answers to legal problems which insistently arise in the shrinking world, a universal legal system may emerge gradually, may shape appropriate institutions for its maintenance, and thus, by an evolutionary process, may in time create a genuine world society without arousing nationalist opposition or stimulating alarm concerning encroachments upon the sovereignty of states.

Such a process, however, while it may at long last create conditions for a world society capable of maintaining peace, cannot provide legal norms and procedures for the authoritative settlement of international disputes now threatening the peace. For a long time the time-honored principles of international law, which assert that no sovereign state can, without its consent, be bound by a new rule of law or subjected to the jurisdiction of an international tribunal, will make the processes of international legislation and international adjudication slow, uncertain, and ineffective. On the other hand, it is clear that organizations which ignore these principles or seek to modify them rapidly cannot function unless supported by organized material power of the world community greater than that of any state. The slow pace of the United Nations in developing disarmament agreements and international policing forces suggests that such power of the world society to enforce its law is far in the future. For a long time, and perhaps indefinitely, because of essential differences in character between the world society and any national society, it appears that international law will remain largely law between states. It will be sanctioned largely by the good faith, custom, and national appraisal of their interests by states, fortified by an emerging world public opinion and by the cooperative activity of states to frustrate the most serious violations of law—international aggression—by *ad hoc* coalitions with the defender, as in the operation of traditional balance of power politics or by the fulfillment of collective security obligations under the United Nations.

If this is true, the society of nations will continue decentralized and relatively weak. Its law will leave many matters to the domestic jurisdiction of states and it will rely more upon persuasion than upon coercion. In such a situation the role of politics to maintain the peace will be relatively large.

This does not mean, however, that law will be unimportant. It can contribute to establishing the goals, standards, and principles of international politics, and the procedures through which international politics operates even though it cannot subject all controversies to authoritative settlement by its courts and according to its rules.

LAW AND POLITICS IN THE SOCIETY OF NATIONS

A society implies that there is both law, formulating its values and its procedures, and politics, continually adapting these values and procedures to new conditions. Law, drawing its principles, standards, and rules from past experience, seeks stability and order. Politics, shaping its goals and methods from a judgment of future consequences, seeks reform and progress as interpreted by those taking political initiative. Law is the stabilizing and politics is the dynamic element of society. But, through enlarging its sources to embrace considerations of "natural law" both human and physical, law may include dynamic elements. It may have within itself possibilities of adaptation to a changing environment, as has been indicated in the

United States by the history of the Supreme Court. Conversely, by limiting its goals to those defined in a rigid constitution and its methods to those prescribed by such a constitution, politics may become stable and, if such prescriptions are excessive, society may become so rigid that it cannot survive in a changing world, and violent revolution may be anticipated. Thus if law becomes too dynamic it ceases to be law, a virtue of which is to create conditions of predictability, and if politics becomes too stable it ceases to perform its function of adapting society to new conditions.

The problem of statesmanship, national or international, is therefore to maintain the proper balance between law and politics in the existing conditions of the society. If there are wide variations in the cultural or material development of the members of the society or if the speed of technological and ideological inventions demands social change, law must be decentralized, leaving large areas of human relations to politics. On the other hand, if a society is relatively stable and uniform, law will tend to be centralized and comprehensive and politics will play a lesser role.

What should be the role of law in the present society of nations? That society is changing rapidly, under the impact of inventions, shrinking the world in communication and transportation time and rendering all peoples vulnerable to influences difficult to predict, such as military attacks, economic embargoes, and propaganda initiated in any part of the world. The society of nations is also characterized by great diversity of ideology, religion, nationality, culture, economy, technology, and standards of living among its members. The role of politics is therefore necessarily predominant. These conditions, however, make it all the more necessary that law should impose some restraints upon the values and methods of politics in order to prevent the destruction of civilization by the use of war as an instrument of politics and to preserve the fundamental values accepted by all peoples. Conditions require a flexible and decentralized world society but they also require that there be a society capable of maintaining respect for its basic values by its members.

Politics normally proceeds from the parts, law from the whole. Politics is the art by which a group formulates and achieves its ends against the opposition of other groups. In domestic politics the group may be an ambitious leader and his adherents seeking to gain political power against the opposition of rivals; it may be a city, province, or region seeking to achieve local ends against the opposition of the majority in the state; it may be a political party seeking to control agencies of the state against the rival parties, but in any case it functions within the law of the state.

In international politics the groups have been in modern times sovereign territorial states, each seeking to realize national interests against the opposition of others. In the Middle Ages supranational groups, such as the papacy and the empire, and subnational groups, such as feudal lords and commercial cities, functioned in international politics together with the kingdoms. In recent times general international organizations, such as the United Nations, regional organizations, such as the Organization of American States, and collective defense organizations, such as NATO, Warsaw and SEATO, have functioned in international politics together with sovereign states. While international politics functions within the regime of international law, that law has placed few restrictions upon the goals and the methods employed. War has been a major instrument of international politics.

Law may be conceived as a body of rules and principles defining the goals and standards of the society and the relations among its members, and the procedures for maintaining and for changing them. It may also be conceived as the art by which the force of a society can be invoked to compel or induce observance of these rules and principles by the agencies and members of the society. The first is law in books, and the latter is law in action. In either case the society as a whole faces its members and its agencies by its law.

The decentralization of the society of nations means that the principal members—the great states—are more powerful than the society as a whole, which functions through such cooperative institutions as the United Nations, the International Court of Justice, and the specialized agencies; such negotiating and administrative institutions as the diplomatic and consular systems; and such temporary institutions as international conferences and arbitral tribunals. Thus initiative comes mainly from the members. The society as a whole, as organized under the United Nations Charter, can propose and recommend rules of law, procedures, and agreements to settle disputes and can intervene and coordinate the forces of the members to prevent or stop hostilities, but it cannot legislate, decide disputes, or directly administer services except in a few areas or exceptional circumstances.

This does not imply that international law is unimportant or that an increase in its role is either undesirable or impracticable. It would seem that an increase in the role of law in the present world is desirable for the same reason that more traffic control is necessary as vehicles become more rapid and more numerous. The shrinking and changing world of today requires more legal regulations if collisions of unbearable destructiveness are to be avoided. A suitable balance of law and politics seems to require a larger role for law, although the very conditions cited make that enlargement difficult. Times of rapid change tend to become revolutionary. In such times politics escapes the control of law but revolution implies violence, and international violence under present conditions might destroy civilization. Only if the role of law is increased can politics effect the changes necessary to adapt the society of nations to the changing conditions of technology and ideology. Only within a framework of law can a continuous evolutionary process direct mankind toward a clearer formulation of values, a peaceful adjustment of differences, and a realization of generally accepted goals.

It is generally said that a sovereign state is bound by a new rule of law or the decision of a dispute only if it has consented. A more precise statement of this principle of existing international law would assert that a sovereign state is bound only by general rules, principles, and standards which it has tacitly or expressly accepted, which are established by jural sources which it has tacitly or expressly accepted, or which have been declared by a procedure which it has tacitly or expressly accepted as competent to make law within defined limits. It is bound only by concrete decisions which it has expressly accepted, which have been declared by a tribunal whose jurisdiction it has expressly accepted, or which have emerged from a procedure which it has agreed is competent to decide the matter. Accepting this definition, much can be done to improve the legislative, judicial, executive, and administrative procedures of the society of nations. Because of the general requirement of consent by the subjects of law there is a hesitancy to apply to international law these terms current in municipal law. Some would prefer to speak of the law developing, dispute settling, peace preserving, and cooperation assuring procedures of the society of nations. It is believed, however, that with the establishment of the United Nations as a central body, with certain powers over its members, the terminology familiar to municipal law is justifiable although the differences arising from the far greater centralization of national societies should always be borne in mind. Attention will be given in the successive sections to these four aspects of law—legislation, adjudication, execution, and administration—in the community of nations.

INTERNATIONAL LEGISLATION

The legislative process in the society of nations can be improved by procedures to assure that proposals for codifying international law, for adapting it to new conditions, and for extending it to new areas are such, in form and substance, as to induce easy acceptance and ready observance of the proposals by states. The process can also be improved by procedures to facilitate and encourage such acceptance and observance, as well as by full utilization of the legislative authority which states have conferred upon the United Nations and other international organizations.

The General Assembly is authorized to "initiate studies and make recommendations for the purpose of promoting international cooperation in the political field and encouraging the progressive development of international law and its codification" (Article 13). To assist it in this function the General Assembly has established the International Law Commission and that body has been engaged in preparing statements of law in many fields without attempting to state what is "codification" of existing law and what is "development" of new law. These statements, when approved by the Commission after considering the comments of governments and scientific institutions, are published and submitted to the General Assembly, which may return them to the Commission for further study, may take note of or adopt them for the benefit of governments, jurists and people, may recommend them to members with a view to the conclusion of a convention, or may convoke a conference competent to formulate them as conventions for signature and ratification by states.

These alternative procedures appear desirable, and it would seem that the last should not be undertaken until a draft has enlisted a high degree of informal consent as manifested by Assembly debate and the comments of governments. Premature effort at formal codification may result in failure of agreement because of diverse political interests of states at the moment, thus making the customary law on the subject less certain than it was before. This was illustrated by the failure of agreement, both in the Hague Conference of 1930 and the Geneva Conference of 1958, on the limits of the territorial sea.

The Commission originally consisted of fifteen jurists, largely from countries of European civilization, and its financial support has been such as to permit sessions of only limited duration. It is believed that the limitations under which the Commission has worked indicate insufficient appreciation of the importance of its function, which is less that of codifying law than of adapting that law to new conditions.

Among these conditions are the entry into the community of nations of a number of Communist states and many Asian and African states most of which were formerly colonies. These states, which constitute half the members of the United Nations, profess ancient or modern religions, philosophies, or ideologies different from those of the states of Western Europe, which evolved international law since the sixteenth century from cultures based on Greek philosophy, Roman law, and Christian religion and from political practices of colonial expansion, Machiavellian politics, and capitalistic economy. It is clear that if international law is to be a law which commands the confidence of all states it must take account of the diverse philosophies and institutions of justice of the states of non-European civilization. The Asian and African states believe existing international law gives too much weight to colonialism, racialism, legalism, and militarism; the Communist states believe it gives too much weight to capitalism; and the Latin-American states have long believed it gives too much weight to economic imperialism.

Another condition is the development in all parts of the world of democracies, giving a larger role to public opinion, to individual liberty, to general welfare, and to constitutional limitations upon government than did the absolute monarchies of sixteenth- and seventeenth-century Europe whose relations international law was originally designed to regulate. Furthermore, many people, even in the Western countries, believe that traditional international law gives too much weight to the authority of government and the sovereignty of territorial states and not enough to human rights, international trade, and social and economic progress.

Still other conditions are the unparalleled destructiveness of weapons, the extraordinary reduction of communication, travel and transportation time, the increase in economic and social interdependence of peoples, and the vulnerability of every state to military attack, economic embargo, seditious propaganda, and subversive infiltration from distant areas. All peoples are convinced that international law has been too permissive of military aggression and other forms of intervention, sometimes called "indirect aggression," and that it must give more effective protection to states against such action.

If the International Law Commission is to perform the task of adapting international law to these new conditions, it should engage the full time of its members. In 1957 its original membership of fifteen was increased to twenty-one in order to make possible an adequate representation of the main forms of civilization and of the principal legal systems of the world as required by the constitution of the Commission. At present the Commission includes seven persons from Western Europe and North America, four from Latin America, seven from Asia and Africa, and three from Communist countries. Persons expert in comparative civilizations, comparative law, political science, economics, and technology might be attached to the Commission as advisers to emphasize the Commission's function in "developing" international law. The Commission itself consists mainly of jurists, supposedly expert in the rules of traditional international law and thus emphasizing its "codification" function.

It would appear that the very diversity of national cultures requires that primary weight be given to the autonomy of territorial states. There should be a presumption that states are free to make and enforce law each within its own territory, but the new conditions may require some modification of this sovereignty in the interest of the outlawing of war, the regulation of transnational propaganda, international trade, self-determination of peoples, the responsibility of states for injury to aliens, fundamental human rights, and cooperation in the use of atomic energy, of international rivers, of the high sea, the bed of the sea, polar regions and outer space, and of unequally distributed economic resources.

It is particularly important that in developing international law the problem of the areal extension of rules of law should be considered. Some rules, such as those concerning war and subversive intervention, should be universal while others may be susceptible of effective operation among a limited number of states of similar culture or economic development or occupying a particular region. The Commission should make it clear what scope of acceptance should be necessary to make a rule effective, and what rules are susceptible of reservation and what are not.

Furthermore, draft conventions should consider that the enforcement of rules of international law is facilitated if the rules apply to individuals rather than to states. International law has assumed that states are its only subjects, but the practice of holding a state responsible for injury to aliens within its territory; the making of conventions in the interest of aborigines, minorities, labor, women, and other groups of persons; the provisions of the Charter concerning human rights; and the war criminal trials after World Wars I and II indicate a trend toward extending international law to the individual. While states are presumed to be sovereign each in its own territory, there is nothing to prevent a state assuming obligations to protect or punish individuals in its jurisdiction or even permitting international agencies to protect or punish such individuals. In this matter the superior efficiency of extending the law to individuals must be balanced against the reluctance of states of very diverse cultures to accept regulation of their internal action by universal standards or by international agencies functioning in their territory.

The United Nations Charter gives the Security Council responsibility for formulating plans for the regulation of armaments and for making agreements with members for international security forces, and the General Assembly has power to make recommendations on any question or matter within the scope of the Charter (Article 10), on general principles of cooperation for the maintenance of international peace and security including the principles governing disarmament and the regulation of armaments (Article 11), on political cooperation and the codification and development of international law, and on the promotion of international cooperation in the economic, social, cultural, educational, and health fields and the realization of human rights and fundamental freedoms (Article 13). It also has power to supervise the administration of trusteeship areas and non-self-governing territories and to apportion contributions and approve the budget of the United Nations (Article 17).

The effect of resolutions in pursuance of these powers is controversial but in some cases, especially in regard to trusteeships and the budget, resolutions may be of binding effect. In other cases, if approved with substantial unanimity, they may amount to general recognition of a new state or government, a threat to the peace, breach of the peace or act of aggression, or a rule of law, in which case, according to customary international law, the decision or rule is generally binding. The International Court of Justice has considered the effect of General Assembly resolutions and further juristic consideration should be given to the possibility of this process of international legislation. Such consideration may suggest increased use of this procedure of lawmaking, but in the main it is probable that the development of international law will have to rely not on authority but on intelligence. Formulations should be self-executing because they are of a quality to command voluntary support of states by convincing them that general observance would contribute to realizing national interests and the conceptions of justice of each. General treaties prepared in international conferences and establishing international organizations and rules of law binding only the states that ratify them have this character and will probably continue to be the principal method of international legislation.

INTERNATIONAL ADJUDICATION

The judicial process can be improved by a more extensive utilization of the advisory jurisdiction of the International Court of Justice by United Nations agencies, by more frequent recommendation by such agencies that states accept the Court's jurisdiction or that of an *ad hoc* arbitral tribunal for the settlement of disputes, and by improvement of procedures of the Security Council and the General Assembly for investigating, mediating, conciliating, and inducing agreement in disputes or situations before them. More important, however, for this purpose may be the development and codification of international law and improvement of the composition and procedures of agencies of adjudication so that the states will be more willing to accept obligations to submit to adjudication and more certain to carry out the decisions of such agencies.

The use of the International Court of Justice, whether for advisory opinion or for the decision of disputes, has been less frequent since World War II than in the interwar period, as has acceptance without destructive reservation of the optional clause of the Statute of the International Court of Justice. Resort to *ad hoc* arbitration or acceptance of recommendations of international political agencies also has been less frequent.

The United Nations has been more effective in stopping fighting than in settling disputes. Consequently, many situations have arisen since World War II in which cease-fire lines have been established but the disputes remain, continually threatening a new outbreak of hostilities. Such lines *de jure* or *de facto* exist in Germany, Korea, Vietnam, Palestine, Kashmir, Indonesia (according to that state which claims West Irian), and China (both governments of which claim that Formosa and the coastal islands of Quemoy and Matsu are part of China). Similar situations of longer duration may be noted in the continued claims of Argentina to the Falkland Islands, of Guatemala to Belize, of Iran to Bahrein Island, and of the trusteeship territory of Somaliland to adjacent territories in Ethiopia and British Somaliland. Claims of Greece and Turkey in respect to Cyprus have, for the moment been settled, but the claim of Algeria to independence has not been settled nor has fighting been stopped.

Clearly better procedures for the settlement of disputes are needed. The Charter suggests that in case a dispute threatens international peace and security the parties "first of all, seek a solution by negotiation, enquiry, mediation, conciliation, arbitration, judicial settlement, resort to regional agencies or arrangements, or other peaceful means of their own choice." The Security Council is authorized to "call upon" the parties to settle their dispute by these means (Article 33) and if they fail to do so may, on its own initiative or that of a member or a nonmember or of the Secretary-General, investigate to determine whether the dispute is likely to endanger international peace and security (Article 34). If it discovers such a danger it may go further and "recommend" appropriate procedures or methods of adjustment (Article 36) and if these fail it may "recommend such terms of settlement as it may consider appropriate" (Article 37). Even if there is no danger to international peace and security it may make such recommendations at the request of the parties (Article 38). These procedures, which look toward settlement by agreement of the parties rather than by the application of law, are available to the General Assembly in any case in which the Security Council does not function (Articles 11, 12). Settlement by agreement is deemed to be preferable because the process of making is more flexible and the settlement if made is more likely to be observed. Procedures for effecting such an agreement can doubtlessly be improved by broader commitments of states to permit investigatory and conciliatory agencies to function within their territory, by more skill in the application of mediatorial or conciliatory procedures, by better understanding of the circumstances under which confidential negotiations or the invocation of world public opinion is desirable, and by the segregation of the factual, legal, political, and ideological aspects of the dispute in order that the most suitable procedure can be utilized for each aspect.

Procedures dependent upon persuading the parties to agree may not result in settlement, in which case the utilization of adjudication may be useful. The Charter provides that the Security Council (or the General Assembly) "should also take into consideration that legal disputes should as a general rule be referred by the parties to the International Court of Justice" (Article 36). This does not provide a procedure of compulsory jurisdiction, but it would appear that when both parties rest their contentions on issues of fact or law the United Nations might more frequently exert strong pressure to induce them to submit the issue to adjudication. If they refuse to do so, the United Nations may frequently find it possible to submit questions for advisory opinion, though this also requires consent of the parties if the question concerns primarily an issue between the parties rather than an issue of United Nations procedure (Eastern Carelia Case). As indicated in the Mosul Case, the two may be so closely related that the Court will be willing to deal with the substance of the dispute in answering a procedural question.

A claim of domestic jurisdiction is usually of this type because it involves an issue of United Nations competence to intervene, though its determination may involve the issue in dispute between the parties. The United Nations has not asked for advisory opinions on this issue as frequently as did the League of Nations, justifying itself by the different phraseology of the article on the subject in the Charter as compared with the Covenant, with the unfortunate result that the organs of the United Nations, exercising a political judgment, have often passed resolutions on matters which the state criticized considers within its domestic jurisdiction and consequently has refused to observe the resolution. It seems clear that the question of whether a matter is within the domestic jurisdiction of a state is a question of international law. Its answer depends on whether the discretion of the state claiming domestic jurisdiction is qualified by obligations under general international law or a treaty to which it is a party. In so far as that is the case the matter is not domestic, because in principle no state can determine its own obligations under international law. For this reason it would seem advisable for United Nations organs to adopt the practice of the League of Nations of asking for advisory opinions on claims of domestic jurisdiction. This is true not only because it might contribute to the settlement of the dispute but also because it would contribute to settling one of the most important questions of international law, namely, the juridical line determining, on the one hand, the limits of state sovereignty and, on the other, the limits of intervention by the United Nations and by other states.

While the rule of law may be increased by improved practices of United Nations organs in dealing with the settlement of disputes and situations, it may also be increased by improved practices of states. The reason for the diminished use of adjudication in the postwar period as compared with the interwar period appears to be that states have less confidence in the Court and the law it applies and are more reluctant to risk an adverse decision on interests which they regard as vital to their security or their faith. The factors of change in the world, already referred to, seem to account for these changes in attitudes. The Asian, African, and Communist states, which are more numerous and important in the recent period, believe the Court and the law it applies reflect in too great measure concepts and values indigenous to the civilization of Western Europe. Improvements in international law of the type already referred to and improvements in the Court giving a larger weight to Asian, African, and Communist judges would doubtless increase the willingness of these states to submit controversies to its jurisdiction but it might at the same time decrease the willingness of the Western states to do so.

In this situation of great ideological differences among different states and among different areas of the world it may be that arbitral tribunals established by the parties to a dispute, in some cases applying rules of law agreed to by the instrument of submission, might be more suitable than the International Court of Justice. While such arbitral awards would not be as valuable for stabilizing international law as would opinions of the International Court of Justice, they might prove more useful for settling disputes and might inject into international law ideas better adapted to the changing world. It is to be noted that because of the extensiveness of the sources from which it can draw, not only treaties and customs but also "general principles of law recognized by civilized nations" and the opinions of jurists

and judges, the Court has a considerable opportunity to develop the
law. In proportion, however, as it utilizes these less precise sources
the results of its adjudication become less predictable and less acceptable to states which fear that their basic ideologies will not be
given due weight. The Soviet Union has tended to give major weight
in international law to treaties. Arbitral awards would also have the
advantage that the parties would be more able to discount defeat
in advance and thus would be less likely to resist an adverse award.

Efforts should, however, continue to extend the compulsory jurisdiction of the International Court of Justice by inducing a wider
and less reserved ratification of the optional clause. The United
States reservation on questions which it deems domestic has been
followed by several states although it is contrary to the spirit of the
Statute and probably to the letter. The Statute provides explicitly
that "in the event of a dispute as to whether the Court has jurisdiction, the matter shall be settled by the decision of the Court"
(Article 36, paragraph 6). The American reservation of a veto on the
interpretation by the Court of general treaties to which the United
States is a party is equally destructive.

Progress in developing the Court's compulsory jurisdiction is retarded not only by the skepticism of Eastern states and traditional
isolationism of the United States Senate but also by the cold war,
which has developed exaggerated fears among the great states that an
adverse decision may deteriorate their power or prestige, by the fear
of new states that their recently won sovereignty may be impaired,
and by fear of all states, in an age of exaggerated concern for national-
isms and ideologies, that their national way of life and ideological or
religious faith may be qualified. This situation has given new force
to the old reservation of vital interests and national honor in agreements to submit to arbitration. Moderation of these obstructions to
the advance of adjudication can only be brought about by political
tranquilization, more tolerant attitudes, more perfect adaptation of
international law to national interests and world conditions, and
greater confidence in the capacity of the United Nations to fulfill
its prime purpose of maintaining international peace and security.

INTERNATIONAL EXECUTIVE AUTHORITY

The executive procedures of the society of nations might be improved by a clarification of the Charter provisions defining the obligations of members to refrain from the use or threat of force, to cooper-

ate for the maintenance of these obligations, especially by contributing to a permanent international force, and to accept the investigatory and coordinating authority of the United Nations organs for this purpose.

The executive competence of United Nations organs is limited. It consists of the authority of the Security Council to determine the existence of any threat to the peace, breach of the peace or act of aggression, to call upon the parties concerned to comply with such provisional measures as it deems necessary or desirable, to decide what measures of nonmilitary or military coercion are to be employed to maintain or to restore international peace and security, and to call upon members to apply such measures, in the case of military actions, only in accord with explicit commitments which they may have made. These specific grants of authority are buttressed by the general provision that the members confer on the Security Council primary responsibility for the maintenance of international peace and security and agree that in carrying out its duties under this responsibility it acts on their behalf (Article 24). The members also agree to accept and carry out decisions of the Security Council in accordance with the Charter (Articles 25, 48). Terms of the Charter indicate that the General Assembly has a secondary responsibility in the field of international peace and security, and this responsibility was implemented by the Uniting for Peace Resolution of the General Assembly in November, 1950, utilized not only in the later stages of the Korean incident but also in the Suez and Hungarian incidents of 1956 and the Lebanese and Jordan incidents of 1958. It seems clear that the General Assembly can make recommendations (but not decisions) like those prescribed for the Security Council, but only in case the latter body, in the judgment of the General Assembly itself, is unable to function in a particular situation. The frequent incapacity of the Security Council to function because of the veto has cast the major burden upon the General Assembly in executing United Nations functions for the maintenance of peace.

The value of an embodied UN force to patrol cease-fire lines, protect UN agencies, and tranquilize disturbed areas is widely recognized. Such a force has been used in Kashmir, Palestine, and Sinai, and there is little doubt of the capacity of the Security Council and the General Assembly to provide such a "subsidiary agency" if the General Assembly is ready to make the necessary appropriations.

The fact that the General Assembly cannot decide but can only recommend often leaves the ultimate decision for effective executive action with the governments of states and makes it important that the concept of aggression should be clearly defined in order that member states shall have no doubt when the purposes and principles of the Charter impose upon them a moral, if not a legal, duty to act.

Such a definition is less important if provisional measures called for by the Security Council or the General Assembly succeed in bringing about a cease fire or armistice. But under the Charter such measures can be recommended only if there is a threat to, or breach of, international peace, and consequently the appropriate United Nations organ is faced by the problem of whether hostilities or threats are domestic or international. Only in the latter case may the United Nations intervene. States are obliged to refrain from threat or use of force only in international relations. If a government threatens or uses force to maintain internal order, the state is presumably under no international obligation and consequently the matter is domestic in principle. However, internal hostilities may threaten international hostilities; if they do, then an international obligation is involved and the United Nations may intervene. Such a judgment depends on consequences and is necessarily political rather than legal. It is a striking fact that in the majority of cases in which the United Nations has called for a cease fire it has been contended that the hostilities were domestic. This was true of the situations in Palestine, Indonesia, Kashmir, and Korea.

If provisional measures fail and hostilities proceed, the United Nations must face the issue of aggression in order to determine on which side UN forces should be used. This is a legal issue. The problem must be solved whether one or both of the governments engaged in hostilities has violated its obligation not to use force in international relations.

The practice of United Nations organs, as of the League of Nations organs, makes it clear that if one party accepts and the other rejects provisional measures the latter is presumed to be the aggressor. The presumption may, however, be overthrown, and it may be necessary to decide in principle which is the aggressor. Opinions of war crimes tribunals, of the International Law Commission, and of many jurists and the practice of United Nations agencies indicate that aggression refers only to an illegal use of armed force, thus excluding subversive propaganda, infiltration, embargo, or other forms of nonmilitary intervention sometimes called "indirect aggression." These opinions indicate that any use of armed force, authorized or tolerated by a *de facto* or a *de jure* government, across an international frontier or an internationally recognized armistice line is aggression, unless it can be justified by a necessity for self-defense, by authority of the United Nations, or by invitation of the state in which the armed forces operate.

These three justifications require elaboration. Probably defensive necessity may go beyond "an armed attack" referred to in Article 51 of the Charter to an "instant and overwhelming" danger of such attack, recognized in customary international law. It also seems probable that the authority of the United Nations may be sufficiently manifested by a recommendation of the General Assembly as well as by a decision of the Security Council. The invitation by a government can justify armed invasion only if at the moment the government is capable of representing the state. Such capacity seems to imply actual control of the state's territory. A *de facto* or a *de jure* government in time of insurrection or civil war cannot speak for the state in this matter. International law does not forbid domestic revolution. Consequently, if foreign governments were permitted to intervene on the invitation of either faction in such circumstances they would be impugning the independence of the state. On the other hand, if a government has lost control of much of its territory because of external aggression or subversive intervention, there can be no doubt of the right of other states to respond to an invitation for assistance. Thus in situations such as that of Lebanon in the summer of 1958 the justifiability of intervention on the invitation of a *de jure* government would depend on whether that government was at the moment faced primarily by domestic rebellion or by foreign intervention. However, as already noted, this principle should not prevent intervention to preserve the peace by United Nations organs in a domestic rebellion which in its judgment is likely to endanger international peace and security.

The need of assuring the willing cooperation of states in suppressing aggression makes it important that there be no doubt when aggression has occurred, and this implies clear definition. The United Nations has failed to achieve general agreement on such a definition because of the insistence by important states that "indirect aggression" be included. It seems clear, however, that if propaganda, subversion, or infiltration were regarded as forms of aggression and therefore as justifying armed reaction in defense, all barriers to war set up by the Charter would be eliminated. These forms of hostile intervention may require regulation, but the methods must be very different from those appropriate to stopping armed invasion. The term "aggression" should therefore be confined to cases where there has been a breach of the peace or an immediate threat to the peace in the military sense.

This discussion indicates that international executive authority is at present very limited. It may be that under Article 94 of the Charter the Security Council may decide upon coercive measures to give effect to judgments of the International Court of Justice and that either the Security Council or the General Assembly may make recommendations to this effect, but this conclusion is doubtful unless the situation is such that defiance of the Court's judgment endangers international peace and security. In general the Charter permits coercive action either by the United Nations or by its members only to preserve the peace. Peace, as has been noted, takes precedence of justice. States are not permitted to engage in reprisals or other coercive measures to remedy what they deem injustices nor are United Nations organs authorized to recommend that they do so. In the theory of the Charter the maintenance of justice and of law depends upon good faith and persuasion rather than coercion in so far as relations between states are concerned. It is for this reason that it is desirable that international law be extended in larger measure to individuals against whom it is easier to enforce the law than against states.

INTERNATIONAL ADMINISTRATION

The administrative processes of the society of nations might be improved by the continuous development of the procedures of the United Nations and the specialized agencies for studying social, economic, and cultural problems and for assembling, analyzing, and distributing information so that governments and peoples will be more aware of the social, economic, and cultural problems of the world, more certain of the obligations of the state in this field, more enlightened in appraising their national interests, more aware of the requirements of the changing world, more informed of the actions and negligences of states and international agencies which obstruct progress, and more willing to cooperate with other nations to realize common goals.

Such improvements of governmental and public opinion should contribute to the negotiation and general ratification of conventions for realizing the social, economic, and cultural objectives of the United Nations and the specialized agencies and for increasing the appropriations for, and efficiency of, the administrative services of these organizations, thus assuring better drafting and more effective administration of such conventions as well as more effective investigatory and informative services.

Some competent students of international relations believe that the development of effective international cooperation and administration in "nonpolitical matters" is the essential means for developing a sense of world community among governments and peoples which is a necessary prerequisite of an international legal order. Others point out, however, that so long as the world is divided by political rivalries and expectations of war the progress of nonpolitical cooperation will be limited because each power, or power bloc, will seek to mobilize its economic, social, and cultural resources for the augmentation of its own power or prestige and the elimination of those of its rival rather than for contributing to human progress and welfare. Furthermore, powerful nationalistic convictions which regard the maintenance of the national culture, ideology, and way of life as more important than human progress and welfare are likely to be suspicious of international cooperation which would tend to subordinate national values to universal values and perhaps to disintegrate the national culture.

These considerations suggest that the so-called "nonpolitical" objectives of the Charter are in reality highly political. This suggestion is supported by the reluctance of states affected by vigorous national ideologies, such as communism, to engage in international cooperation for such objectives and their original desire to exclude such objectives from the scope of the United Nations. The Soviet Union has indicated that it fears that international cooperation in nonpolitical matters may encroach upon its Communist ideology and its national policy even more than cooperation in such political matters as the prevention of aggression, the pacific settlement of international disputes, and disarmament. However, its eventual acceptance of the Charter provisions for nonpolitical cooperation, its eventual entry into many of the specialized agencies, and its recent interest in cultural exchanges and economic agreements indicate a possible shift in this position.

In any case it seems clear that a moderation of claims to absolute sovereignty, of rising international tensions, of excessive political rivalries, and of exaggerated sentiments of nationalism is a necessary prerequisite of effective cooperation in nonpolitical matters.

This might be facilitated by more careful study of proposed administrative activities of the United Nations to ascertain whether the United Nations action is indispensable to the function, whether it would be convenient but not indispensable, or whether the matter can best be left to each state. While in the legal sense domestic jurisdiction refers to all matters in which a state has not undertaken international obligations either by treaty or under general international law, in the political sense it refers to those matters in which international action is neither indispensable nor convenient and which should, therefore, be left to the states. A more careful consideration by United Nations committees of the degree of indispensability or convenience of United Nations action before recommending further study or resolution might reduce the fear of states that their proper sphere of domestic jurisdiction may be encroached upon.

The United Nations Charter gives first place in its objectives to political activities such as the preservation of peace, the settlement of disputes, and the self-determination of peoples, but it attaches great importance to promoting "social progress and better standards of life in larger freedom" and to achieving "international cooperation in solving international problems of an economic, social, cultural or humanitarian character." A large proportion of its revenues and effort is devoted to these objectives which constitute the main purpose of the dozen specialized agencies and the International Atomic Energy Agency.

The General Assembly is authorized to "initiate studies and make recommendations for the purpose of . . . promoting international cooperation in the economic, social, cultural, educational, and health fields, and assisting in the realization of human rights and fundamental freedoms for all without distinction as to race, sex, language or religion" (Article 13).

A more detailed statement of these objectives is offered in Chapter IX of the Charter and "all Members pledge themselves to take joint and separate action in cooperation with the Organization" for their achievement (Article 56).

The Economic and Social Council is established as a principal organ of the United Nations to study and recommend in this field, to set up specialized and regional commissions, and to coordinate the activities of the specialized agencies. Regional arrangements primarily for political purposes are authorized by the Charter and these arrangements, such as the Organization of American States, have also engaged in extensive programs of nonpolitical cooperation.

The administrative problems of the United Nations, the specialized agencies, and the regional agencies in recruiting, organizing, and instructing the more than ten thousand international civil servants engaged in promoting nonpolitical international cooperation cannot be discussed here. But in so far as these problems are solved and result in effective action toward stated goals the effort undoubtedly contributes to the development of the solidarity of the society of nations and thereby establishes conditions favorable to increasing the role of law in that society. The balanced program of the United Nations giving due emphasis to political and nonpolitical objectives is well calculated to "establish conditions under which justice and respect for the obligations arising from treaties and other sources of international law can be maintained." A moral solidarity of the community of nations cannot be developed unless political rivalries are moderated and, on the other hand, such rivalries cannot be moderated unless there is some development of moral solidarity throughout the entire community. The two efforts must go hand in hand and through their success they will develop both the society and the law of nations.

CONCLUSION

The foregoing considerations suggest that legislative procedures of the United Nations might be improved by increased support of, and technical advisors for, the International Law Commission, and by increased recognition of circumstances in which resolutions of the United Nations General Assembly have legal authority.

The adjudicative procedures of the United Nations might be improved by a greater use of advisory opinions by the political organs of the United Nations, especially when the plea of domestic jurisdiction is raised, by withdrawal of destructive reservations to acceptances of the optional clause of the World Court Statute by states, especially by the United States, and by continued development of procedures of fact-finding, mediation, conciliation, and arbitration for the settlement of international disputes.

The executive procedures of the United Nations might be improved by a General Assembly definition of aggression, confining it to illegal use of armed force, and by the establishment of an embodied United Nations force. The problems of indirect aggression, referring to subversive propaganda, infiltration and economic pressure, are important and might be dealt with by a United Nations monitoring of radio communications when complained of. The concept of "indirect aggression" should not be confused with the concept of "aggression," which is significant because it implies counteraction by defensive use of armed force clearly not permissible under Article 51 of the Charter in response to "indirect aggression." It would seem desirable, therefore, to designate the latter concept by a different name, such as "subversive intervention."

The administrative procedures of the United Nations might be improved and made more palatable to members by distinction of the meaning of domestic jurisdiction in the legal and political senses. Concern lest a creeping process of international legislation and administration unduly encroach upon a state's domestic jurisdiction in the political sense might be mitigated if United Nations organs and committees carefully studied the indispensability and convenience of United Nations action on a proposed subject before making recommendations. Fear of actual United Nations "intervention" should be relieved if actions of United Nations political bodies directly critical of a state's behavior were always preceded by obtaining an advisory opinion in case the state pleads that the matter is, in a legal sense, within its domestic jurisdiction.

These suggestions, designed to increase the role of law in international relations through improved functioning of the United Nations, are apart from political measures within or outside of the United Nations aimed directly at reducing international tensions, settling international disputes, stabilizing the power equilibrium, moderating the arms race, and ameliorating the atmosphere of fear and suspicion between states of diverse ideology which has characterized the world since World War II. The success of diplomacy in achieving these objectives would contribute immeasurably to the carrying out of these suggestions.

THE ROLE OF POLITICS IN THE

ORGANIZATION OF PEACE

by Arthur N. Holcombe

THE QUEST FOR PEACE IN THE NUCLEAR AGE

This study in the organization of peace begins with the assumption that the quest for peace in the nuclear age will continue to be based on the purposes of the United Nations and the principles set forth in its Charter. Though the Charter was framed by statesmen who could not know what the nuclear age had in store for mankind, their purposes are the right purposes for an age in which war is "unthinkable," as President Eisenhower has bravely declared, meaning of course war between powers armed with the most modern weapons. The principles of the Charter are likewise well suited to these purposes and will continue to be well suited to them as long as the liquidation of so-called sovereign states also is unthinkable. To look forward to a more distant future is untimely. The Organization under the Charter, together with the affiliated specialized agencies forming the United Nations family, is a going concern. The immediate problem is to keep it going and to make it a more serviceable instrument of the purposes of mankind in this new and terrifying age.

By assumption the problem of keeping the United Nations family alive and active is not too difficult. In fact there is plenty of evidence to support the view that this assumption is both realistic and valid. The independent states of the world, with the sole exception of Switzerland, which have been in a position to apply for membership have done so. No state has sought to withdraw from the Organization. The Soviet Union for a time withdrew its representative from the Security Council in order to emphasize its dissatisfaction with the refusal of that body to seat a representative of Communist China. But the fighting in Korea quickly brought him back. The French delegation has walked out of the General Assembly to indicate its displeasure at a decision to consider the Algerian problem, but there has been no disposition to give up membership in the Organization. The Union of South Africa sulked for a time in the face of universal hostility to its racial policies, but it held on doggedly to its rights under the Charter. At the Thirteenth General Assembly in 1958 there was a larger attendance of prime ministers and foreign ministers than ever before, attesting a general disposition to take its work seriously. The Organization is more than holding its own under the strenuous conditions of the modern world.

But the problem of making the Organization a more serviceable instrument of the purposes of mankind in the nuclear age is more troublesome. To be sure, there has been no third world war since the establishment of the United Nations Organization. But talk of war between the major powers has not ceased; indeed it has grown unconscionably since the beginning of the nuclear arms race between the superpowers. Along with the growing talk has gone the mounting fear of another world war. It is impossible to end the fear without abating the talk and it is impossible to abate the talk without checking the arms race. Persistent attempts to check the arms race have been followed by a rapidly expanding production of arms and a corresponding growth of tension. It requires no profound insight into the causes of war to foresee the end of an unchecked and ever-accelerating arms race. The arms will be used. To prevent this result the United Nations Organization was created. Up to now, however, the world's diplomats and politicians who have attended the meetings of the Security Council and the General Assembly, the organs charged with the principal responsibility for keeping the peace, have not been able to make effective use of the facilities for peacemaking under the Charter.

There are many opportunities under the United Nations Charter for peace-loving politicians, even if politics be defined in the narrowest sense of the term. In this sense politics may be conceived as concerted efforts to influence elections and appointments to the offices within the Organization and also to influence the deliberations of the organs charged with responsibility for determining its policies.

The principal elective offices are the Secretary-General, the President of the General Assembly, the nonpermanent members of the Security Council, the vice-presidents of the General Assembly and the chairmen of its standing committees, and also the judges of the International Court of Justice. Others, less important, are the members of the Economic and Social Council and the nondesignated members of the Trusteeship Council. These elections make much work for United Nations politicians. A glance at the record shows that the same tendency exists to form factions and parties in United Nations elections as in those of member states with representative institutions operated under a system of free enterprise in politics.

Consider, for example, the elections to the Security Council. Ever since the outbreak of the cold war the parties to this conflict have exerted themselves to obtain as much representation as possible in this principal organ of the United Nations. The Communist party, if the delegations from the Communist member states may be so described, possesses one permanent seat and in addition has always contended that Eastern Europe, a region from which most of the delegations have been Communist, was entitled to one of the elective seats. This contention has been successfully challenged since the early years of the cold war by the combination of delegations which has been headed by the United States. In the year 1958 the Soviet Union was the only Communist state with a vote in the Security Council. Eight votes were controlled by the United States and military allies of the United States under the NATO and SEATO treaties and other treaties or agreements of a similar character. One vote was controlled by Iraq, a party to the Baghdad Pact, with which the United States maintained an informal relationship until the July revolution in Iraq ended Iraqi participation in the Pact. The only Security Council member in 1958 which maintained its independence of both the major parties throughout the year was Sweden. Yet there were thirty member states which professed to be neutrals in the cold war. It is evident that the American party, if that be the proper term for the combination which has acquired such disproportionate representation in the Security Council, had played politics in Security Council elections with impressive results. At the next Security Council elections Sweden was replaced by Italy, a member of NATO, and Iraq by Tunisia, one of the most Western-oriented of the Arab states. In 1959, but for the Soviet veto, a system of military alliances, holding a bare majority of the votes in the General Assembly, would have possessed complete control of the Security Council.

The record of elections to other offices also is significant. Perhaps the most impressive exhibition of American leadership in this branch of United Nations politics was the filling of a vacancy in the International Court of Justice, caused by the death of a Chinese judge, at a special election in December, 1956. Elections to this Court require an absolute majority of the votes in the Security Council, regardless of the distinction between permanent and nonpermanent members, and in the General Assembly, each body voting separately. The United States delegation supported a Nationalist Chinese to succeed the deceased member of the Court. The opposing candidate was a Japanese jurist, nominated from a country which had just been admitted to the United Nations after a long and hard struggle. The Nationalist Chinese candidacy symbolized one of the most divisive issues in United Nations politics. The Japanese was a symbol of reconciliation. By means of the most resolute arm-twisting, as high-pressure electioneering is called in the jargon of contemporary diplomacy, the election of the Chinese was procured. The margin of victory in the General Assembly was as narrow as possible, but the combination of states under the leadership of the United States was eventually successful.

The influence of politics on the policies of the United Nations is less easy to measure. One test is to analyze the process of pursuing the primary purpose of the Organization, the maintenance of international peace and security. The framers of the Charter provided three principal methods of maintaining peace and security, each of which calls for investigation. The first of these was to give the General Assembly a general, though not unlimited, commission to inquire into situations constituting threats to the peace and to recommend measures for reducing tension. The experience of the General Assembly with this method during the years since the Organization was first established should throw light on the role of politics in the formation of policy up to now and help in determining what it should be in the future.

The record shows that the system of majority party politics, as practiced in the United States, does not produce the same results in terms of General Assembly recommendations as in the filling of elective offices. In the first place, a two-thirds vote is necessary for important actions in the General Assembly and such a majority is ordinarily beyond the capacity of a majority party. In recent years American leadership has scored some extraordinary successes in the General Assembly, such as keeping out the representatives of Communist China; but these successes did not require a two-thirds vote. The outstanding American triumph in the General Assembly was the adoption of the Uniting for Peace Resolution in November, 1950, by means of which member states supporting the international police action in Korea assured themselves of the practical capacity to maintain their control of that and similar operations at all times if they possessed a two-thirds majority of the votes. Six years later the necessary two-thirds majorities were readily forthcoming to condemn the Soviet Union for resorting to military force in Hungary, but there was no support for an international police action in this case as in Korea. In the Emergency Special Session of the Assembly, called in August, 1958, to consider the situation resulting from the American and British military interventions in Lebanon and Jordan, the United States was no more able than the Soviet Union to win a two-thirds majority for its proposals. The winning recommendations had to be initiated by member states not affiliated with either of the major parties and gained general acceptance under leadership operating outside the framework of a two-party system.

In measuring the influence of American leadership on the policies of the General Assembly it is necessary to distinguish between positive and negative action. To defeat an important measure in the General Assembly only one more than a third of the votes is needed. In preventing undesired action, such as the establishment of a special United Nations fund for the economic development of underdeveloped regions by the investment of venture capital in large amounts, the United States has seemed to be uniformly successful, though the practice of abstaining from doubtful votes, such as those on issues arising from the cold war between the colonial powers and the anticolonial states, makes any general statement inappropriate. The record of action on positive policies is more difficult of appraisal. Some apparent American triumphs, as on recent proposals to set up special commissions on disarmament and outer space, were rendered fruitless by the refusal of the Soviet Union to participate in the work of commissions the composition of which was unsatisfactory to it. Under the existing conditions in the General Assembly, as will be shown later in greater detail, the member states which profess to be neutral in the cold war between Communist and anti-Communist states, possess a veto over the policies of the major parties to that war and thereby constitute a third force of substantial, though unpredictable, importance in United Nations politics.

Moreover, the fact that important actions of the General Assembly in matters of policy take the form of recommendations greatly influences the role of politics as practiced by the major parties. A recommendation is merely a provisional action and depends for its efficacy upon its acceptance by the governments of the member states. The practical utility of recommendations is contingent upon their moral force, and after their adoption by the General Assembly the indispensable moral forces are still to be mobilized and put into effective operation. Hence the unequal results of General Assembly recommendations in different cases. In dealing with the Chinese "volunteers" in Korea in 1951 or with the Soviet Union's "regulars" in Hungary in 1956, the record of the General Assembly looks very different from that relating to the interventions at Suez in the same year or two years later in Lebanon and Jordan. The moral force of its recommendations is not the same in the Communist dictatorships as in the Western democracies. Under such conditions action upon General Assembly recommendations cannot be definitive and therefore cannot enter into the calculations of United Nations politicians in the same way as does action upon proposed measures in the normal legislative process. Instead of normal politics there is propaganda.

The second method of maintaining international peace and security provided by the framers of the Charter is the pacific settlement of disputes under the authority of the Security Council. This method is even more unworkable by a majority party within the Council than that of recommendations by the General Assembly. Any proposed action can be blocked not only by the veto of one of the permanent members of the Council but also by what amounts to a veto in the hands of any five of the six elective members. Minorities of one major power or five lesser states may render the majority of the Council helpless to proceed in accordance with the expectations of the framers. Any combination of major powers and lesser states, amounting to five, can defeat a measure without invoking a major-power veto. It is not surprising, therefore, to find the record of the Security Council in the pacific settlement of contentious cases so nearly a blank. Effective action requires the consent of all the nuclear powers and the requirement of such consent in contentious cases, involving the interests of the two major parties, is incompatible with a system of majority rule. Again, instead of normal politics—if by normal politics is meant a system of effective leadership by a majority party—there is propaganda. The Security Council, like the International Court of Justice, can dispose of disputes of the kind the parties do not wish to fight over but it cannot maintain peace by the method of pacific settlement in those cases where there is a serious threat of war. On the record there is some evidence of useful mediation in minor disputes and abundant evidence of aggressive, though inconclusive, propaganda.

The third method of maintaining international peace provided by the framers of the Charter is that of decisions by the Security Council in cases involving breaches of the peace or acts of aggression. Just what constitutes an act of aggression has never been authoritatively determined, and now, since the events leading up to the landings in Lebanon and Jordan, comes the new category of indirect aggression to make confusion worse confounded. Breaches of the peace seem to be somewhat more readily recognizable, but the area of undefined, or ill-defined, discretionary authority on the part of the Council is further broadened by the provision that it may act in situations which constitute threats to the peace. What constitutes a threat must be a matter of opinion, and opinions in the Security Council are bound to differ in contentious cases. It is not surprising to find the record of the Security Council in dealing with these cases even more nearly a blank than in those involving attempts at pacific settlement. Instead of effective action there has been more propaganda and, naturally, more bitter propaganda. Apparently only the "unthinkability" of war, involving the use of the most modern weapons, restrains the major powers from letting these situations get out of control. Instead of atomic or nuclear war there is cold war.

It is evident that in the United Nations the role of politics, as politics is understood in countries where there is a system of free enterprise for party leaders, has been narrow. In the Security Council, which was intended to be the principal organ for keeping the peace, there can be no effective action in contentious cases involving the interests of the major powers except by unanimous consent of those powers. This means that either the rule of action to enforce peace by unanimous consent of the major powers must be abandoned or the effort to operate a partisan system of politics must be directed into other channels than those with which party politicians in the Western democracies are familiar. The former alternative is so unlikely to be adopted under the existing or anything like the existing circumstances that it may as well be dropped from further consideration. The latter alternative is more promising, but requires some fresh thinking on the part of Western politicians.

Meanwhile the United Nations Organization becomes a theater of aggressive propaganda instead of the scene of effective decisions promoting international peace and security. It is well suited to the conduct of a cold war, so well suited indeed that it has long contributed to keeping the war cold. Since the system of politics in the United Nations is so well suited to a world at cold war, it is doubtful if the cold war can be ended under such a system. To be sure, it is a great service of the United Nations that it has contributed so much toward substituting cold war for atomic or nuclear war. This is an achievement for which the world should be grateful, since the military experts are agreed that no department of defense can protect its people against devastation by the most modern weapons if war actually breaks out. They can only promise that the enemy will suffer even more than their own people, which is cold comfort in the nuclear age. Under such circumstances the maintenance of a state of cold war registers an important advance in civilization.

But the state of cold war is bound to be precarious. National leaders are irritated almost beyond endurance by the ceaseless bombardment of aggressive propaganda which always puts the actions of their opponents in the best possible light and their own in the worst. When they reject their opponents' diplomatic communications because of the alleged rudeness of the language employed therein, the strain on their nerves is obviously beginning to tell. The tension between their respective peoples mounts, and the cold war grows warmer. Moreover, the maintenance of peace is left too much at the hazard of the cheerless gloom of chance, a nervous radar operator misinterpreting a shadow on his screen, a mentally distraught bombardier dropping a bomb at the wrong moment, or a tragically misguided air force or ballistic missile commander accepting a self-imposed mission to bring intolerable suspense to an end.

Men who believe that by taking thought they can become masters of their fate will naturally turn to the problem of ending the cold war by a genuine peace. If atomic or nuclear war can be superseded by cold war, why cannot cold war in turn be superseded by something less precarious and more satisfying? Is it really necessary to endure the cold war until it gets superheated and the arms race ends in a universal holocaust? Why not try to make better use of rational political methods in the proceedings of the United Nations? In short, why not enlarge the role of politics in the organization of peace by suitable changes in the Charter or in the practices under the Charter?

The theme of this study is that the solution of the problem of keeping the peace in the nuclear age lies in expanding the role of politics in the organization of peace. The scope of United Nations politics must be made consistent with a role for United Nations politicians which will discourage aggressive propaganda in the Security Council and General Assembly and encourage constructive action in the interest of mankind. What changes in the structure and processes of the United Nations this may involve will be considered more closely in the following pages. The conclusion of this study, however, may be suggested here. It is that by suitable measures, designed to expand the role of politics in the activities of the United Nations, the Organization can be made a more serviceable instrument of human purposes in the years ahead. Its representative character can be so improved that it will command the confidence of the peoples of the world. Its procedures also can be improved so that parties to a serious dispute will expect a timely and reasonable decision on the merits of the case. The scene of its action can be made hospitable to the operations of a rational system of politics instead of merely furnishing constant incitement to aggressive propaganada. In short, the cold war can be ended by making the United Nations a more efficient instrument of the purposes embodied in the Charter.

THE ESSENTIAL NATURE OF INTERNATIONAL POLITICS

Every student of international politics is familiar with Clausewitz's often-quoted aphorism on the nature of war. The nature of peace can be described in a similar manner. If modern war is the continuation of national politics by other means, that is, by military operations instead of strictly political measures, modern peace is the continuation of international war by other means, that is, by political measures instead of military operations. Such verbal acrobatics is obviously a vain exercise unless one or the other of the basic terms is independently intelligible. Clausewitz seemed to assume that the politics of peace was generally understood. In modern times it is the politics of war which seems to be most familiar. Hence we speak of cold war rather than of cold or hot peace. The point is that there are important resemblances between the politics of war and the politics of peace. This is the second point in the study of the role of politics in the organization of peace.

The next topic for the student of international organization, therefore, is neither the nature of war nor the nature of peace, but the nature of politics, bellicose or pacific as the case may be. This is a topic concerning which the widest differences of opinion have been expressed. On the one hand, there are those writers who have contended that the essence of politics is always the perennial struggle for public office and an influential part in the management of public affairs. In other words, the essence of politics is the struggle for power. Whether those engaged most actively in this struggle do so out of regard for the public interest or merely in pursuance of their own private interests, these writers would assert, is a matter of secondary importance. These self-styled realists in the study of politics indeed often deny that there is such a thing as a public interest. The important reality in politics, according to their understanding of the nature of politics, is the contest between persons, or groups of persons, with conflicting interests for control of the powers of government in order the better to protect or promote their own particular interests. The victors in the struggle may speak of the triumph of the public interest over adverse private interests but, if so, their purpose is merely to cloak with a garment of respectability the naked reality of one special interest, or group of interests, dominating the scene of the struggle and exploiting its position for its own private gain.

At the opposite pole of opinion are those writers who defend the idea of a genuine public interest. They assert that the interests of the whole body of people in any political community are always as real as those of any part of the people and that they are or may be even more important. Through democratic processes the people of such a community can adjust the conflicts of interest between individuals or groups within it in such a manner as to protect or promote the general interests of the whole body. The standard list of public interests for Americans is that contained in the preamble to the United States Constitution. Justice, domestic tranquillity, the common defense, the general welfare, liberty: these are concepts which are full of meaning to Americans. These general concepts can be, and should be, particularized in more explicit forms; but, despite controversy over the particular forms, the conviction that governmental action ought to be, and often is, in the public interest is basic in the political faith of the American people.

It is not necessary to prove that governmental action always is in the public interest in order to maintain the belief in the validity of the concept. What is necessary is faith in the capacity of democratic peoples to establish political processes which offer acceptable assurances that the public interest can be made to prevail over the private and special interests which compete for political influence. Politics in a modern democracy, Americans think, is an art by which the people may promote the public interest if they can equip their state with suitable political structures and processes and can procure the services of enlightened and public-spirited statesmen. It is not unreasonable, therefore, in a modern democracy to regard public office as a public trust and not merely a specially favorable opportunity for those in power to pursue private ends at the expense of those out of power. In a well-constituted democracy this view is no less realistic than the so-called political realism which denies the existence of a genuine public interest.

In modern times the most insistent of political realists have been the Marxian Communists. The Marxian creed makes a virtue out of its denial of such concepts as national interest, national duty, and national honor. Its dogmatic repudiation of obligations resting upon the moral force of such concepts leaves no room whatever for the idea of a world-wide public interest. The idea of the common interests of mankind, the Marxists contend, is an illusion, more iridescent perhaps but also more empty, if that be possible, than the ordinary idea of national interest or the idea of the interests of any other group than a ruling class or a class destined to become a ruling class. According to their way of thinking, it is only when the state, regarded as an instrument of class rule, withers away and ceases to exist that a true public interest can emerge from the welter of contending private and special interests.

This extreme partisan view, repugnant as it is to the political instincts of genuinely democratic peoples, contributes to a better understanding of the true nature of the public interest. For the Marxists claim that in the classless society, which they believe will follow a proletarian dictatorship, private interests will disappear with the classes to which they belong. When the state, regarded as an instrument of class rule, ceases to exist only the public interest, they assert, can remain. Under such conditions the public interest would be as real, the Marxists concede, as "bourgeois" political scientists contend it may be in any rightly constituted state. The important difference between the Marxist and the bourgeois view of the public interest is that the Marxist dreams of the public interest as the catastrophic and definitive product of the last revolution, thereafter to be enjoyed by all survivors, world without end, whereas the better bourgeois political scientists think of it as a natural product of historical processes gradually broadening and deepening with the progressive development of political institutions down through the years.

It is evident that the concepts of national politics and international politics are closely related. The idea of a universal interest of mankind is no less realistic than that of a national interest. It may be less familiar to the people in modern so-called sovereign states than that of a national interest but its essential nature must be the same. To be sure, the adjustment of conflicting interests in the general interest of all parties to the conflict necessarily takes different forms in different areas, large or small, where the conflicts may develop. In modern times the principal area in which the most important adjustments have been made, and hence in which the leading politicians have operated, has been the so-called sovereign state. But politicians may operate at all levels of political accommodation if the conditions are favorable to the employment of political methods. In principle world politics is as real, that is, as natural, as national politics.

The great difference between national politics and world politics springs from the different conditions under which politicians must operate on the two levels. The national politician possesses the inestimable advantage of established political structures and processes at the national level, to which people are accustomed and in which they may place a relatively high degree of confidence. For the would-be world politician there are no corresponding institutions, and those institutions which do exist are less capable of commanding the con-

62 Organizing Peace in the Nuclear Age

fidence of the peoples of the world. What are called in sovereign states
civil wars, therefore, while still excessively frequent, at least in undemocratic countries, leave a wide scope for the political accommodation of interest conflicts. But world civil wars, or what we ordinarily
call international wars, are a greater threat to peace, that is, to the
adjustment of interest conflicts by the methods of political accommodation, under the conditions in which world politicians must now
operate. At the national level pacific politics is the normal method of
adjusting interest conflicts and the resort to physical force and official violence, at least in the democratic countries, is abnormal; at the
world level, unhappily, bellicose politics has been more usual. But
the forms of politics remain always and at every level the same.

In recent years the international Communists seem to have understood the nature of politics, and hence also of war and peace, better
than the politicians in the genuine democracies seem to have done.
The Marxist doctrines of class struggle and class war offer a far from
adequate explanation of all the facts of political life, but they have
helped to clarify the ideas of war and peace. The Marxists' over-
emphasis on the conflicts between classes, however classes may be
defined, and their neglect of other forms of conflict unduly simplify
the problems of politics at all levels but they do see clearly the
elementary truth that the principal distinction between war and
peace is a technical one, namely, the employment of organized
physical force as an instrument of official policy. The ends of policy
remain the same. Both war and peace are forms of politics, rightly
understood.

The Marxists' grasp of the true nature of war and peace enables
them to approach the problems of a cold war with more confidence
than is shown by many politicians in the genuine democracies. They
understand that the distinction between cold war and hot war, like
that between any kind of war and peace, is technical and depends
principally upon the choice of weapons. The appropriate weapons for
cold war are propaganda, infiltration, subversion, and other forms of
indirect aggression. The latter term is new, and even less well defined
than direct aggression, but presumably does not include the use of
economic weapons, not even in the form of so-called trade wars.
The non-Marxist peoples, less clearly understanding the distinction
between war and peace, are apt to think of cold war, like hot war,
as something evil, to be won and ended as soon as possible. But

this is a mistake, since cold war, like peace and hot war itself, is but a form of politics, to be pursued with the appropriate instruments and methods until its aims can be better secured by other instruments and methods or can be abandoned as not worth the efforts and sacrifices required for the continuance of that kind of struggle.

Politics is a natural product of the conditions under which men live. It is something not to be ended but to be improved, in order that conflicts between interests of all kinds may be suitably adjusted with a minimum of effort and sacrifice. The objection to cold war, like that to hot war, is not that it is a form of struggle but that it is waged with weapons involving needless losses and suffering. Cold wars may be fought with less fire and slaughter than hot wars, but they are capable of producing much sweat and many tears. Cold war, regarded as an instrument of national policy, may be preferable to hot war, but better still are the methods of adjusting interest conflicts which do not seek to exploit the fears and hatreds of mankind. Peace should not be defined negatively as the mere absence of war, hot or cold. Peace is that form of politics in which conflicts of interest are adjusted by appeals to reason, not involving organized violence or intimidation, or are endured as patiently as possible until rational methods of adjustment can be effectively employed.

THE ALIGNMENT OF FORCES IN THE UN ORGANIZATION

With this insight into the nature of war and peace and of politics, both bellicose and pacific, the recent history of the United Nations becomes more intelligible. It must not be supposed that the political regimes which are committed to international communism, and hence to a course of action in world politics which they regard as genuinely realistic, are unable for that reason to find any good in the United Nations. On the contrary, they have always recognized that the meetings of the Security Council and the General Assembly afford convenient and attractive opportunities for aggressive propaganda, that is, propaganda designed to impose the will of the propagandist upon his adversary rather than to appeal to the latter's reason. Moreover, the veto power of the Soviet Union in the Security Council and the votes of Communist delegations in the General Assembly are defensive weapons which, although of limited efficacy, are not to be despised. Furthermore, the facilities of the United Nations headquarters are well suited for use in private negotiations with spokesmen for rival political regimes. The adherence of the Communist bloc to the United Nations rests on the solid basis of a fixed conviction that participation in its proceedings can be made to serve the special interests of international communism everywhere. The Communist leaders presumably believe that in reality there can be no higher loyalty to the United Nations than theirs.

The spokesmen for non-Communist regimes in the United Nations may try to be equally realistic in their attitude toward the Organization. But they do not seem to have been equally successful in applying their political ideas to the actual problems of the cold war. Statesmen who represent genuinely democratic states in the United Nations do well if they make the Organization serve the special interests of their own particular states. They do better when they identify their national interests with the universal interests of mankind. For they may then count on the ungrudging aid of statesmen from other countries with a similar understanding of the broader interests to be served. Anyone can understand the practical utility of an organization which can stop yellow fever or bubonic plague, wherever it may be found, before it spreads abroad and contaminates other nations. Anyone can understand the utility of an organization which can stop a little local war before it spreads and embroils a whole world in fratricidal slaughter. Anyone should be able to understand the desirability of utilizing a general international organization to protect and cherish all the universal interests of mankind. But the spokesmen for the "free world" seem not to have been clear in their own minds concerning the relations between national interests, universal interests, and the conduct of international affairs in the United Nations.

The pattern of conflicting interests in contemporary international affairs may be conveniently observed in the proceedings of the Twelfth United Nations General Assembly. The accession of Ghana and Malaya in the course of the year 1957 had raised the total number of member states to eighty-two, making the Organization more nearly representative of the whole world than ever before. (The union of Egypt and Syria in 1958 reduced the number temporarily to eighty-one, which was raised again at the end of the year to eighty-two by the admission of Guinea.) Among the independent nations of noteworthy political importance only Switzerland and the divided states, Germany, Korea, and Vietnam, remained outside the fold.

China also remained divided, but only Communist China was excluded from the Organization; Nationalist China continued to occupy the Chinese seat in the Security Council and other UN organs. In the previous year the British, French, and Israelis had resorted to war as an instrument of policy for dealing with Nasser's Arab nationalism. Bellicose prevailed over pacific politics also in the Soviet Union's harsh measures to check Hungarian independence. Never since the establishment of the United Nations had the leadership of peace-loving politicians in international affairs been put to so severe a test.

Analysis of the political scene begins with the distribution of the member states among the military alliances which have been formed since the beginning of the cold war to sustain the influence of the leading parties in international politics. Supporting the leadership of the United States were (1) the Organization of American States with its even score of Latin-American members, (2) the North Atlantic Treaty Organization with eleven members (not counting the German Federal Republic) in Western and Southern Europe together with Canada in North America and Turkey in Asia, (3) the South East Asia Treaty Organization with five additional members in Asia and Australasia, and (4) Nationalist China and Japan, which were associated with the United States under special arrangements. Including two virtual, though not formal, allies in South West Asia under the Baghdad Pact, Iran and Iraq, there were altogether forty-three members of the United Nations in the grand military alliance of the so-called free world. On the opposite side in the cold war stood the Soviet Union and its Communist allies under the Warsaw Pact, accounting for nine of the United Nations member states. The remaining member states were uncommitted to either of the two sides in the cold war and maintained a diversified and precarious neutrality. Twenty-two of these states, which had attended the great conference of Asian and African states at Bandung in 1955 and were not affiliated with any of the special military alliances, may be described as the "Bandung neutrals" and eight—Austria, Finland, Ireland, Israel, Spain, Sweden, Union of South Africa, and Yugoslavia —may be described as the "independent neutrals."

The leadership of the United States, as reflected in the elections to the Security Council, seemed to be firmly established. In the Security Council, as it was constituted in 1957, the Soviet Union stood alone. Eight of the Members—two from Latin America, three from NATO, one from the Baghdad Pact states, and two from the Far East—were American allies or associates. There was no chosen representative of the Bandung neutrals, and only Sweden maintained a position of independent neutrality in the perennial struggle between the two superpowers. If the command of voting majorities were the clue to politics in the Security Council, the American position would have been impregnable.

The leaders of the American forces in the United Nations have been former senators, trained in a democratic system of majority rule and apt to practice on the bank of the East River in Manhattan what they had learned on the bank of the Potomac. Senator Austin was a peace-loving politician who never reconciled himself to the hard facts of the cold war. Senator Lodge was always more realistic and has proved an adept partisan in cold-war politics. But in organizing a partisan majority in the Security Council the United States delegation seemed to have overreached itself. The alignment of forces in the Security Council had little relation to the actual distribution of interests in international affairs. Under the voting formula adopted at Yalta the American bloc could use its majority of the votes, as the Soviet Union could use its veto, for defensive action but it could not make its votes count for constructive decisions on controversial cold-war issues. A Security Council more generally representative of all the various interests in the United Nations would have served equally well as an arena for the propaganda battles of the cold war and might even have contributed something to the performance of its peacemaking functions.

The proceedings in the General Assembly are more instructive for the student of international politics. Though the voting system in the Assembly underrepresents the major powers as flagrantly as that in the Council overrepresents them, at least all the member states possess a voice there and can obtain a hearing for whatever interests, national or universal, they may choose to speak. The proceedings do serve as a mirror of the various interest conflicts in contemporary international affairs. Inspection of the roll calls on some leading controversial measures, therefore, should throw light upon the true nature of cold-war politics. There were a half dozen such measures before the Assembly in the autumn of 1957, which can be conveniently utilized to test the actual alignment of forces in the struggle between the superpowers.

The first of these measures, the resolution accepting the report of the Special Assembly Committee appointed to investigate the military intervention of the Soviet Union in Hungary, was actually adopted at a resumed session of the Eleventh General Assembly, ending in September, 1957. The vote on this measure recorded the maximum strength of the anti-Communist forces in the cold war. In favor of its adoption were sixty member states, including all the members of the various American military alliances and most of the neutrals, both Bandung and independent. Opposed were the Soviet Union and its allies under the Warsaw Pact, together with Yugoslavia, casting altogether ten votes. There were also ten votes recorded as abstentions, nine of which were cast by Bandung neutrals and one by an independent neutral, Finland.

This roll call affords an excellent illustration of one of the peculiarities of United Nations politics. Under the United Nations voting system, which records abstentions as freely as yeas and nays, there can be three sides to a question. Being present but not voting on a controversial measure may, and usually does, mean more than mere indifference to the measure or inability to choose a side. In a deliberative body possessing important legislative powers, those who are not for a measure, when it comes to a final vote, are presumably against it. But in a body like the United Nations General Assembly, which ordinarily does not legislate but only expresses opinion or recommends action by its Members, an abstention can be a deliberate expression of a positive preference for a different policy than that embodied in the measure or favored by its principal opponents. The abstainers in the vote on the Hungarian resolution were not ready to condemn the Soviet Union for an act of aggression contrary to the principles of the Charter. Neither did they wish to let the intervention of the Soviet Union stand unchallenged as a precedent for the future. Numerous abstentions are a sign of weakness in an ordinary legislative body. In a body whose most important function is to mobilize the moral forces of mankind provision for recording abstentions, as if the abstainers were not only present but actually voting, gives a flexibility to the proceedings which enhances their political value.

The vote on the second test measure in the autumn of 1957, which came early in the twelfth regular session of the Assembly, marked the minimum strength of the anti-Communist forces. This was the American proposal to postpone action on the claim of Communist China to a seat in the General Assembly as the proper Chinese representative. The balloting on this proposal showed a decrease of the ayes to 47, an increase of the noes to 27, and 7 abstentions. The United States held the support of all its military allies and associates, including the Baghdad Pact members, with only three exceptions. Denmark and Norway, which had recognized the Communist government of China long before, voted no, and Portugal, with an eye perhaps on its interest in Macao, abstained. But American support among the neutrals almost vanished. Among the Bandung neutrals most of those which, following the lead of India and Egypt, had abstained on the Hungarian question now voted no and many of those which had voted with the United States on the Hungarian question now abstained. Those which stood beside the United States were Ethiopia, Lebanon, Liberia, and Libya, now joined by newly admitted Malaya. Among the independent neutrals only Spain and Austria continued to support the American position, Yugoslavia adhered as before to the Communist bloc, Sweden, Finland, and Ireland went over to the opposition, Israel abstained, and the Union of South Africa continued to take no part in the proceedings. It is evident that other interests than the "containment" of communism weighed heavily with most of the neutrals.

The next two test votes introduced a greater complication of interests. In November the General Assembly turned its attention to the general problem of the limitation of armaments. On the 14th it voted on fresh instructions to the Disarmament Commission, expressing confidence in American leadership of the negotiations at the London Conference which had ended in the previous August in a deadlock. On the 19th it voted on a separate resolution calling for the immediate and unconditional suspension of nuclear bomb tests. The first vote registered support for the anti-Communist position almost as widespread as that on the Hungarian question. The second vote disclosed a disintegration of the non-Communist forces even more striking than that on the seating of Red China. On the fresh instructions for the Disarmament Commission there were 57 ayes (supporting American leadership), 9 noes, and 15 absentions. On the suspension of nuclear bomb tests there were 24 ayes (opposing American leadership), 34 noes (supporting the United States), and 20 abstentions. On these two votes the NATO and SEATO blocs held fast, but there was a wide break in the ranks of the Latin-American states, led by Mexico and Guatemala, on the question of suspending nuclear bomb tests.

The trend of the voting among the various kinds of neutrals, including on these ballots the Baghdad Pact states, Iran and Iraq, was the same as on the first two test ballots. Of the three states which supported American leadership on the Hungarian question and refused their support on the question of instructions, two were Bandung neutrals, Sudan and Ghana. The third was Japan, which, as a disarmed state under its postwar constitution, had its own reasons for a more positive policy on disarmament. On the question of suspending bomb tests, the United States suffered a net loss of 13 votes from the total it had been able to hold on the question of Communist China's representation in the General Assembly. Losses of support were suffered both among America's military allies and among the neutrals. In fact there was no support among the neutrals for the American position on nuclear bomb tests except by Spain and Israel. Thirteen voted against the United States and 15 abstained. This was a virtual abdication of leadership by the United States.

The last two test votes showed the consequences of an actual abdication of American leadership. One of these votes came on November 29, when the Bandung neutrals forced a showdown on their proposal that negotiations between the Netherlands and Indonesia over the possession of the former Dutch New Guinea, now called West Irian, be resumed. The other came on December 14, when the Greek delegation forced a showdown on their claim to the whole of Cyprus despite the Turkish delegation's objections in the interest of the Turkish minority and British objections to so controversial a settlement of the Cyprus problem. The United States delegation, deeply embarrassed by the bitter conflict between the colonial powers, all of whom were its allies in NATO, and the anticolonial Asian and African states, many of whom steadily followed its leadership on other issues, declined to commit itself to a choice of sides in either of these ballots. The results of the voting clearly showed that, whatever the United States might think, anticolonialism was as real and as important an issue as anticommunism in the minds of many members of the United Nations.

The United States found little support for its policy of complete abstention in the vote on the two colonial questions. The ballot on the question of West Irian showed 41 ayes, 29 noes, and only 11 abstentions. That on the Cyprus question showed 31 ayes, 23 noes, and 24 abstentions. The colonial issue was clearly defined in the West Irian voting, but the conflict between Greece and Turkey over Cyprus was embarrassing to many others besides the United States. The Arab states were helped to choose sides by their traditional hostility to Turkey, but the rest of the Bandung neutrals generally took refuge, like the United States, in uneasy abstentions. The NATO members, except Greece, Turkey, Iceland, and the United States, supported the colonial powers on both ballots. The SEATO members were divided and the solidarity of the Latin Americans was completely disrupted. Those who, like the United States, abstained on both ballots were widely scattered: Mexico, Venezuela, and Paraguay among the American allies; Finland, Liberia, and Cambodia among the neutrals. The Philippines, one of the most loyal of the American allies, abstained on the Cyprus question but took no part whatever in the voting on the question of West Irian. The leadership of NATO on these votes passed definitely to the British and French, who were supported also by Australia, New Zealand, South Africa, Spain, and Sweden. The American effort to play the part of a neutral on the colonial issue seemed to be less successful than that of the Bandung states to make an issue of neutralism in the cold war. The interest conflicts in international affairs manifestly required closer study than they had received by those American politicians who would stake American leadership in world politics on their interpretation of the containment-of-communism issue.

The pattern of leadership at the twelfth session of the United Nations General Assembly may be better understood by analyzing the composition of the various power blocs. The most solid of the blocs was that led by the Soviet Union. All the Warsaw Pact members always voted with their leader. In addition there were those states which never voted against the Soviet Union, though abstaining on one or more of the test votes. Conspicuous among these abstainers was Yugoslavia, which abstained once, on the question of the instructions to the Disarmament Commission. There were no less than ten other Members of the United Nations which never voted against the Soviet Union, though abstaining on several votes. Finland abstained four times, as did Afghanistan and Saudi Arabia. India, Ceylon, and Nepal abstained three times, as did also Yemen. Egypt, Syria, and Indonesia abstained twice. In these cases abstention obviously meant unwillingness to support the leadership of the Western powers, but it did not indicate unqualified subservience to the Soviet Union. The issues were more complex, the distinctions of policy more subtle, than is suggested by the simple formula that those nations which are not against the policies of the Soviet Union must necessarily be for them.

The power bloc led by the United States lacked the solidarity of the Communist bloc. Only two of the more than forty American military allies and associates supported the leadership of the United States on all six of the test ballots. These two, Venezuela and Paraguay, were dictatorships whose rulers may well have had private reasons for accepting American leadership straight down the line. There were in addition three member states which never voted against the United States: the Philippines and Liberia, with one abstention each, and Cambodia, with two abstentions. There were also seventeen states which managed to get through the session without voting against the United States on the test ballots more than once, but these are reluctant witnesses to the effectiveness of American leadership. Eight of these were Latin-American states, headed by Brazil and Mexico. The others were widely scattered. There were China, Japan, Turkey, and Thailand from the allies and military associates of the United States, Iraq from the Baghdad Pact members, the Federation of Malaya and Laos from the Bandung neutrals, and Austria and Israel from the independent neutrals. It was a disappointing showing for a superpower which had spent so many billions on economic and military aid.

The achievements of British and French leadership, measured by the same six test votes, were more impressive. The two leaders of the colonial powers enjoyed the full support of most of NATO and did at least as well as the United States in the other parts of the so-called free world. Of course they received no support from the Bandung neutrals on the colonial issues, but on the other issues the correlation of votes between the English and French and other members of the free-world military alliances is higher than between the United States and the same free-world states. Despite American efforts to avoid antagonizing the anticolonial bloc on the ballots dealing with their own special interests, the United States did not attain a higher correlation with the members of the anticolonial bloc in the other test votes than did the English and French. These contrasting results suggest that American policy had not been as realistic as that of the two major colonial powers. Fortunately for the United States relations with the United Kingdom and France, notwithstanding the strain caused by the Suez misadventure, were on the whole surprisingly good.

The outstanding leader of the Bandung neutrals was India. But the Bandung neutrals were not easy to lead. Only Ceylon and Nepal voted with India on all six test ballots. Afghanistan never voted against India, but this state held an exposed position on the borders of the Soviet Union and by means of numerous abstentions escaped identification with any particular leadership. Six other Bandung neutrals—Indonesia, Burma, Egypt, Syria, Saudi Arabia, and Yemen —voted against India no more than once each, but the four Arab states were manifestly preoccupied with their own special problems. A majority of the Bandung neutrals rejected the leadership of India more frequently. Regarded as a power bloc, they possessed even less solidarity than the bloc led by the United States.

The independent neutrals were even less responsive to leadership by any one of their group. Sweden, because of its relationship to the Secretary-General, might have tried the role of administration leader, but none of the other members of the group voted with the Swedish delegation on all six test ballots. The independent neutrals indeed acted like true independents, each going its own way when the votes were cast. The Spanish and Yugoslav voting records were almost exactly contrary to each other, and the Union of South Africa differed so far from all the others that it seemed close to the point of seceding from the Organization. Regarded as a bloc the independent neutrals were not only less numerous than the Bandung neutrals but also less coherent.

The most cursory inspection of the voting record of the Twelfth General Assembly discloses a kaleidoscopic variety of conflicting national interests represented in the United Nations. Some of them stood out conspicuously in the ballots on the resolutions relating to

West Irian and to Cyprus. The anticolonial states were not always able to present a united front to the colonial powers, as the vote on the Cyprus resolution plainly revealed, but when they did stand together, as on the West Irian issue, they could make effective propaganda against the colonial powers.

The conflicting national interests were less apparent in the votes on the two resolutions relating to disarmament. It may well be that representatives of the major powers in negotiations for the reduction of armaments are primarily interested in gaining an advantage over their principal opponents and can give only incidental attention to the universal interests of mankind that are involved in the proceedings. But where the technical advisers of the negotiators are professionally competent it is impossible for both sides to gain any substantial advantage from such negotiations. Unless one side makes a mistake in its calculations, which is unlikely, the real stakes in the negotiations must lie in the field of propaganda. Regarded from the realistic viewpoint, the United States scored a propaganda victory on the resolution relating to the instructions for the Disarmament Commission and the Soviet Union scored on the resolution relating to nuclear bomb tests. But the universal interest in the prevention of active military hostilities involving the use of the most modern weapons was also served by a process which kept the struggle between the superpowers within the bounds of cold-warlike propaganda.

The influence of the universal interests of mankind was more evident in the first two votes of the test series. The vote on the Hungarian civil war issue did not alter the actual relations between the principal parties, as established by the armed intervention of the Soviet forces, but it did assert the moral supremacy of the universal interests of mankind and thereby contributed something to the creation of a more pacific code of international behavior for the future. The impressive shift of votes on the Chinese representation issue likewise contributed something to the growth of respect for the universal interest in having all significant bodies of people effectively represented by authentic spokesmen in the organs of the United Nations. The proceedings of the Twelfth General Assembly surely marked a forward step, though perhaps only a short step, in the development of an international political system capable of securing consideration for the universal interests of mankind.

The most convincing evidence of such progress in international politics was the final action at the Emergency Special Session of the General Assembly in August, 1958, on the cases of the military intervention of the United States and the United Kingdom in Lebanon and Jordan. This action was not altogether agreeable either to the intervening powers, whose landing of troops by sea and air was obviously hasty and ill-considered, or to the Soviet Union, which had objected most strenuously to their intervention, or to the leading neutrals, which had sought to vindicate the universal interest of mankind in greater respect for the processes of the United Nations by the adoption of some less ambiguous resolution than that finally concocted by the spokesmen for the Arab League. But the Arab League's resolution was adopted unanimously, and thus was set a valuable precedent which surely tends to secure greater respect in the future for the principles of the Charter and the interests of mankind.

The alignment of forces in United Nations politics as exhibited in the Twelfth General Assembly was maintained in the Thirteenth. American and Soviet policy, despite tactical talk about summit meetings, remained substantially unchanged and sharp skirmishes in the cold war were fought on the General Assembly floor. Three roll calls at the end of the regular session can serve well enough as test votes. The first of these came on the estimates of the cost of maintaining the United Nations Emergency Force on the border between Israel and its Arab neighbors; the second, on an American proposal relating to the membership of a committee to study the peaceful uses of outer space; the third, on an Arab resolution recognizing the right of Algeria to independence. The first vote tested the ability of the United States to lead a majority of the General Assembly in support of the established United Nations policy concerning the problem of Israel; the second, the ability of the United States to defeat the Soviet bloc in a direct contest between the two superpowers; the third, the influence of the United States in its policy of neutralism in the cold war between the European colonial powers and the Asian and African anticolonial member states.

On the first test vote American leadership was sustained by a narrow majority. The record of the roll call shows 42 ayes, 9 noes, and 27 abstentions. Voting with the United States were seven of the twenty Latin-American members of the Organization of American

States, sixteen of the twenty members of NATO and the Asiatic and Pacific military alliances and consultative pacts, all of the eight independent neutrals, and ten of the Bandung neutrals. The Soviet bloc cast nine votes against the American position. Twenty-seven other member states, including a majority of the Latin Americans and a majority of the Bandung neutrals, abstained. The Latin Americans generally disliked the method of apportioning the costs. Continued presence in the Near East of an Emergency Force was detested by many of the Bandung neutrals.

There was general agreement upon the importance of ensuring the peaceful use of outer space, but bitter disagreement between the American and Soviet delegations over the composition of the investigating committee. Voting with the United States were all twenty Latin Americans, all twenty members of NATO and the other military alliances and consultative pacts, six of the eight independent neutrals, and the same number of Bandung neutrals. The Soviet bloc cast its nine votes against the American proposal. Seventeen Bandung neutrals, together with Finland and Yugoslavia, abstained. The American party polled 53 out of a total of 81 votes. The United States easily gained the necessary two-thirds majority for its proposal, but the refusal of the Soviet Union to participate in the work of Committee made the American triumph a hollow victory. It was a frustration of American leadership and a defeat for the general interest of mankind.

In the vote on the Algerian question the French delegation refused to participate, but the vote of Guinea, which had been admitted to the United Nations the preceding day, kept the total at eighty-one. Voting for the motion were 22 Bandung neutrals, 2 independent neutrals, Ireland and Yugoslavia, 2 American military allies or associates, Greece and Pakistan, and the 9 members of the Soviet bloc. Voting against it were 6 Latin Americans, 9 members of NATO and other American military alliances or pacts, 2 independent neutrals, Israel and the Union of South Africa, and 1 Bandung neutral, Laos. Abstaining, along with the United States, were 14 Latin Americans, 8 other military allies or associates of the United States, 4 independent neutrals, and 1 Bandung neutral, Cambodia. On this vote American leadership failed conspicuously to hold together its following on either of the other test votes. NATO and the other military alliances were badly split. The combination of Bandung neutrals with the Soviet bloc led the field, but could not control the action of the General Assembly.

Analysis of the most significant roll calls in recent sessions of the General Assembly shows that there are two paramount issues in United Nations politics, the extension or containment of communism and the preservation or liquidation of colonialism. Since there are three sides to each issue under the United Nations system of voting and the alignment of forces is radically different in the test votes on communism and on colonialism, respectively, there are many possible combinations of factions among the eighty-two member states. Pro-Communists, anti-Communists, and neutralists, pro-colonialists, anticolonialists, and again neutralists, can combine with and against one another in kaleidoscopic variations. American critics of United Nations politics have shown great impatience with the neutralists in the cold war between capitalism and communism, but when, as in the equally cold war between colonialism and anti-colonialism, the Americans have essayed the role of neutralists the critics have been no less impatient with the nations which have tried to force a choice of sides on the Americans. The task of leadership, regarded from the viewpoint of politicians with experience in operating systems of responsible party government, seems excessively complicated and difficult.

American leadership in United Nations politics is likely to be tested by its success in getting desired action, or at least in preventing objectionable action, in the General Assembly. The claim has been made that the American coalition of forces has never been defeated in an important test vote. This claim is not supported by the evidence. In the cold war between colonialism and anticolonialism, the record of American leadership of the neutralists is negative. In the cold war between capitalism and communism combinations of factions large enough to produce the two-thirds majorities required for action on important questions can be formed for the containment of communism when the issue is clear, but not otherwise. When the issue is less clear, as in the exclusion of representatives of Mainland China from the General Assembly, it is increasingly difficult to hold together the bare majority needed to prevent action by the General Assembly on the merits of the question. It is in order to consider whether the organization of a permanent majority party is the proper aim of intelligent leadership in United Nations politics.

THE PARTY SYSTEM IN UN POLITICS

The record of international politics at recent sessions of the General Assembly of the United Nations provides useful material for a study of the political methods most suitable for adjusting conflicting national interests in the general interest of all the nations. The spokesmen for the democratic powers naturally prefer the methods with which they are familiar in the conduct of public affairs in their respective home countries. This means a preference for some form of the party system. Politicians from the English-speaking countries generally prefer the two-party system. Politicians from the countries where the French model of parliamentary government has exerted a greater influence might prefer some form of the multi-party system. Either system implies habitual respect for the principle of majority rule. The rules of procedure in the General Assembly have accordingly been framed upon the assumption that this rule will be respected as far as the principles of the Charter and the prescribed system of voting permit.

Whether or not an expanded role for politics in the organization of peace calls for the introduction of the party system in one of its freely competitive forms into the United Nations General Assembly and Security Council is an important question, which cannot be answered without some preliminary inquiries. In the first place, how are the parties to be formed? An often-quoted explanation of the formation of political parties is that offered by the talented French politician and historian Alexis de Tocqueville, in his widely read treatise *Democracy in America*. "All the skill of the actors in the political world," de Tocqueville wrote, "lies in the art of creating parties. A political aspirant in the United States begins by discerning his own interest, and discovering those other interests which may be collected around and amalgamated with it. He then contrives to find some doctrine or principle which may suit the purposes of this new association, and which he adopts in order to bring forward the new party and secure its popularity. . . . This being done, the new party is ushered into the political world."

The classic illustration in American history of the formation of a political party by the method described by de Tocqueville was furnished in his own time by the founders of the Whig party. Clay, Webster, and Calhoun assembled the components of an effective opposition to the Jacksonian democracy by framing a program of policies calculated to bring together all the principal interests which found Jackson's vigorous measures not to their liking. But there is another way of forming a political party, capable of managing public affairs in accordance with the principle of majority rule, which was impressively illustrated by the Jacksonian democracy itself. That is the method of gathering around a magnetic personality a body of followers, who esteem the gift of leadership above any program of policies. Actually the Jacksonian democracy proved more successful at the polls than its Whig opponents. The most important fact, however, about the American party system, described by de Tocqueville, was that it was a two-party system.

The original model of all two-party systems was developed in England, whose politicians showed the world three solid advantages to be derived from such a system when in good working order. The first is that it offers to a democratic-minded people a choice of candidates for the highest offices in the land which can satisfy them that they are playing a suitable part in the process of government. Another advantage is that it enables an organized majority to carry into effect any legislative program upon which its leaders are able to agree. The third is that it puts a premium on temperate leadership and moderate measures and makes the way hard for extremists of all kinds, radical or reactionary. In short, it supplies an acceptable substitute for the right of revolution of which so much was heard in England in 1688 and in the United States in 1776.

In the United States the existence of a comparatively rigid written constitution has tended to make the two-party system also more rigid than in Great Britain. In the first place, the method of filling the high office of president dominates the political scene in which the party system operates, making the whole governmental process more democratic than the framers of the Constitution really intended it to be. Moreover, the separation of powers under the Constitution results in a legislative process which works more smoothly when a majority party possesses a well-adjusted program of policies. Furthermore, the emphasis on temperate leadership and moderate measures favors the maintenance of a wholesome system of middle-class rule. This system originated when the people were mainly a nation of independent farmers and has become even more wholesome now that the people are predominantly a nation of wage and salary workers and city dwellers. In short, the American form of the two-party system is a highly serviceable, though unplanned, political development, which has been greatly influenced by the special circumstances of the American way of life and by the peculiar nature of the written Constitution.

The conditions for a useful form of two-party system clearly do not exist in the Organization established under the United Nations Charter. The peoples of the United Nations have nothing to do with the election of the principal officers of the Organization. The Secretary-General is an office manager and universal "trouble shooter," with unprecedented opportunities for greatness but with little temptation to seek personal popularity in the member states. The President of the General Assembly is a shining figure for the year of his incumbency and can exert a statesmanlike influence in its proceedings, but is not in a position to make a strong appeal to the world at large. The President of the Security Council is but a temporary chairman of a body where the system of voting under the Yalta formula precludes the operation of any simple form of majority rule.

The second important advantage derived from the two-party system in the countries where it operates smoothly is equally contingent upon conditions which do not exist in the United Nations. The major parties in the English-speaking countries operate as fairly efficient instruments for the adjustment of the conflicting interests of their principal components, the special interest groups and regional factions which seek to influence the management of public affairs, because control of the legislative powers under a democratic constitution enables the party leaders to give effect to their intraparty arrangements for a common program of policies. In the United Nations there are more than enough conflicting national interests to furnish ample materials for party programs, but under the Charter, when narrowly construed, there is not enough legislative power to put such programs into effect. There is therefore no sufficient inducement for the leading member states to subordinate their special interests and private aims to the requirements of a common legislative program which can command the support of a majority of the members. Under such conditions the limitless opportunities for aggressive propaganda make a stronger appeal to the spokesmen of the major powers than does the barren field for legislative action.

The third advantage of the two-party system is entirely irrelevant under the political conditions governing the operations of the United Nations. The members of the General Assembly and the Security Council constitute a congress of ambassadors, representing governments rather than peoples, and take their instructions from the particular persons controlling those governments. They derive their class character from that of the governments which they represent, and there is nothing that can be done in international politics under the Charter to change that situation. The representatives of most of the middle-class democracies, which exert an important influence in United Nations politics, doubtless do infuse a spirit of moderation and good temper into the proceedings on the bank of the East River in Manhattan. But this conciliatory influence is necessarily limited by the unequal progress of democracy in the world at large.

The persistence of the cold war does not improve the prospects for the two-party system in United Nations policies. A state of cold war means the predominance of the private and special interests of the warring powers in their political planning over the more general interests which the Organization might be made to serve. The Soviet Union has been more interested in brightening the outlook for international communism than in reaching compromises with non-Communist countries which could form the basis of an effective majority party in the General Assembly. The United States has been more interested in "containing" communism than in creating a partisan basis for constructive action in the organs of the United Nations. Under these conditions the Organization has to compete with other organizations which are primarily military in character, such as NATO and the Communist alliance under the Warsaw Pact, for the active allegiance of the cold-warring powers.

These considerations go far to explain the violent intervention of the Soviet Union in the Hungarian civil war. The triumph of the Hungarian revisionists threatened the solidarity of the Warsaw Pact. The disintegration of this organization threatened to defeat the purposes of the Soviet Union in waging the cold war. The Hungarian intervention prevented the Soviet Union from gaining new recruits for the Communist bloc in the United Nations. But this failure did not prevent the Soviet Union from exploiting its membership in the United Nations for its aggressive propaganda. At the same time it strengthened its defensive position in the event of a hot war, or so it must have seemed to the Kremlin leaders, when they made their decision to intervene in Hungary. Thus the persistence of the cold war confirms the tendency to convert the United Nations into an instrument of aggressive propaganda, and the persistence of aggressive propaganda tends to postpone a peace in the cold war. It is a vicious circle which, it may be hoped, can be broken by sufficiently bold and energetic measures.

These considerations go far to explain also the marked preference of recent American policy for reliance upon NATO and other military alliances rather than upon the United Nations for national security. It is questionable, however, whether this preference can be justified under the developing conditions for the conduct of a war to be fought with the most modern weapons. The use of intercontinental ballistic missiles with nuclear warheads seems to doom the fixed air force bases, with which the United States through NATO and SEATO and its other alliances has encircled the Soviet Union, as surely as the development of air power during the interval between World War I and World War II doomed the battleship and the super-dreadnought. But whatever may be the ultimate verdict of the military experts upon the strategy underlying the policy embodied in NATO, there are other reasons for questioning the preference for military over political weapons in a period of cold war. These other reasons make the outlook for NATO, regarded as a principal agent of American defense policy, as uncertain as that for the Warsaw Pact.

It is significant that the leading members of NATO make little use of that organization when they find occasion to resort to military measures as instruments of national policy. The British and French, when planning their Suez misadventure, not only neglected to consult their NATO allies before taking the action which provoked the Soviet Union to threaten the peace of the world but even failed to give them advance notice of their bellicose intentions. The Americans and British, when determining upon their naval and air operations in Lebanon and Jordan, likewise neither consulted their NATO allies, who would have been involved in any hot war which might have ensued, nor gave them notice of their intentions. The negotiations for a restoration of peace, or perhaps it should be said for a resumption of the cold war of aggressive propaganda without violence, took place not between the NATO and Warsaw Pact Powers but between all the members of the United Nations at the seat of the Organization in New York. It was a great triumph of the United Nations over NATO and other regional military organizations.

There are good reasons for such a triumph. The emerging role of politics in international affairs is necessarily hostile to the use of military force as an instrument of national policy. The classical theory of war, expounded by Clausewitz and other influential writers, is no longer applicable to wars between nations armed with the most modern weapons. It is doubtful whether any war, even one beginning as a war for limited objectives, can be confined to limits which are compatible with the true interests of the modern superpowers. Wars between weak countries, armed only with old-fashioned weapons of limited potency, might still be waged with some prospect of profit to the victor if they could be prevented from spreading and involving also the superpowers. But how can their spread be prevented? The answers to this question are painfully unconvincing. The actions of the superpowers when confronted with a serious threat of a major war, in taking their problems to the United Nations, regardless of the existence of NATO and other military alliances, speak for themselves. It is not a predilection for theoretical pacifism which blights the future of NATO and the Warsaw Pact. It is the actual conditions under which international politics, bellicose or pacific, must be practiced that compel resort to the facilities of the United Nations by the powers which possess greater military strength than they dare to use.

In default of permanently satisfactory alternatives to political action under the auspices of the United Nations the leading powers are forced to reconsider the case for the organization of political parties in the United Nations General Assembly. Under the existing circumstances this means an attempt to exploit the opportunities for a multi-party system. The foundations of such a system already exist. The Communist bloc is well organized. The NATO powers have no formal organization in the General Assembly but in practice have been able to work together more consistently than any other group except the Communists. The outlook for more limited regional parties is perhaps more attractive. The growing efforts toward a European Union, at least in the form of an association of the leading democratic powers in Western Europe, might easily produce a working agreement in the United Nations General Assembly between the members of "Little" Europe, already working together in the Coal and Steel Community, the Common Market Community, and Euratom. Similar opportunities for the development of regional parties present themselves to the Latin Americans and to various groups of Bandung neutrals.

The weaknesses of a multi-party system, regarded as the framework for the operation of an energetic system of government, have been made familiar by the tragic experience of the Fourth French Republic. But such a system is better suited to the United Nations as now constituted, with its emphasis on cold-war propaganda and its lack of opportunity for the formation of major parties of the type described by de Tocqueville. Indeed no better party system can be expected in the existing state of international politics. The preoccupation of the superpowers with the cold war compels concentration in the organs of the United Nations on the opportunities for aggressive propaganda. The coldly militant atmosphere of the Security Council and the General Assembly tends to frustrate the halfhearted attempts to utilize the limited legislative powers of the Organization for the general welfare of all the member nations.

A multi-party system, however, operating under conditions for which it is suited, offers some solid advantages. Minor parties are more easily organized than major parties and, since the conflicts of interest within a minor party are less sharp, are likely to possess greater solidarity. They can form combinations with one another in search of legislative majorities for temporary objectives without compromising their basic principles and can resume their freedom of action readily enough when their temporary objectives have been gained. They form a more faithful mirror of opinion among the body of peoples which they represent and are less likely than the more artificial major parties to suffer sudden and wide fluctuations of popularity in consequence of changing conditions which may be beyond control by political action. They make for greater stability in a representative body and, if the executive is not too dependent on their continuing support, the price that must be paid for such a party system in terms of governmental energy and zeal for action in the public interest may not be too high.

The conditions that are most favorable to the serviceability of a multi-party system are associated with the United Nations as it has operated heretofore under the Charter. The Secretary-General enjoys a substantial degree of independence during the earlier part of his term and, unless excessively eager to hold his office for more than one term, may maintain his independence until the end. The limited legislative authority of the Organization reduces to a minimum the need for highly organized major parties as permanent instruments of legislative policy. The paramount function of the General Assembly—the framing of appeals to public opinion with a view to mobilizing the moral forces of mankind—can be performed more effectively under a multi-party than under a two-party system. In short, the multi-party system is well suited to the requirements of international politics in a period of cold war. It is likely, if given a fair trial, to operate more or less satisfactorily as long as favorable operating conditions continue to exist.

The multi-party system, as it might operate in the United Nations, offers the further advantage that it could provide an opportunity for the gradual development of an Administration party. It must not be supposed, however, that such a party would come into existence by the process of gathering a band of personal followers about a strong personality in some administrative office. In the United Nations the only personality about whom a party could be formed is the Secretary-General. But in the present state of world politics he would have to be an extraordinarily strong personality. The conflicting interests are too numerous and complex, the leading contenders for control of the Organization are too deeply interested and too powerful, to permit any person who could ordinarily get elected to the office of Secretary-General to make it the instrument of effective party leadership in international affairs. Trygve Lie possessed the necessary insight into the nature of politics at the international level and the necessary ambition, but adverse circumstances were too much for him. Dag Hammarskjold also possesses the necessary insight, is more politic by nature, and is working under increasingly favorable circumstances, but the organization of an effective Administration party, even if the Secretary-General deemed it desirable, seems still to be impracticable. It is unlikely that so politic a leader deems it desirable under the existing type of Charter. The Jacksonian method of party organization may be dismissed as presently outside the field of practical international politics.

An Administration party could come into existence by the method described by de Tocqueville if some enterprising member state, perhaps an independent neutral, would take the lead in insisting that the universal interests of mankind must take precedence over the national interests of particular member states. Such a party would aim at stopping the cold war by improving the opportunities for the practice of pacific politics in the Security Council and the General Assembly. It would bring to bear the moderating influence of even-tempered politicians upon the more emotional operations of aggressive propagandists. It would support moderate measures of all kinds in preference to the extreme proposals of intensely nationalistic politicians. It would encourage resort to the services of the Secretary-General as the instrument of the general purposes set forth in the Charter and would employ him for pacific missions on all suitable occasions. In short, an Administration party under the multi-party system could be one of the most promising means of maintaining the principles of the Charter and enhancing the prestige of the Organization in the practice of international politics. Long before such a party could command the systematic support of a majority of the member states it might gain control of the balance of power among the principal contending factions and utilize its strategic position in international politics to strengthen the influence of all genuinely peace-loving nations.

The conclusion is irresistible that the Charter of the United Nations, as interpreted up to now, is more suitable to cold-warlike politics than to the adjustment of conflicting national interests in the universal interest of mankind. The International Court of Justice is capable of adjudicating minor conflicts not involving the vital interests of nations, or what tradition calls the national honor. But the adjustment of the kinds of conflicts that used to cause sovereign nations to resort to war as an instrument of national policy is beyond its powers. War, however, regarded as an instrument of policy for nations possessing the most modern weapons, has become "unthinkable," as President Eisenhower rightly declared. It is clearly necessary, therefore, to consider how the Security Council and the General Assembly may become the stages for more fruitful international politics conducted in accordance with the purposes of the Charter by politicians who are free to act in pursuance of universal rather than merely national interests.

These observations lead directly to recognition that there are some general principles of international politics. One is that the role of politics in international affairs is dependent on the form of international organization. Another is that such a political system as that embodied in the present United Nations not only presents the superpowers with an unrivaled opportunity to wage cold war but tends to compel them to do so. It is unlikely therefore that the cold war can be ended except by arrangements for endowing the Organization with greater practical capacity for managing international affairs in the general interest of all its Members. The form of the Organization must become more favorable to an expanded role of politics in international affairs.

Already the role of politics in the organization of peace is greater than is commonly realized. The United Nations has virtually succeeded in substituting cold war for the kind of war the nations once proposed to renounce under the Kellogg Pact. If the Organization were strengthened, as it might easily be by appropriate changes in the interpretation of the Charter or in the Charter itself, would it be capable of ending the cold war by substituting for cold-war politics the more rational politics of genuine peace? More specifically, can the United Nations substitute the politics of peace for cold-war politics by introducing into the Organization a suitable form of the party system? To answer these questions it is necessary to investigate further the structure and powers of the Organization.

THE INTERNATIONAL LAWMAKING PROCESS

The beginning of a practical solution of the problem of expanding the role of politics in the organization of peace lies in the improvement of the international lawmaking process. There has been a great deal of international lawmaking in recent years, but the process has been dominated by traditional habits of political thought. It has consequently been excessively slow, laborious, and uncertain. The adaptation of traditional rules to the changing circumstances of the coming age has been excessively difficult. The growing conflict between tradition and reason has not been readily enough resolved in favor of reason.

The nature of the difficulties is well illustrated by the proceedings of the International Law Commission, established by the United Nations to codify the existing body of law. The need for codification was clear. The law had grown up haphazardly in response to the troublesome lack of uniformity in the practices of the nations in their dealings with one another and to the imperative demand for rational standards of international behavior which could protect the better practices against subversion by the worse. It could be found only by searching the records of diplomacy, the writings of scholars, the opinions of members of arbitral tribunals and of judges of courts of various jurisdictions, the agreements between heads of states, and the formal treaties in which leading states sought to put their relations with one another on a more rational basis. The precedents were often conflicting and there was no convenient way of reconciling them. Treaties were binding only on those states which agreed to them, and no state could be forced to treat except by war or the threat of war. As long as resort to war as an instrument of national policy was the acknowledged right of every sovereign state the strong could find ways of accommodating themselves to the defects of the international lawmaking process. The weak might hope to save themselves from the perils of their situation by their wits, if not by their arms. *Inter arma silent leges* were the last words of the international lawyer.

The International Law Commission began its work in 1949. After ten years of preparatory studies it had covered four of the fourteen sections of international law originally chosen as suitable for codification. A United Nations Conference held at Geneva, February to April, 1958, and attended by representatives of eighty-six nations used the Commission's draft articles on one of these four sections, the law of the sea, as the basis for four conventions respectively on the high seas, on territorial waters and contiguous zones, on fishing and the conservation of the living resources of the high seas, and on the continental shelf. These conventions would become effective when ratified by a prescribed number of states and would be binding on those states which ratified them. That would be the end of this particular phase of the lawmaking process relating to the law of the sea.

But the ratification of these conventions will not be the end of the effort to make a satisfactory set of laws regulating the use of the seas in the nuclear age. The four conventions were written by specialists in international law and experts in the use of the seas and were necessarily restricted to matters concerning which these persons were competent to treat. They could reach agreements on technical matters, which were not the subjects of serious disputes between different states, but controversial matters, which might lead to international friction or give rise to a dispute likely to endanger the maintenance of international peace, were beyond their powers to settle. Thus they could make no contribution to the settlement of the serious dispute between Iceland and the other states claiming an interest in the Icelandic offshore fisheries concerning the extent of the waters in which the people of Iceland have an exclusive right to fish. Agreements concerning the law applicable to situations constituting a threat to international peace can be made only by persons competent to speak for the policy-determining agencies of the nations concerned with the situation. The technical expert and specialist in jurisprudence must give way to the political lawmaker and specialist in politics. A better lawmaking process must be found than that available to the United Nations International Law Commission.

This Commission, or conferences assembled to deliberate upon the Commission's legislative drafts, can of course refer a project of law to the United Nations General Assembly instead of submitting it for ratification to the states of the world. This is the proper procedure in cases where the project deals with topics of a highly controversial nature. The General Assembly can then recommend suitable measures to the Members of the United Nations. If two-thirds of the General Assembly can agree upon an acceptable convention, the convention becomes binding upon those member states which may adopt it. It is conceivable that the International Court of Justice, acting in cases duly brought before it, might extend the application of such conventions to states which had not ratified them. Thus general rules of law might eventually come into existence by this roundabout lawmaking process. But obviously it would be slow, laborious, and uncertain.

Much international law is now being made by the specialized agencies belonging to the United Nations family. This branch of the international lawmaking process in its simplest form produces by-laws or administrative regulations applicable to the internal operations of the agencies. It concerns the employees of the agencies but not as a general rule the public at large. It may even take the more complex form of establishing standards for the guidance of international officials engaged in activities which involve the exercise of wide discretionary authority of a technical nature. For example, the International Atomic Energy Agency has power to require the operators of approved nuclear power projects to observe health and safety measures prescribed by the Agency. This grant of power to the

Agency could result in the production of an important body of administrative law designed to protect the public health and safety against radiation hazards and other dangers arising from the operation of nuclear power plants. This kind of international lawmaking is becoming ever more important in this increasingly technical age, but it does not ordinarily involve legislative action in situations which constitute threats to the peace.

The process of international administrative lawmaking has been further developed by specialized agencies charged with the responsibility for developing higher standards of practice in technical situations of a more controversial character. For example, the International Labor Organization has long been actively engaged in drafting conventions for the better regulation of terms of employment and working conditions in factories and other industrial establishments. These conventions have become effective only in countries whose governments have ratified them, and have been studiously ignored in countries like the United States, which prefer their own methods and standards of labor legislation. To the extent that they are ratified they enter into the general body of international law, and in fact a substantial body of law of this kind is now in existence. But again the process is slow, laborious, and uncertain.

All these processes of international lawmaking are further complicated by the problem of amendments. Ordinarily amendments must be made by the same process as the original law itself and in those cases where ratification is necessary for effectiveness are binding only upon those states which ratify them. This leads to greater uncertainty concerning the actual law effective in different states. The framers of the Statute of the International Atomic Energy Agency were mindful of this difficulty and accordingly provided that duly ratified amendments should apply to all the states which belong to the Agency, including those which do not ratify, but a state which finds an amendment unacceptable is permitted to withdraw from membership. This in effect gives a veto over proposed amendments to the Statute to states which, like the United States, are indispensable if the Agency is to serve its purpose with success. This privileged position may be justified in this particular instance, since the United States furnishes the bulk of the nuclear fuels for use by the Agency. In general the problem of a suitable amending process cannot be solved so easily.

The outstanding example of international lawmaking in modern times is of course the multilateral treaty establishing the United Nations Organization. Other important recent instances of international lawmaking are the treaties establishing the various specialized agencies, which together with the United Nations Organization constitute the United Nations family. The latest treaty of this kind is that establishing the International Atomic Energy Agency, which is the subject of Professor Stoessinger's excellent case study in international lawmaking printed in this volume. In each case every effort was made by the promoters of the legislation to obtain for their project the free and full consent of the participating states. How uncertain such projects may be is attested by the failure of some of them, notably the treaty establishing the International Trade Organization, to obtain the ratifications necessary for putting them into effect.

All these important treaties were made by a similar process. One or more interested nations took the lead in developing the demand for legislation. Preliminary studies were made, consultations were held, and a tentative plan for a legislative project was prepared. There followed a general conference at which agreement was obtained upon the details of the project and a draft of the proposed legislation was completed and signed. Thereafter ratifications of the treaty by the requisite number of signatory states were procured and the treaty was duly promulgated and put into effect. The process is patently slow and laborious. In the case of the treaty establishing the United Nations Organization the formal proceedings extended over a period of more than four years, beginning with the meeting between Roosevelt and Churchill in August, 1941, in Argentia Bay and ending with the ratification of the Charter by the government of the Soviet Union on October 24, 1945 and the deposit of the necessary papers with the government of the United States. The proceedings culminating in the establishment of the International Atomic Energy Agency followed a similar course, took almost as long, and were hardly less laborious. In general the proceedings resulting in the establishment of the specialized agencies, though quicker and easier, required extensive preparations by the initiators of the legislation and elaborate efforts to bring the process to a successful conclusion.

The most constructive legislative process at the present time for making international law is that for amending the Charter of the

United Nations. By this process legislation may be enacted which will be binding upon all Members of the Organization, regardless of the opposition of a minority of the Members. Amendments may be proposed by a two-thirds majority of the General Assembly and become effective when ratified by two-thirds of the member states, including all five Members with permanent seats in the Security Council. Nothing is said in the Charter about a right of secession, though a right of expulsion is explicitly provided, but presumably a right of secession is implied. Apparently any project of law whatever, provided only that it is in harmony with the purposes of the United Nations, may be adopted in the manner in which the Charter may be amended and will be binding on all member states, unless they should secede. This is a legislative process with interesting possibilities.

The possibility of utilizing such a legislative process under the United Nations Charter as a means of making laws in the interest of the whole family of nations opens a ready prospect of enlarging the role of politicians in the organization of peace. For the lawmaking process at any level of political organization, next to the electoral process, offers the politician the most attractive opportunities for performing an essential function in the management of public affairs. Without the possibility of lawmaking in matters of importance the United Nations General Assembly and Security Council will continue to be suitable theaters of operations for diplomats and propagandists, but will offer little scope for the talents of the men who shine brightest in the legislative halls of so-called sovereign states. With such a possibility the principal organs of the United Nations are capable of attracting the ablest men in national politics from all parts of the world. The chief special limitation upon the activities of the most skillful lawmakers is the necessity of obtaining the consent of the spokesmen for all five of the Members with permanent seats in the Security Council.

Since the voting formula in the Security Council excludes from the lawmaking process the partisan legislative practices which are associated with the two-party system in the English-speaking countries, international lawmaking by a process similar to that of amending the United Nations Charter must be based upon the method of consensus among the five major powers. It is widely believed that this method is impracticable on account of the ideological differences between the Communist and the non-Communist states. The method doubtless is impracticable during the continuance of the cold war. It becomes practicable only by agreement between the principal Communist and non-Communist powers that the cold war should be ended. Such an agreement is no less conceivable in the nuclear age than an agreement to end a hot war in the age that is passing away. In view of the nature and predictable effects of a war between great powers armed with nuclear weapons and of the near certainty that a cold war cannot go on indefinitely without turning into a hot war, such an agreement is not only possible but also more likely than the irrational and suicidal alternative. The outlook for international lawmaking by the method of consensus among the nuclear powers, if they can keep the technically less advanced and politically less responsible states from forcing war upon them, is good.

There is no inherent incompatibility between legislation by the method of consensus and a greater role for politics in the United Nations. Lawmaking at Washington by the method of consensus is not unusual and in fact is more customary than is commonly supposed. Inspection of the roll calls upon controversial measures in both the Senate and the House of Representatives shows that a substantial portion of such measures are adopted with the support of a majority of the members of both major parties. Votes in which a large majority of one party are recorded on one side and a corresponding majority of the other party are recorded on the other side are by no means the normal form of the legislative process in national politics. Dissent from the projects of the majority party by a substantial portion of its own members and assent by a substantial portion of the members of the minority party also are frequent phenomena in the national legislative process. The large number of measures of a less controversial character which are adopted by unanimous consent in the Congress further attests the normality of legislation by consensus under the American two-party system. There is no rational ground for fearing that international lawmaking by a similar process cannot develop in the United Nations, provided that there is agreement between the nuclear powers that the cold war should be ended before it turns into a hot war.

A special obstacle to the use of the method of consensus by the nuclear powers as the normal international lawmaking process is the requirement of ratification by two thirds of the Members. This requirement constitutes a standing invitation to aggressive propaganda instead of rational politics in the General Assembly. Since a definitive condition of peace in the nuclear age is an expanded role for politics in the operations of the United Nations, it is manifestly necessary to exploit the opportunities for international lawmaking in the Organization by methods that do not require an appeal to the members for their express approval of each project of law after its adoption by the appropriate United Nations organ. In fact much important legislation is possible under the Charter as it stands, provided the necessary and proper development of the implied powers of the Organization is not hampered by excessively narrow and strict interpretations of the text. It is of course true that little lawmaking power is explicitly conferred upon the United Nations. But there are numerous provisions of the Charter, happily phrased by inspired draftsmen, which justify the belief that the Charter is in general a document well suited to the needs of a fast-changing world and fully capable of serving the purposes of its framers for years to come.

Consider, for example, the logical basis in the Charter for the three constructive functional developments recommended by the Commission to Study the Organization of Peace in its Tenth Report, *Strengthening the United Nations.* One was the establishment of a permanent United Nations Force to assist the Secretary-General in executing decisions of the Security Council, or General Assembly recommendations, respecting situations constituting threats to the peace. A second was the assertion of United Nations jurisdiction over open territory, such as outer space, the Antarctic Continent, and the high seas, for the purpose of adopting timely measures in the interest of mankind to prevent dangerous disputes between rival claimants for special privileges in such areas. The third was the creation of a United Nations Development Agency to direct capital investments into underdeveloped countries on conditions compatible with the general interests of mankind. None of these measures is expressly authorized by the United Nations Charter.

There has been considerable discussion of the constitutional basis for the first of these measures since the establishment of the United Nations Emergency Force in the Suez area in 1956 and of the United Nations Observation Group in Lebanon in 1958. Despite persistent objections from important quarters in the first of these instances, there can be no doubt of the constitutionality of the actions in these two instances by the General Assembly and the Security Council, respectively. In the first place, there is a general grant of authority by Articles 97 and 101 for the provision of such staff as the Organization may require and for its appointment by the Secretary-General under regulations established by the General Assembly. Secondly, there is a special grant of authority by Articles 22 and 29 to the General Assembly and to the Security Council, respectively, for establishing such subsidiary organs as may be deemed necessary for the performance of their functions. The Emergency Force and the Observation Group are such subsidiary organs, and their commanding officers are a part of the staff of the Secretariat.

Similar reasoning leads to a similar conclusion respecting the establishment of suitable organs for administering, or supervising the development of, open territories such as Antarctica and outer space, and for channeling capital funds into underdeveloped countries. Moreover, there is also Article 17, which authorizes the General Assembly to consider and approve the budget of the Organization. The Organization's spending power is legally limited by its purposes, as set forth in the Charter, and is limited in fact by the reluctance of its members to contribute money for these purposes. Nevertheless, the Secretary-General can certainly provide in his budget for whatever he may consider to be necessary and proper expenses and will presumably include the amounts required for carrying into effect the recommendations and decisions of the General Assembly and the Security Council. The extent of the power of decision-making under Chapters VI and VII of the Charter is not altogether clear, but doubtless is broad enough to justify the expenditure of much greater sums of money than the Organization has been able to raise up to now in aid of underdeveloped countries and in pursuance of plans to deal with threatening situations upon conditions to be specified in the appropriation acts. Such acts will have the force of laws and the conditions they impose upon the beneficiaries of such aid and plans will form an important addition to the general body of international law. There is here a lawmaking power of indefinite inherent potentialities.

There is another provision of the Charter, to which little attention has been hitherto directed, which may further broaden the basis of the Organization's legislative capacity. This is the provision in Article 40 authorizing the Security Council, in order to prevent the aggravation of a situation involving a threat to the peace, to call upon the parties concerned to comply with such provisional measures as may be deemed necessary or desirable. The precise meaning of the expression "to call upon" is uncertain, but it doubtless means more than merely to recommend, since it is further provided that the Security Council shall duly take account of failure to comply with such provisional measures. Whether a situation involves a threat to the peace and how long provisional measures may be kept in effect are matters left to the sound discretion of the Security Council. What is needed to make this provision of the Charter a significant factor in the international lawmaking process is not an additional grant of legislative power but such improvements in the representative character of the Security Council and in its methods of transacting business as will enable it to command greater confidence on the part of the Members of the Organization.

It is interesting to speculate on the future of international lawmaking by special international conferences subject to ratification as in the case of a multilateral international treaty. In this connection the history of the Statute of the International Atomic Energy Agency carries an important lesson. In this particular case the United Nations General Assembly, by its criticisms of the proceedings instituted by the original proponents of the Statute, forced the nuclear powers to expand the scope of their preparatory conference, thereby converting it into a general international conference closely resembling in membership the General Assembly itself. If the founding powers had invited the Communist government of China to take part in the conference, thereby making possible the extension of the Statute and of the system of inspection contemplated under the Statute to Communist China, a separate procedure might have been justified. Since no such inclusion was intended of a power whose concurrence in a system of international inspection to prevent the diversion of nuclear fuels to military uses would seem to be indispensable for the success of such a system, the elaborate effort to make the International Atomic Energy Agency as independent of the United Nations as earlier specialized agencies seems ill-advised. Happily it was not wholly successful. In general it is clear that future international statutes of universal interest and comparable importance may better be enacted by a process wholly within the framework of the United Nations.

If there be objection to giving to the United Nations, which is not yet a universal organization, a practical monopoly of the international lawmaking process, the answer is clear. The membership of the Organization should become universal as quickly as possible. It may be conceded that, while the cold war rages, the admission of representatives of Communist China to the General Assembly and the Security Council and the admission of Germany to the Organization itself will be difficult to bring about. But the primary purpose of giving the United Nations a practical monopoly of the international lawmaking process is to help bring the cold war to an end. Doubtless important provisions of a peace agreement capable of ending the cold war are the recognition of the government of China at Peiping by all the nuclear powers and the adoption of some suitable arrangement for dealing with the division of Germany. These indispensable measures seem unlikely to be adopted until there is a determination among the nuclear powers to end the cold war. When there is more general understanding that the nuclear powers are unlikely to survive long in the nuclear age without such a determination, the desirable improvement of the international lawmaking process and the concomitant expansion of the role of politics in the organization of peace will be matters of no insuperable difficulty.

THE SOLUBLE PROBLEM OF THE SECURITY COUNCIL

The framers of the Charter conferred on the Security Council primary responsibility for the maintenance of international peace and security. To this end they expressly provided that this Council should be responsible for formulating plans for the establishment of a system for the regulation of armaments. These plans were to be submitted to the Members of the United Nations, presumably for their approval but, if not approved by all of them, they could be made effective for all by means of a Charter amendment, that is, with the approval of two thirds of them, including the five powers with permanent seats in the Council. The intention was clearly to make the Security Council a principal factor in the management of a more peaceful world. This intention has manifestly not yet been achieved.

An important reason for the failure of the Security Council to fulfill the expectations of the framers is disclosed in the correspondence between Premier Khrushchev and President Eisenhower concerning the control of nuclear weapons tests. Writing to the Presi-

dent on May 11, 1958, the Premier included the following reflections
with reference to the Security Council:

> I must dwell upon yet another question on which we should like
> to have everything cleared up between us. Of late the U.S.A. has
> been reproaching the U.S.S.R. for not agreeing to the United States
> proposal to establish an inspection zone in the Arctic area, although
> the majority of the Security Council had voted for that proposal. I
> must tell you frankly that the method used by the U.S.A. in the
> Security Council during the examination of the question tabled by
> the U.S.S.R. about the need to end the flights of United States
> nuclear-bomb-loaded planes in the direction of the Soviet frontier,
> in our opinion, does not testify to a serious desire to reach agreement
> on a mutually acceptable basis, but testifies to attempts to pressure
> the U.S.S.R. by using the majority in the Security Council. It is
> common knowledge that the majority in the Security Council is
> composed of the votes of countries dependent, in one way or an-
> other, primarily economically, on the U.S.A. Thus, the Security
> Council in its present composition can not be regarded as an impar-
> tial arbiter, and that is why it has of late ceased to play the impor-
> tant role in the maintenance of international peace and security
> which devolved upon it by virtue of the United Nations Charter.

This communication was treated by the United States Government
as a dialectical skirmish in the cold war and disposed of accordingly
without any attempt to discuss Khrushchev's question on its merits.
Such treatment was doubtless an admissible procedure in a cold war,
but if the cold war is to be ended the Security Council must be
rehabilitated. This will call for an inquiry into the reasons for the
Security Council's failure and some consideration of measures for
improving its representative character and restoring its lost prestige.

The basis of Khrushchev's complaint about the composition of
the Security Council appears clearly in the record of Security Council
elections. At the time when he wrote his letter there was no member
of the Security Council upon whom Khrushchev could count for support of the Soviet Union. At the Thirteenth General Assembly in
the autumn of the same year the changes made by the fresh elections
of Security Council members, as has already been pointed out, were
favorable to American interests. The subordination of the Soviet
Union to the United States in the Security Council has never appeared to be more complete than in 1959.

This is a satisfactory position for the United States as long as the principal function of the Security Council continues to be the production of cold-war propaganda. But if the Security Council is to function according to the design of the framers it is necessary that its composition be satisfactory to all five of the major powers. This can be achieved only by improving its representative character. It is not enough for the United States to procure the election of as many as possible of its military allies and political friends. The Security Council does not operate by the method of majority rule and cannot be used effectively by a majority party for its private purposes.

The scheme of representation in the Security Council devised by the framers of the Charter seemed at the time both realistic and reasonable. The strongest powers would have permanent seats and the other Members of the United Nations were to be represented with due regard primarily to their contributions to the maintenance of peace and to the other purposes of the Organization, but also with some consideration for equitable geographical distribution. The record shows that every one of the seventeen Members whose financial contributions amount to at least 1 per cent of the Organization's budget—a rough but convenient measure of contributions to the purposes of the Organization—if not provided with a permanent seat, has been elected at least once to the Security Council. Most of the Members in this group without permanent seats have been elected more than once. Of the thirty-four Members who contribute less than 1 per cent each, but not less than one-tenth of 1 per cent, fifteen have been elected to the Security Council at least once, and of the thirty Members who contribute less than one-tenth of 1 per cent, five have been elected. In 1959 no less than nine members of the Security Council belonged to the group of largest contributors and two members belonged to the group of smallest contributors.

It is evident that much attention has been paid to the first requirement for membership in the Security Council. The major powers with permanent seats contribute altogether 67.59 per cent of the Organization's ordinary income under the current budget and the eleven other member states, whose separate contributions amount to at least 1 per cent of the total, contribute collectively an additional 19 per cent. (For purposes of this calculation the Ukrainian and Byelorussian Soviet Socialist Republics are included with the Soviet

Union.) The thirty-three Members who fall into the second group of states, measured by the scale of financial contributions, collectively account for only 11.92 per cent of the total and the thirty Members in the third group account for no more than 1.49 per cent of the total. These ordinary and small states together, though possessing more than three-fourths of the votes in the General Assembly, do not seem hitherto to have taken for themselves an undue portion of the seats in the Security Council. There has been in the Security Council elections a striking show of respect for the major contributors.

The consideration shown for the claims of equitable geographical distribution has been less manifest. Including both Members with permanent seats and elected Members, the geographical distribution of the seats in the Security Council in 1959 appears in Table I.

TABLE I [1]

REGION	NUMBER OF STATES	CONTRIBUTIONS Per Cent	SEATS
1. Northern America	2	35.62	2
2. Middle & South America	20	4.89	2
3. Western Europe	13	22.61	3
4. Eastern Europe	13	20.46	1
5. Asia	22	12.87	2
6. Africa	9	1.34	1
7. Australasia	2	2.21	0
	81	100.00	11

[1] The African state of Guinea, admitted in December, 1958, is not included in this and the following tables.

The Soviet Union has charged that Eastern Europe is underrepresented; India, which in fourteen years has been elected for only a single term and then as a representative of the British Commonwealth rather than of Asia, would like better Asian representation; and from various quarters have come complaints that there are not enough elective seats to go around comfortably. There seems to be a strong case for a larger number of elective seats to satisfy the requirement of an equitable geographical distribution.

The truth is, however, that geographical distribution is not the important issue. The Soviet government wants more representation for Eastern Europe because it wants more representation for the Communist bloc, India wants more representation for the Bandung neutrals, and all the score and more of recently admitted states want more representation for the newcomers. The General Assembly has always recognized the importance of political factors by giving one of the elective seats to the British Commonwealth regardless of the geographical distribution of its membership. If the Security Council is to regain the confidence of the United Nations, it will be necessary to pay more attention to political considerations, even at the cost of geographical distribution. The problem is difficult of solution because of the complexity of world politics.

The distribution of Security Council seats among the military alliances and political groups existing in 1959 is shown in the following Table II.

TABLE II

POLITICAL GROUP	NUMBER OF STATES	CONTRIBUTIONS Per Cent	SEATS
I. American Group			
1. American Members of NATO	2	35.62	2
2. European Members of NATO	12	20.95	3
3. SEATO and other Asian Allies	7	10.40	2
4. Latin-American Members of OAS	20	4.89	2
Total	41	71.86	9
II. Russian Group (Warsaw Pact)	9	19.09	1
III. Bandung Neutrals	23	4.73	1
IV. Independent Neutrals	8	4.32	0
Grand Total	81	100.00	11

If the United Nations were a sovereign state, governed according to the principle of majority rule, the American group would constitute the majority party and the opposition groups would have to get together in order to make a realistic struggle for power. But the United Nations is not a sovereign state and its affairs are not administered according to any system of majority rule. The existing alliances, blocs, and groups reflect only one of the possible patterns of political alignment. Further analysis of the political scene is necessary to determine the kind of representation that is needed in the Security Council if politics is to supplant propaganda in its proceedings.

A basic fact in estimating the success of an experiment in international organization such as the United Nations is the kind of political education possessed by the representatives of the member states in the General Assembly and the Security Council. The performance of a political body is not likely to be better than the quality of the material of which it is composed. The political education of a delegate from, say, Iceland, with generations of experience in local self-government behind him, is radically different from that of a spokesman from the Imamate of Yemen, where the political traditions have come down through centuries of an utterly different kind of experience in the management of public affairs. Since the General Assembly and Security Council are not only diplomatic gatherings but also representative bodies, training in representative institutions at the national level should be a valuable asset for public men engaged in the business of the United Nations. If the expansion of the role of politics in the organization of peace is to serve the interests of mankind, the influence of democratic politicians in the proceedings of the United Nations should be strong and, if possible, preponderant.

Democracy is a word with different meanings in different parts of the world. The ancient Greeks, who invented the word, cannot be acquitted of the charge of imprecision in its use. Aristotle, who used words more carefully than most classical writers, seems to have meant by it something more closely resembling a modern dictatorship of the proletariat than what Western peoples understand by democracy today. He distinguished between democracy and what the modern West would call a democratic constitutional government. Before saying more about the influence of democracy in contemporary world politics I will explain what I mean by the word.

By democracy I mean more than merely a form of government based on universal suffrage and a system of majority rule. I mean a kind of state in which there is a general respect for basic human rights and fundamental freedoms. In such a state governments will derive their just powers from the consent of the governed and will maintain political processes by means of which the men at the head of public affairs can be changed, when the people wish a change, without resort to force and violence. In modern times this means some form of party government, in which party leaders operate under a system of free enterprise for politicians and those in power can trust their opponents to succeed them in office, when duly elected, without jeopardizing their own right to take the places of their opponents at a future election. The foundations of such a democracy are informed self-reliance on the part of the people and sturdy good faith on the part of their leaders.

It is not easy to draw the line between mature democracies, where the foundations are well laid, and emergent democracies, which offer less assurance that democratic processes of government will be maintained through periods of extraordinary political stress and strain. In general there cannot be the same confidence in the durability of democratic institutions in a state which has been trying to act like a democracy for the first time since the Second World War as in one with longer experience in operating democratic institutions. To qualify a state as a mature democracy there should be convincing evidence that the party in power will conduct honest elections and, if defeated at the polls, will yield control of the government to its political opponents without a violent struggle. Besides the new and comparatively untried democracies, other states which must be included among the emergent democracies are those with constitutionally elected governments actually in office but also with traditions of political instability and recurrent violence in the selection of their rulers. In the emergent democracies competitive party systems exist but have not demonstrated that they are firmly established. Some of them will eventually qualify as mature democracies; others will slip back into the ranks of the party or personal dictatorships; still others may remain emergent democracies for many years. The so-called free world is not a world in which mature democracy is the only kind of state.

There is another class of self-styled democracies, in which a political party dominates the government of the state but tolerates no rival and allows no change in the party system without resort to force and violence. Such a monopolistic party system possesses some, but not all, of the advantages of a true democracy. There might conceivably be a form of democracy within the dominant party, and if the party were open to all who might properly wish to join it the system could evolve into a true democracy. But in practice these monopolistic party systems are dictatorships; in the Communist states they are class dictatorships. They may even verge on some form of

military dictatorship. They cannot qualify even as emergent democracies. But they may possess a latent capacity, if they can keep out of
war and thereby escape the most serious stresses and strains on democratic institutions, to evolve into one of the freer kinds of state.

Besides the various forms of party government among the United
Nations there are two forms of personal rule. One is military dictatorship, where changes in the control of the government are accomplished by fighting, and the other is hereditary monarchy. The former
is apt to be more energetic and efficient but also more violent and
oppressive. The fighting which accompanies changes of government
is always a threat and sometimes ruinous to the prosperity of the
country. Hereditary succession offers the hope of peaceful change in
the control of the government but less promise of sustained political
capacity at the head of affairs. Hereditary monarchy is not incompatible with the actual control of affairs by a military dictator or by
some form of party government, in which case it ceases to be a form
of personal rule. The spokesmen for personal rulers may function as
effectively as representatives of other kinds of government in a
strictly diplomatic assembly. But in the organs of the United Nations
in the nuclear age, if there should be an expanded role for peace-
loving politicians, they are not likely to feel equally at home.

The present distribution of these various forms of government
among the Members of the United Nations, together with their
contributions to the budget and their representation in the Security
Council, are shown in Table III.

TABLE III

KIND OF STATE	NUMBER OF STATES	CONTRIBUTIONS Per Cent	SEATS
1. Mature Democracies	19	61.36	5
2. Emergent Democracies	14	9.78	3
3. Party Dictatorships	11	24.45	2
4. Military Dictatorships	25	4.47	1
5. Hereditary Monarchies	12	.94	0
	81	100.00	11

The leadership of the democracies in the United Nations, when
measured by contributions to the purposes of the Organization, is
apparent, but their control of the organs of the United Nations is
less certain. The existing governments in too many of the emergent

democracies are excessively unstable. If a larger role for politics in the organization of peace is to mean a larger role for democratic politicians, the right solution must be found for the problem of representation in the Security Council.

The road to the improvement of the representative character of the Security Council may be further explored by viewing the distribution of the different kinds of states, classified by their forms of government, among the different classes of states, measured by their financial contributions to the Organization (see Table IV).

TABLE IV

KIND OF STATE	MAJOR AND MIDDLE POWERS	MINOR POWERS & ORDINARY STATES	SMALL STATES
1. Mature Democracies	9	8	2
2. Emergent Democracies	4	6	4
3. Party Dictatorships	4	6	1
4. Military Dictatorships	0	11	14
5. Hereditary Monarchies	0	3	9
	17	34	30

The mature democracies are strongest among the major and middle powers, that is, the states whose respective contributions to the revenues of the Organization amount to 1 per cent or more of its ordinary income. They are weakest among the small states which contribute less than one-tenth of 1 per cent each to the Organization. The military dictatorships and hereditary monarchies are not represented among the major and middle powers and are most strongly represented among the small states.

The significance of these facts is evident. An obvious way to expand the role of democratic politics in the organization of peace is to strengthen the influence in the Security Council of the larger contributors to the purposes of the Organization. The Commission to Study the Organization of Peace has already recommended in its Tenth Report (*Strengthening the United Nations*) that the Security Council be enlarged by the addition of a number of seats to be determined by the Security Council and the General Assembly. This would require an amendment to the Charter, but not necessarily a Charter Review Conference in order to prepare the amendment. The enlargement of the Security Council can readily be accomplished by the ordinary process of Charter amendment. The General Assembly was actually planning to add two seats to the Security Council by an

amendment under consideration in 1955, when the membership of
the Organization was increased from sixty to seventy-six, but was
restrained by opposition from states with permanent seats in the
Security Council. With the subsequent and prospective increases of
membership a greater increase in the size of the Security Council
would doubtless be deemed desirable.

Advantage should be taken of the enlargement of the Security
Council to improve in other ways its representative character. Service
in the Security Council should be made more attractive to the middle
powers by authorizing the election of additional members who are
large contributors to the purposes of the Organization, without regard
to geographical distribution, and by making them eligible for immediate re-election at the expiration of their terms. As long as such a
state as India is the actual leader of a substantial group of Members,
it should be possible to keep it in the Security Council while it continues to command the confidence of its followers. Additional permanent members of the Security Council with a veto are not wanted,
but the opportunity should be created for group leaders to have a
voice and vote there as long as they maintain their leadership. To
increase the participation of the middle powers in the Security Council means to enlarge the opportunities for the democracies to influence its actions.

The vision of a polarized world, in which all the nations are
gathered around Washington or Moscow, is a beguiling one for some
democrats. It involves the establishment of a two-party system in
world politics, which would seem to ensure the supremacy of the
American group in the United Nations. Closer inspection of the
materials for a majority party under American leadership, however,
discloses that the organization of a powerful democratic party is
impracticable. The political composition of the present American
majority in the General Assembly is shown in Table V.

TABLE V

KIND OF STATE	AMERICAN GROUP	RUSSIAN GROUP	BANDUNG NEUTRALS	INDEPENDENT NEUTRALS
1. Mature Democracies	14	0	0	5
2. Emergent Democracies	9	0	4	1
3. Party Dictatorships	1	9	0	1
4. Military Dictatorships	17	0	7	1
5. Hereditary Monarchies	0	0	12	0
Total	41	9	23	8

The American group is dependent for its majority upon the support of substantial numbers of military dictatorships. No majority party is possible which does not include numerous dictatorships of some kind or small Oriental monarchies.

In fact the two-party system in any form is unsuitable for United Nations politics. To yield to the temptation to work for the establishment of such a system would be a great mistake. It could not be established without the complete abolition of the veto in the Security Council and other changes in the direction of a much more centralized form of government for the United Nations. Such changes are not necessary in order to end the cold war. Indeed, if they were possible, they would make its ending more difficult. What is necessary is a fixed determination by the nuclear powers to operate the institutions which have been established under the Charter in accordance with the intentions of its framers. The method of consensus supplies the basis of a workable system of politics under the appropriate conditions. The creation of the appropriate conditions is not beyond the capacity of the nuclear powers. Those who really wish a firmer organization of peace should give the method of consensus in United Nations politics a fair trial.

To give the method of consensus a fair trial the most important condition is a fairly representative Security Council. To satisfy this condition it is desirable to assure adequate representation to those dutiful middle powers which not only make substantial financial contributions to the work of the United Nations but also furnish efficient contingents to the emergency forces and observer corps which are occasionally needed to give effect to the decisions and recommendations of the Organization. Some of the additional seats in an enlarged Security Council should of course be made available for geographical areas not equitably represented therein, but others should definitely be reserved for large contributors to the Organization's purposes. Such an enlarged Security Council could command the confidence of the various divisions of mankind. The growth of confidence is the indispensable basis for an expanded role of politics in the organization of peace.

THE POLITICAL IMPERATIVES OF THE NUCLEAR AGE

The organization of peace in the nuclear age will mark the end of a gradual evolution in accepted thinking concerning the problem of keeping the peace in the family of nations. Time was when the best thinking concerning this problem was represented by the doctrine of the balance of power. The problem was conceived to be one of coercing sovereign states which threatened to exercise their legal right to make war. The method of coercion was to organize a combination of states, bent on peace, strong enough to resist successfully any state or combination of states bent on aggressive war. If the states prepared to meet force with force were manifestly strong enough to overpower the aggressors, the peace was likely to be preserved as long as other things remained unchanged. But in the longer run other things were likely to change. Particularly the relative strength of different states was likely to change. The system of peace-keeping therefore needed one or more states ever willing to support the weaker side against the stronger in a warlike situation and capable of giving the weaker side sufficient additional strength to deter the stronger from breaches of the peace and acts of aggression.

In the nineteenth century the British government essayed the role of peace-keeper through manipulation of the balance of power. On the whole it did so with impressive success. There were plenty of petty wars, mainly incidental to imperial expansion by major European powers, but no great wars between the major powers themselves. Local wars, which might have spread and become great wars, were successfully limited and ended before they became great international disasters. But a price had to be paid for the success of the system. The government which undertook to hold the balance of power had to be able and willing to intervene in any threatening situation on the weaker side regardless of the merits of the particular controversy. Thus its policy might appear in a particular case to be immoral. The British government defended its manipulation of the balance of power with the plea that its interventions were justified by the greater good of general peace, even though they might appear to involve some injustice in cases where the weaker side might seem to be in the wrong. It could even change sides, if necessary, to preserve the balance of power, regardless of the special interests of former associates. The appellation "perfidious Albion" could be borne with dignity as long as the system continued to serve the general interest in peace.

What Woodrow Wilson and the other founders of the League of Nations sought to do was to put a moral foundation under the balance-of-power system of peace-keeping. They rejected the idea that the keepers of the peace should intervene in a threatening situation regardless of the merits of the particular controversy but retained the idea that a threat of aggressive war should be countered by a threat of overpowering defensive war. The danger of violent aggression was met by the assurance of forcible coercion and, if necessary, aggression itself would be met by officially sponsored and organized enforcement-action. The founders of the League accepted the implied obligation to determine the merits of international disputes, threatening to lead to breaches of the peace or acts of aggression, by suitable proceedings in an open forum of the nations and devised what they hoped would be effective processes of collective action in the interest of collective security.

The League Covenant marked a great advance in the organization of peace over the traditional balance-of-power system. But it did not abandon the basic principle that the peace was to be kept by holding the threat of coercion over sovereign states planning aggressive use of their legal right to make war. Unhappily the reluctance of the major powers to perform their duties under the Covenant, together with defects in the structure and procedures of the League, prevented this more moral system of keeping the peace by manipulating the balance of power from achieving its objectives.

Franklin D. Roosevelt and the other founders of the United Nations took another great forward step in the thinking about the problem of peace. They rejected not only that part of the traditional balance-of-power system which had already been rejected by the founders of the League but also the idea that sovereign states possessed a right to make aggressive war. The sanction for this act of renunciation, as far as the holders of permanent seats in the United Nations Security Council were concerned, consisted in their own good faith. As far as other states were concerned, international police action, authorized by the Security Council, was to be substituted for war as a means of coercing states which might be unmindful of their obligations under the Charter. Member states may still wage defensive war under the Charter, but aggressive war is outlawed. The coercion of bellicose states, if they are not dangerously powerful, remains a part of the new system of organizing the peace. The framers of this system of peace-keeping obviously assumed that the major powers had learned the folly of war among themselves by their hard experiences in the two world wars. Possessing collectively a strong preponderance of power, the major powers, the framers seemed to believe, would have no need for any form of the traditional balance-of-power system of keeping the peace. Responsibility for maintaining international order was at last to be combined with adequate powers for dealing with irresponsible states which might still require coercion.

How the system of peace-keeping under the United Nations Charter might have operated if there had been no major advance in the art of war cannot be known. In fact the outbreak of the cold war showed that the major powers had not fully learned the lessons of their hard experience. As long as the United States retained its monopoly of the atomic bomb it could hope to operate a balance-of-power system within the framework of the United Nations. When that monopoly was broken, the cold war ceased to make sense for either of the principal combatants. Efforts to intimidate an opponent armed with nuclear weapons were bound to fail. Intimidation was mutual, and the threat of massive retaliation lost its potency. If the cold war did not tragically turn hot, it was clearly destined to fade away in the dawn of a genuine peace.

In short, the development of the most modern weapons has ushered in a new stage in the organization of peace. The principles of the United Nations Charter, rationally interpreted, are so clearly compatible with the interests of the nuclear powers that it should no longer be necessary to rely upon their good faith to make the new system of peace-keeping work effectively. Recognition by the nuclear powers that cold war, like hot war, is obsolete does not necessarily put an end to the danger of war. War between the nuclear powers might break out by accident. A clearer and more imminent danger to peace comes from the lesser states which may still hope for tangible gains from a victorious war fought with the old-fashioned weapons. The classical theory of war is not wholly obsolete in a world where there are many states with ungratified ambitions, weak neighbors, and no access to the new weapons. Under these circumstances the adaptation of the United Nations to the requirements of the nuclear age is an urgent piece of unfinished business.

The first imperative of the new system of peace-keeping is that the party system in international politics must be adapted to the needs of the nuclear age, an age, it must be kept in mind, in which the lawmaking authority under the United Nations Charter will be broadly construed and the annual budgets of the Organization and its affiliated international agencies will deal with expenditures running into many billions of dollars and with corresponding revenues. This means the rejection of the two-party system in the Security Council and the General Assembly and the adoption of some form of the multi-party system. It seems likely that there will be at least as many parties as permanent members of the Security Council and that the method of consensus, at least among the nuclear powers, will become the normal procedure in international politics. While the cold war rages, the American and Soviet efforts to operate a two-party system seem necessary and proper. But the end of the cold war must bring the beginning of an effort to operate a more flexible and sensitive party system.

The principle of simple majority rule cannot be an acceptable substitute in world politics for agreement by the nuclear powers. The traditional sanction for the principle of majority rule is convenience. Democrats do not have to believe that the majority is always right. To accept such a belief is to acknowledge that might may make right. Superiority of numbers at the polls is no more a guarantee that truth prevails over error than superiority of arms on the battlefield. It is the convenience of a rule, under which there can be prompt decision and effective action in ordinary matters, that commends it to the people of modern democratic states. But wise constitution makers provide for longer deliberation and broader agreement before definitive action in matters of extraordinary importance. The preservation of peace in the nuclear age is such a matter. The Yalta voting formula, with some modification in those Security Council proceedings which take place under the provisions of the Charter for the pacific settlement of disputes, is convincing evidence of the wisdom of the framers.

The method of consensus in international lawmaking has already demonstrated its practicability. In the international conferences, which have produced the great statutes under which the International Court of Justice and the specialized agencies operate, those major powers which were concerned with the purposes of the proposed agencies have been able to reach agreement without too much difficulty. The consent of the minor powers and lesser states has often proved as difficult, or even more difficult, to obtain. The method, though slow, laborious, and uncertain, is capable of making law for situations of exceptional importance. The problem of the nuclear powers, which must take the lead in developing a suitable legislative process within the United Nations, is to adapt it to the kind of situation with which the Security Council is likely to be concerned. The indispensable condition is that the nuclear powers understand that mankind has no rational alternative to superseding the politics of war by the politics of peace.

Politics, conceived as the practical business of arranging consent to proposed actions in a policy-determining body, is an essential function of human organization at all levels. The true relation between politics and law at any level of organization is not that in which law displaces politics but rather that in which improved political processes produce more ungrudging consent to better laws. The role of the politician in a democracy is not to impose ill-considered laws upon reluctant subjects but to contrive arrangements by means of which his fellow citizens obey a prescribed rule of action as the most effective means of accomplishing their own purposes. International organization on the eve of the nuclear age has already reached a stage where it should be possible to attract to the Security Council and the General Assembly of the United Nations statesmen who are intellectually and temperamentally capable of putting to good use the opportunities which these bodies will increasingly afford for practicing the art of politics. To mediate successfully between contentious powers and thus to prevent war is good; to persuade them to agree upon common action in the general interest of mankind is better.

The great difficulty in expanding the role of politics in the organization of peace is that the politicians cannot ordinarily deal directly with the people of the so-called sovereign states which make up the family of nations. They have to deal with the particular persons who operate the governments of those states, and these persons unhappily are apt to put their continued control of power ahead of the interests of the rest of the people for whose benefit such power exists, or is presumed to exist. There is the ever-present temptation to appeal over the heads of the men in power to the people behind them, but yielding to this temptation leads to subversive propaganda and other political practices better suited to the requirements of cold war than of genuine peace. If the international politicians in the Security Council and the General Assembly are to make the best use of their great opportunity they must aim at obtaining the consent of the men who have a right to speak for the member states. It is a great advance in the organization of peace that unanimous consent is no longer required except in the cases of the spokesmen for the five powers with permanent seats in the Security Council.

It is clear that under the Charter, as originally designed, the United Nations was to be primarily a diplomatic body. The Security Council, instead of conducting its deliberations in open meetings and in the manner best suited to the needs of aggressive propaganda, could have met in private, thereby greatly facilitating the process of diplomatic accommodation. In fact the popular yearning for "open covenants, openly arrived at" fostered the development of a kind of parliamentary diplomacy, a new political art for which practical politicians may be better qualified than professional diplomats. Nevertheless, the facilities which the Organization affords for the practice of conventional diplomacy constitute an important improvement in the organization of peace. There are the ready opportunities for informal negotiations between representatives of the member states, which have already been put to good use in critical times. There is a growing body of experienced diplomats in the Secretariat itself under the skillful leadership of the Secretary-General. There are interesting possibilities for the further development of a diplomatic corps to serve as agents of the United Nations wherever international tensions may form threats to the peace.

It is also clear that parliamentary diplomacy promises to become an invaluable advance in the organization of peace. Though it has contributed to the perversion of the Security Council into an instrument of aggressive propaganda, in the General Assembly it has been more than a convenient device for use in the cold wars. It is already making the recommendations of the General Assembly considerably more influential than was originally anticipated. Even without recourse to legislation the Organization can make a solid contribution to the preservation of peace. But, to a greater extent than is commonly recognized, the Organization is capable under the Charter of becoming an important agency for the adjustment of disputes between member states by the potent process of lawmaking.

The second imperative of the new system of peace-keeping is that the international lawmaking process must be adapted to the needs of the nuclear age. It is not necessary that the Security Council and the General Assembly become legislative chambers of the conventional type in national states or that in the beginning of the nuclear age the Charter be radically amended in order to confer additional legislative authority upon them. The Organization already possesses a substantial quantity of lawmaking power. To say nothing of the power to enact administrative regulations, applying to its own officers and employees, it can adopt budgets, levy assessments upon member states, and spend money for the purposes proclaimed in the Charter. The power to spend money, as Americans have learned from the history of their own Federal Union, implies the power to finance activities not even dreamed of by the framers of the Charter. There is no limit, except that imposed by the difficulty of raising revenue, to what the Organization can try to do by the expenditure of money to promote the general welfare of mankind. Moreover, decisions by the Security Council, taken primarily in order to deal with particular situations threatening to lead to serious disputes, give notice to all nations what they may expect to happen to them in similar situations. Such decisions may include elaborate arrangements for adjusting disputes between member states. If these arrangements prove efficacious, the decisions acquire the force of precedents. The accumulation of precedents produces law.

Both the decisions of the Security Council and the recommendations of the General Assembly in disturbing situations must carry with them the assurance of sufficient support to make any ordinary state pause before treating them with contempt. With sufficient weight of authority behind them recommendations should generally serve as well as decisions, and the General Assembly therefore should be able to act almost as effectively as the Security Council in cases involving the possibility of lawmaking by this process. In the nuclear age the indispensable sanction for such a legislative process must be a consensus among the nuclear powers. When such a consensus exists, skillful international politicians should not find too much difficulty in procuring the necessary additional support among the lesser powers and other member states. Though the legislative powers expressly conferred upon the Organization seem modest, its practical capacity to make acceptable adjustments between the conflicting interests of member states by what is in effect a kind of legislative process may eventually prove to be one of its most important attributes.

When there is a recognized need for greater certainty in making international law than is possible under the decision-making and recommendation-making procedures in the Security Council and the General Assembly, the Organization can have recourse to the procedure for amending the Charter. This procedure is more difficult than the traditional processes for making international conventions, since it requires unanimous agreement among the five major powers, but it possesses the important advantage that legislation adopted by the amending process is binding upon all member states, whereas the legislative product of the traditional processes binds only those states which ratify it. Like the Statute of the International Court of Justice, amendments can be annexed to the Charter and become integral parts of it without actually cluttering up the basic document with masses of ordinary legislation. The history of the Statute creating the International Atomic Energy Agency shows the practical utility of an international lawmaking process which is independent of that provided by the Charter in time of cold war. An agreement among the nuclear powers, however, to end the cold war, which is so greatly in their interest, would clear the way for the adoption of important international statutes by the amending process. Whether a simpler legislative process, such as the enactment of laws by the concurrence of the Security Council and the General Assembly, should be introduced for lawmaking in particular fields of international politics is a question which can be left for the future. It is enough to know at the beginning of the nuclear age that the Charter, as it has been written, provides a workable legislative process for international politicians whenever there may be a general disposition to make use of it.

The third imperative of the new system of peacemaking is that the international administrative process must be adapted to the needs of the nuclear age. This means that the principle of personal responsibility for official acts must be applied to the men in power in so-called sovereign states and that the coercion of such states must give way to the disciplining of offending individuals. The Nuremberg and Tokyo war-criminal trials at the close of World War II set a precedent for proceedings against persons who may be responsible for disturbing the peace in the nuclear age. Robert A. Taft was not the only thoughtful statesman to feel misgivings about the execution of offenders against a law which did not clearly provide for a process of trial and punishment. But the war-criminal trials did establish the fact that the renunciation of war as an instrument of national policy by the Pact of Paris, proclaimed at Versailles in August, 1928, was an enforceable part of the law of nations eighteen years later.

The provision of suitable procedures for dealing with individuals who may disturb the peace of nations in the future is an important piece of unfinished business for the United Nations. The Charter, rightly construed, gives power to the Security Council to provide such procedures if it finds that the lack of them is likely to lead to situations which may give rise to dangerous disputes. The Security Council should decide in advance of the next emergency how war criminals shall be tried and punished. Statesmen who control powerful national armaments and meditate their employment in offensive warlike operations should have no ground to complain, if eventually brought to justice, as did certain war criminals in 1946, that they were victims of victors' justice, administered without due notice by no other right than that of conquest. The accent in the nuclear age should fall upon peace through enforcement of law instead of peace through victory in war.

Peacemaking in the nuclear age calls for the collaboration of statesmen capable of perceiving the general interests of mankind and willing to put these interests ahead of the special interests of particular states. Who speaks for man? should be not a rhetorical question but a realistic inquiry. What a war-weary and frightened world needs most at this phase in the development of international organization is a better opportunity for leadership, animated by an intelligent concern for the general welfare of all nations and bent on framing and carrying into effect constructive international programs and policies. The annals of the United Nations already record a lengthening list of skillful politicians who have responded to the challenge of provocative events and have achieved such successes under the present Charter as justify the expectation that an improved and strengthened Organization would supply a firmer foundation for an orderly world. It is easy to understand the nature of the measures that would improve and strengthen the Organization. To bring about action in the light of this understanding is more difficult. Effective action, however, need not wait for a United Nations Charter Review Conference.

What is now in order is prompt action to improve the opportunities for leadership in international politics by the middle powers. The major powers, those with permanent seats in the Security Council, rely too much upon violence or intimidation as an instrument of national policy. In the most recent years they have shown themselves too quick to employ their arms in military adventures, either forgetting their obligations under the Charter or seeking to justify their military operations by strained interpretations of its language. The middle powers are less tempted to engage in such adventurism and more apt to combine some necessary idealism with the proper realism in international affairs. The honor roll of the member states in the United Nations is headed by Canada, which took the lead in the organization of the Emergency Force at Suez. Others on the honor roll are those which instantly responded to the call for serviceable contingents: the three Scandinavian states, India, Brazil, Colombia, and Yugoslavia. It is such states as these whose influence in world affairs needs to be strengthened.

The great objection to the arms race, and to the cold war of which the arms race is the most conspicuous feature, is not the fantastic waste of money which it involves. It is the practical certainty that if the race is long continued the arms will be used. The middle powers, not yet possessing the most modern weapons but competent enough in the use of weapons suitable for putting down occasional disturbances created by irresponsible ordinary and small states, command the confidence of the nations. They will more easily than others be elected to the Security Council, if room is provided there for additional members of the United Nations regardless of geographical distribution. This is the open road to improving the representative character of the United Nations and to expanding the useful role of politics in the organization of peace.

It is of course true that mere changes in the form of an organization are not enough to bring about important improvements in the quality of its product. There must also be the will to put the better organization to good use. But in the nuclear age the will to substitute the politics of peace for the politics of war follows closely on the discovery of the ruinous potential of the most modern weapons. A new system of peace-keeping is as inevitable as it is rational. War between nuclear powers is indeed unthinkable. The immediate practical problem is to protect them against involvement in war without thinking. For this purpose there must be an expanded role for peace-loving politicians in the United Nations.

ATOMS FOR PEACE:

THE INTERNATIONAL ATOMIC ENERGY AGENCY

by John G. Stoessinger

ACKNOWLEDGMENTS

I wish to thank the Commission to Study the Organization of Peace. Through a generous grant, it enabled me to make an on-the-spot analysis of the International Atomic Energy Agency in Vienna and to attend the Second United Nations Conference on the Peaceful Uses of Atomic Energy in September 1958 in Geneva.

I owe many debts of gratitude to the officials of the International Atomic Energy Agency. Members of the Agency's Board of Governors and its Secretariat took time from their pressing duties to share their experience and impressions with the author. I am particularly indebted to Mr. Sterling Cole, Director-General, Dr. Paul Rudolf Jolles, Deputy Director-General, and Mr. Roger M. Smith, Director of the Division of Safeguards, for their patience and generosity.

Another debt I owe to Professors Arthur N. Holcombe, Inis L. Claude, Jr., Leland M. Goodrich, Lawrence S. Finkelstein, John H. E. Fried, and George Liska, who gave the author the benefit of their counsel and who are responsible for numerous substantive improvements in the text.

I am grateful for many constructive suggestions to my colleagues in the Department of Political Science at Hunter College: Professors Ruth G. Weintraub, Frederick L. Zimmermann, Robert D. Hayton, Melvin Richter, Robert S. Hirschfield, James F. Tierney, and Blanche D. Blank.

Miss Barbara K. Davidson assisted in the compilation of important data. Finally, I wish to thank Miss Elinor C. Fuchs for valuable editorial assistance.

117

Mankind has discovered the genius to disintegrate the atom. It must now find the genius to reintegrate mankind.

—*Representative of Brazil to the International Atomic Energy Agency*

INTRODUCTION

Atomic power, like other discoveries of genius, is inherently amoral. It does not guarantee human progress, merely change and process. Man imposes purpose and direction and may choose welfare or warfare.

The present study attempts an analysis of the International Atomic Energy Agency. This new member of the United Nations family represents a concerted effort by the world community to impose an international purpose and policy upon a process of fundamental change at its very beginning. The Agency is the first global organization pledged to enlist the discoveries of the new science in the cause of peace. Such initiative is rare in the history of both discovery and statecraft.

The IAEA was established only a short time ago. A complete analysis may therefore be made only of the legislative process which led to its establishment. Part I attempts to do this. International legislation is always complex, and the highly controversial issues with which the IAEA deals made its birth particularly difficult. For this reason the Agency's genesis is perhaps of special interest to the student of diplomacy and international organization.

Part II deals with the Agency in action: its responsibility to encourage the diffusion of atomic energy for peaceful purposes and its equally important task of preventing the diversion of nuclear technology and materials to the uses of war. Evolving patterns of the Agency's policy-making process, functions, and operations are examined; the negotiations leading to the creation of a special niche for the Agency in the United Nations system are traced; and the Agency's relations with bilateral arrangements and regional organizations dealing with the peaceful uses of atomic energy are discussed. Any assessment must, of course, be tentative. Part II concludes with an analysis of the dilemmas of universality and regionalism, especially problems of coordination in atomic development and control.

Part III is an attempt to evaluate the Agency in the context of the international struggle for power and peace.

PART I

THE ESTABLISHMENT OF
THE INTERNATIONAL ATOMIC ENERGY AGENCY (IAEA)
A CASE STUDY IN INTERNATIONAL LEGISLATION

THE LEGISLATIVE PROCESS

Three years of legislative labor culminated in the unanimous adoption by eighty-two states, on October 26, 1956, of the Statute of the International Atomic Energy Agency.[1] The negotiation of the Statute was arduous, complicated, and unique in the emergence of international legislation under United Nations auspices. The fact that unanimity ultimately prevailed with respect to a document dealing with a subject as controversial as atomic energy lends special significance to the genesis of the Agency.

When President Eisenhower first launched the idea of the Agency in his address "Atomic Power for Peace" delivered in the United Nations General Assembly on December 8, 1953, he proposed that "The United States would be more than willing . . . to take up with others 'principally involved' the development of plans whereby peaceful use of atomic energy could be expedited." [2] The President further stated that, "of those 'principally involved,' the Soviet Union must, of course, be one." [3]

While it is clear that the United States hoped for universality of membership in the Agency to be born, it is equally clear that the initial negotiating process was to be reserved for the powers "principally involved" in atomic energy. These "atomic powers" fell into three categories. The first group comprised those countries which were producing substantial quantities of fissionable materials.[4] It included the United States, the United Kingdom, Canada, and the Soviet Union. The second category included those powers in a position to produce and supply substantial quantities of "source material," especially uranium and thorium: [5] France, the Union of South Africa, India, Brazil, Belgium, Czechoslovakia, Portugal, and Australia. The third group, the Netherlands, Norway and Sweden, had attained technical skills in the field of atomic energy but did not produce either source or fissionable material.

Until the discussion of the Agency Statute in the Ninth General Assembly in the fall of 1954, those powers with neither technical skills nor source materials were excluded fom the drafting process despite the fact that the majority of states which were to constitute the membership of the projected Agency would fall into this category.

In early 1954 the United States planned to prepare a draft Statute for bilateral negotiations with the Soviet Union. The two main atomic powers would then invite a representative group from the producer powers to participate in the drafting process. Finally, the draft Statute was to be presented for comment to all other interested powers in the Ninth General Assembly. All three features of this plan, however, were to be radically changed.[6]

The United States first revealed an outline of a statute for an agency of the kind envisaged in President Eisenhower's proposal of December 8, 1953, in a Department of State memorandum handed to Soviet Ambassador Zarubin on March 19, 1954.[7] During the following five months five similar memoranda followed. All were rejected by the U.S.S.R., the last one on September 23, 1954. It is significant that these early outlines contained many features of the Agency Statute to be adopted two years later by eighty-two states including the Soviet Union.[8] The U.S.S.R. at first rejected the entire idea of an atoms-for-peace agency, claiming that the American plan evaded the problem of nuclear weapons and would tend to intensify the atomic armament race. In Mr. Molotov's words:

> The level of science and technique which has been reached at the present time makes it possible for the very application of atomic energy for peaceful purposes to be utilized for increasing the production of atomic weapons.[9]

The Soviet government, during the first six months of diplomatic correspondence with the United States, described the issues of disarmament and the peaceful uses of atomic energy as inseparable. Mr. Molotov's solution to the dilemma was a restatement of the Soviet position on the disarmament problem: prohibition of nuclear weapons would have to precede the creation of the Atoms for Peace Agency.[10] The American position steadfastly insisted on the separability of the two issues:

> In reality, ways can be devised to safeguard against diversion of materials from power producing reactors. And there are forms of

peaceful utilization in which no question of weapon grade material arises.[11]

The mid-1954 deadlock was a reflection in miniature of the struggle between the two great powers over disarmament. According to the Soviet government, only the prohibition of nuclear weapons would guarantee the birthright of an Atoms for Peace Agency. In the American view, effective international control of nuclear weapons would have to precede prohibition. In the words of Inis L. Claude, Jr.:

> The United States began by regarding prohibition [of nuclear weapons] as the element more costly to itself, while the Soviet Union considered control as the more onerous burden for itself. Hence, the United States insisted upon the priority of control, for fear that the USSR would never permit the realization of control if it first succeeded in imposing prohibition upon its rival; the American plan postponed the American sacrifice until the Soviet sacrifice should have been made. Contrariwise, the Soviet Union demanded that prohibition should come first, for fear that the United States would never actually move to the prohibition stage if it first succeeded in securing the development of a control system; the Soviet plan delayed the Soviet sacrifice until the American sacrifice should have been made.[12]

Thus the first stage of the American plan—to interest the Soviet Union in participation in the Agency—seemed thwarted in the summer of 1954 by having come under the cloud of the general disarmament debates. At this juncture the United States decided to proceed to the second stage of its plan: the negotiation of a draft statute without the Soviet Union. Ambassador Morehead Patterson, representative of the U.S. Department of State, issued invitations to seven other "atomic powers." Delegations from Australia, Belgium, Canada, France, Portugal, the Union of South Africa, and the United Kingdom met in Washington in the summer of 1954. While this eight-power negotiating group was engaged in its drafting labors, the United States government stated again that it kept the door open for the Soviet Union to join the group. It reserved the right, if necessary, to continue negotiations without the Soviet Union.[13]

On September 22, 1954, in a dramatic about-face, the Soviet Union indicated its willingness to separate the issues of disarmament and peaceful uses of atomic energy and to accept the eight-power draft as a basis for further negotiations.[14] This sudden Soviet reversal was greeted with surprise and ambivalence by the eight Western powers negotiating the draft Statute. They felt that the U.S.S.R. had calculated—as it had probably done on the question of United Nations membership—that its interests were better served inside than out.

As a power with great scientific accomplishments and potential, it is likely that the U.S.S.R. could not afford to ignore an organization which seemed to be assuming concrete form with a membership closely resembling that of the North Atlantic Treaty Organization.[15] By participating in the drafting of the Statute the Soviet Union could prevent the Agency from taking on the aspect of a hostile alliance. Most important, the Soviet Union perhaps foresaw and hoped to exploit the developing rifts between the atomic powers and the atomic "have-nots." The specter of a new atomic colonialism imposed by a small group of producer powers upon the underdeveloped countries of the world promised to justify the Soviet's role as self-appointed champion of the oppressed and exploited. Finally, Soviet absence from the Agency would have identified the United States in the eyes of the underdeveloped countries as the leading nation in the scientific and technological development of nuclear energy for peaceful purposes.

The Soviet Union's role as catalyst between the eight negotiating atomic powers and the atomic have-nots became manifest when the question of the Agency came up for the first time for general international discussion in the Ninth General Assembly in the fall of 1954. In the First Committee the Soviet delegation expressed consternation at the small size of the group that was to set up the Agency. It was composed "exclusively of European or quasi-European powers." [16] The discussions in the First Committee subsequently turned upon this question and proceeded to place the United States delegation on the defensive. Mr. Barrington, the Burmese delegate, expressed the sentiment of the majority when he stated:

> It is regrettable that Asia and South America had not been called upon to take part in the origin of the Agency. A new undertaking should be in fact, not only in appearance, a genuine United Nations effort. True, it had been promised that the draft treaty would be circulated to interested governments before it came up for ratification. But the difficulties in the way of changing agreements already signed are well known. It would be better, therefore, to place the

various states on an equal footing by making them all "founding fathers." [17]

Mr. Lodge replied by stating that the American government would invite

All governments to submit their views to Washington for serious consideration. The document would not be presented to the Assembly as a *fait accompli*. But the Assembly [was] not the appropriate place to draft the Agency Statute—a long and complex document.[18]

Mr. Menon, delegate of India, once more expressed the view of the majority when he countered that

The General Assembly is precisely the place for drafting the Statute. All nations should have an equal part in the actual elaboration of the Agency.[19]

As a result of these criticisms and the pressure of the General Assembly, the United States government, on July 29, 1955, decided to make the draft Statute the subject of multilateral negotiations. First, Brazil, Czechoslovakia, India, and the U.S.S.R. would be invited to join the original eight sponsors and, second, the completed new twelve-power draft would be submitted to all members of the United Nations and its specialized agencies at a conference on the final text of the Statute.[20]

The twelve-power negotiations in Washington from February 27 to April 18, 1956, were the crucial stage in the evolution of the Statute. During these six weeks a delicately balanced compromise document emerged which received the unanimous support of the drafting powers. A study of the negotiations reveals a minimum of voting *per se*. Unacceptable proposals were withdrawn rather than adopted over minority opposition. The accent was placed upon bargaining proposals which were tailored to meet the interests of the minority. In view of the serious disagreements not only between East and West but even more frequently between the atomic powers and the underdeveloped countries, this final unanimity was a remarkable accomplishment. The final report of the twelve-power group concluded:

The Group reviewed each article of the Statute, together with the proposed amendments, taking into account the comments advanced during the proceedings of the tenth regular session of the United

Nations General Assembly . . . At the final plenary session on
April 18, 1956, the Negotiating Group approved, *ad referendum*,
the revised text of the draft Statute . . . At the same session, the
Group agreed that a conference should be convened at the United
Nations Headquarters in New York in the latter part of September
1956 to discuss, approve and open for signature the Statute of the
International Atomic Energy Agency . . .[21]

In accordance with the recommendation of the working level
group, an International Conference on the Statute convened for five
weeks in September and October, 1956. The Conference exhibited
a high degree of initiative. The vast majority of the amendments to
the Statute offered at the International Conference were proposed by
those powers with neither highly developed nuclear technical skills
nor source materials. Approximately half the amendments brought
to a vote at the Conference were adopted.[22] Although there was
little unanimity on individual items, the Statute as a whole was
adopted unanimously on October 26, 1956. Three years of labor had
given birth to a constitution.

Three features thus characterized the negotiating process. First, discussions on the Statute ended, but did not begin, as genuine multilateral diplomacy. The United States in 1954 made no effort to
include atomic have-nots in the negotiations, and the eight-power
group was therefore highly unrepresentative of the ultimate membership of the Agency. Second, the General Assembly of the United
Nations exerted considerable influence upon the legislative process.
The Assembly criticized the American proposal that comments on
the Statute be communicated by interested powers directly to Washington and insisted on multilateral diplomacy in the formulation
stage of policy. Many delegates felt that communications to Washington could have been disposed of one by one in a series of bilateral
discussions, without the collective will of the General Assembly ever
being expressed. The twelve-power negotiating group became a small
but representative body including those states most vitally interested
in matters of atomic energy. Finally, it was unprecedented for a special group outside the United Nations committee structure to draft
international legislation. The fact that unanimity on a highly controversial subject prevailed in the group suggested to many delegations
the possibility of using a similar drafting technique in the future.

THE PROBLEM OF MEMBERSHIP

The original eight-power negotiating group recommended in August, 1954, that the initial membership of the Agency be limited to states which were members of the United Nations or any of the specialized agencies. The admission of new states would have to be recommended by the Board of Governors and then approved by the General Conference, the two main organs of the Agency. In accordance with President Eisenhower's intention to establish the Agency under the aegis of the United Nations, membership and admission procedures were closely patterned after those of the parent organization. The American position was supported by the other seven powers and was incorporated without change into the Statute of the Agency at the International Conference in October, 1956.[23]

This position, however, was challenged in the twelve-power negotiations, where it provided one of the few issues on which it was impossible to attain unanimity. It was challenged again with no success during the Statute Conference. The major point of controversy was the admission of Communist countries which were members neither of the United Nations nor of the specialized agencies: the Chinese Communist regime, North Korea, East Germany, Outer Mongolia, and Viet Minh.

During the twelve-power discussions the Soviet and Czechoslovak delegations took the position that Communist China, as a nation possessing both source materials and technical skills in the field of atomic energy, was a power "principally involved" in the affairs of the Agency regardless of membership in the United Nations or its specialized agencies.[24] Any reference to United Nations membership, they held, should be deleted from the Statute, and the sole criterion should be a nation's capacity to participate in the development of the peaceful uses of atomic energy. "In this venture, the existence and aspirations of 700 million people cannot be ignored." [25]

Ambassador James J. Wadsworth, representative of the United States, contended that the Agency would be so closely connected with the United Nations that conditions for membership could not be widely different in the two organizations. The Agency should not revive bitter political controversies, the American argument ran, but should conduct itself in such a way as to further the principles of the United Nations.[26] The American position was carried in the twelve-power group by a vote of 9–2 with India abstaining.

The controversy flared up again during the Statute Conference. Both American and Soviet delegations restated their positions on membership. The delegates seemed to be divided along lines very similar to those that had obtained in the discussions in the General Assembly on the problem of Chinese representation. However, Mr. Lall, the Indian representative, pointed out that the question of membership in the projected Agency included an additional dimension. He implied that Red China's membership was not only a boon to be enjoyed but a responsibility to be shouldered:

> We must remember in dealing with this question that it is intended that the Agency not only will be in charge of the development of atomic energy for peaceful purposes but that it will be the Agency which will protect all countries from seepage of atomic energy for peaceful purposes into the domain of non-peaceful purposes, which, of course, none of us wishes to see happen. Is it then not extremely unwise of us to set up the Agency in such a manner that it excludes from its operations wide territories of the earth and over one quarter of its population? Do we not leave most unjustifiably a large loophole in which the safeguard operations to which I have referred would not be operative and in which we would not be able to make those safeguards operative in those areas? Is this not most unwise in this particular case whatever may be the decisions which have been taken in respect of membership of other agencies? I feel that this reason, which is special to this Agency, is one which should lead us all to agree that we should bring within this Agency all the countries and peoples of the world.[27]

The logic of this argument was not lost upon the delegates. It pointed up the problems inherent in the membership issue. The United States, supported by the majority of delegates, regarded the Nationalist regime's representative as the competent spokesman for China, yet was concerned with Red China when inspection provisions and safeguards on atomic energy were contemplated. A similar contradiction had appeared the year before when the United States supported United Nations Secretary-General Hammarskjold's mission to Peiping on behalf of imprisoned military personnel while at the same time refusing representation to Communist China in the world organization.[28]

The United States wanted to make sure that atomic energy would
be distributed through the Agency only with the most stringent safeguards against diversion for military use, and yet permitted the Communist Chinese regime access to atomic energy without the safeguard of international inspection.[29] Regardless of Agency membership, of course, Red China could be supplied with fissionable material
on a bilateral basis.[30] But, as many delegates at the Statute Conference observed, membership would at least imply the principle of
international inspection of Agency-supplied material.[31]

The final vote of 53–18 with nine abstentions supported the American position but may have sown the seeds of a Pyrrhic victory. The
problem of admitting the five Communist regimes outside the United
Nations family was especially complex because of the dual nature of
the projected organization. The Agency was "to accelerate and enlarge the contribution of atomic energy to peace, health and prosperity throughout the world." [32] In this positive sense it was to aim
at raising standards of living everywhere. But, of equal importance, it
was to have the restrictive function of ensuring, "so far as it is able,
that assistance provided by it or at its request or under its supervision
or control, is not used in such a way as to further any military purpose." [33] In that sense the Agency was to be related to the over-all
problem of disarmament by siphoning off for peaceful uses fissionable materials available for war.

The majority vote on the membership issue portended serious
problems for the Agency about to be born. With regard to the
Agency's first function, the idea might be defended on both political
and moral grounds that an unpurged aggressor power should not
receive the assistance of an international organization closely related
to the United Nations. While this criterion might be applied to Communist China and North Korea, it would not hold with equal validity
in the cases of Outer Mongolia, Viet Minh, and East Germany. The
argument used in the General Assembly—that these powers did not
adhere to the principles and purposes of the Charter—would condemn
the Agency membership policy to ambiguities similar to those which
plagued the United Nations and the specialized agencies.

In regard to the Agency's second function, an analysis of the membership decision must turn upon an assessment of the Agency's role
in disarmament. If one interprets the Statute literally, then international control would become operative only in the case of Agency-

supplied materials and Agency-approved projects. International inspection could not, of course, be applied to the excluded countries. If the hope is nurtured—as it was by the majority of delegates—that habits of international control and inspection could ultimately be transferred to the arena of armaments, then the exclusion of Red China may confine the Agency to a narrower role than might otherwise have been possible. It is paradoxical that the United States, the most articulate power in favor of an exclusive membership policy, was also the power most ambitious in its hopes and plans for the long-range functions and activities of the Agency. The admission debates during the Statute Conference—because of the unique nature of the new Agency—highlighted the dilemmas inherent in the membership problem more dramatically than ever before in the history of the United Nations.

THE EVOLUTION OF THE AGENCY'S STRUCTURE

As early as 1954, during the eight-power discussions, the Statute negotiators had decided that the Agency was to have three organs: a Board of Governors, a General Conference, and an administrative staff headed by a Director-General. But the nature and composition of each of these organs as well as the relationships among them presented the most difficult and stubborn problems that arose during the evolution of the Statute.

The thorniest issue was the composition of the Board of Governors. This organ was to be given preponderant authority "to make most of the necessary decisions for the Agency since the membership as a whole [could not] deal with day-to-day technical problems." [34] The eight-power group visualized an atomic parallel to the United Nations Security Council. The top atomic powers—the United States, the Soviet Union, the United Kingdom, France, and Canada— would be given permanent seats and special voting privileges. Five other powers were to be selected on a rotating basis from the other principal producers and contributors of source materials. Six countries were to be elected to the Board by the entire membership of the Agency through the General Conference. [35] In the words of the American representative this group of sixteen nations was to constitute

> a small Board of Governors in which appropriate recognition [was] given to the indispensable role of suppliers of the essential ingredi-

ents of peaceful atomic energy programs, but in which the interests of recipients of assistance as well as geographic representation are also appropriately weighted.[36]

As the number of negotiating powers increased, this formula came under severe attack. The principle of an "Atomic Security Council" with five permanent powers was criticized as unrealistic by Mr. Bhabha, the Indian delegate in the twelve-power discussions:

> The distinction between suppliers of material and technical assistance and receivers is not a hard and fast one. Some of those who are receivers today may be suppliers tomorrow. Some will be suppliers and receivers at the same time.[37]

Mr. Baxter, the Australian delegate, defended the American position:

> The Agency will be an instrument for putting to the best use contributions made largely by a small minority of the membership. Hence, this small minority should be recognized because otherwise the Agency would be stillborn. A similar system applies in the International Bank for Reconstruction and Development and in the International Monetary Fund where a special voice is accorded through a system of weighted voting.[38]

The debate sharpened when Mr. Bhabha criticized the eight-power draft as undemocratic:

> This service is to be rendered in a spirit of dedication and not in an arrogant take-it-or-leave-it manner. We have to carry the recipient countries with us as equal and enthusiastic partners in this enterprise and not as people who are prepared grudgingly to receive help because some of them have no option.[39]

Mr. Baxter countered by stating that the composition of the Board as suggested in the eight-power draft "would be undemocratic if everyone made the same contribution. But since the contributions [were] *not* the same, it would be undemocratic not to have weighted voting." He was supported by the delegate from Portugal, who added laconically that the Indian position would "make the Agency parallel to a bank whose governing body should be controlled by loan applicants." [40]

At this impasse the Soviet Union in a surprise move supported the Indian position by stating that the Board of Governors must have adequate representation of all parts of the world. A large Board is necessary since it will perform world-wide functions. The current figure of sixteen members proposed by the United States is insufficient.[41]

Mr. Holloway, the South African delegate, attacked the Soviet contention:

The Soviet position overemphasizes the principle of geographic distribution. Such a criterion would subordinate the producers of atomic material to the influence of the consumers. Unless the position of the producer group is adequately safeguarded there will be no incentive to join. On the contrary, such a country would incur risks.[42]

The Belgian delegate supported the South African argument by adding that the producer countries were in fact "the only irreplaceable group in the Agency and hence [were] entitled to a privileged position." [43]

At this point in the negotiations the eight original drafters found themselves solidly arrayed against the four additional delegates invited to the twelve-power discussions. The former insisted that the atomic powers have a privileged and permanent position on the Board while the latter were equally insistent on greater representation of the automatically underdeveloped countries.

The final solution was a delicately balanced compromise resulting in a cumbersome Board of twenty-three members. First, the top five atomic powers—the United States, the Soviet Union, Canada, France, and the United Kingdom—were given what amounted to permanent membership as long as they retained their leading positions in the atomic energy field in their respective geographic areas—North America, Western Europe, and Eastern Europe. It was not stipulated who would decide—and how—on the retention of their status as leading atomic powers. Second, the top atomic power in each of the remaining five geographic areas was to be designated a member of the Board through co-option by the permanent members.[44] Brazil, South Africa, Australia, India, and Japan were in this category. Third, two producers of source materials were to be designated on an annual rotating basis from the following four countries: Belgium, Czechoslovakia, Poland, and Portugal. Czechoslovakia and Portugal were designated to the first Board. Fourth, one nation would be designated on an annual rotating basis as a supplier of technical assistance.

On the first Board this role was given to Sweden. Finally, to meet
the demands of the atomic have-nots, ten members of the Board
would be annually elected by the entire membership of the Agency
through the General Conference.[45]

A unique mixture of self-perpetuation, co-option, and election
thus emerged from the twelve-power discussions on the membership
of the Board of Governors. When the formula was brought up for
debate at the Statute Conference in September, 1956, it was once
more bitterly attacked by the underdeveloped countries as an "atomic
club formula." A series of amendments were proposed, recommending
that the elected members of the Board be equal to the number of
those designated.[46] The Soviet Union now reversed its position and
aligned itself with the United States in defense of the twelve-power
draft:

> The draft article before the Committee seems to be a reasonable
> compromise. In a spirit of cooperation the delegation of the Soviet
> Union has decided not to move any amendments . . . and hopes
> that the same spirit of cooperation will prevail among other delega-
> tions . . .[47]

Mr. Wadsworth, U.S. representative, thanked the Soviet delegate for
his support and added that the formula "[represented] a finely balanced compromise even a small part of which [could] not be changed
without affecting the whole." [48] Nevertheless, criticism by the Afro-
Asian powers continued, and a concession had to be made. It was
decided that the composition of the Board, in particular the special
representation of the producers of source materials, would be placed
for reconsideration on the agenda of the fifth annual session of the
General Conference. This concession placated the atomic have nots,
who claimed that they were rapidly developing their own atomic
power. Mr. Bhabha, the Indian representative and spokesman for
the have-nots, now admitted that "the formula [had] been arrived
at by give and take on all sides." [49] This incident recalls an earlier
compromise at the San Francisco United Nations Charter Conference when the critics of the great power veto were placated in part
by the inclusion of the Charter of a provision for review of this
article.[50]

The evolution of the Board was therefore a record of compromise
between the atomic powers and the atomic have-nots. The Soviet
Union alone radically shifted its position. While it defended the

interests of the latter during the twelve-power discussions, it aligned itself with the former during the Statute Conference. The organ which finally emerged from the legislative struggle was unique in the United Nations family. In composition it resembled most closely the Council of the Intergovernmental Maritime Consultative Organization [51] and to a lesser extent the executive organs of the International Labor Organization, the International Bank for Reconstruction and Development, and the International Monetary Fund.[52] The right of the General Conference to elect ten members to the Board annually—a right insisted upon by the Afro-Asian powers—ensured that the Board would not become a closed shop. The principle of broad representation was to be a guarantor of the Board's strength although fears were expressed that this very principle might inhibit executive efficiency.

The cleavage between atomic haves and have-nots was also reflected in the negotiations determining the relationship of the General Conference to the Board of Governors. While the eight-power draft had placed great power in the hands of the Board, it had nevertheless anticipated future criticisms of this arrangement and had vested two important control powers in the General Conference: complete control over the purse and the election of six members of the Board.[53] When the group of negotiating states expanded to twelve the newly invited powers, including the Soviet Union, insisted that the powers of the General Conference vis-à-vis the Board of Governors be increased. The Soviet delegate maintained:

> The Board is now the highest organ of the IAEA. Hence, the few control the many. This relationship should be inverted. The highest authority should be the General Conference. Its decisions should be binding on the Board.[54]

The Soviet delegation, supported by India, Brazil, and Czechoslovakia, proposed that the number of Board members elected by the General Conference be increased from six to fifteen.[55]

The American delegation restated the arguments used in its defense of the Board's composition and added that as the Agency would be an operational organization its executive arm should be given as much independence as possible.[56]

Once more several concessions had to be made, all of which increased the power of the General Conference. First, the number of elected Board members was raised to ten. Second, it was agreed that,

if the Board was unable to arrive at a decision on a matter which it
would then choose to refer to the General Conference, the latter
body would have not only the power of recommendation but also the
authority to "take decisions." [57] This power to act in case of Board
paralysis was analogous to the "Uniting for Peace Resolution" passed
by the United Nations General Assembly in November, 1950, in
which the powers of the Assembly were increased vis-à-vis the Security Council. Finally, the twelve-power draft gave the General Conference the authority to "discuss any questions or any matters within the
scope of the Statute . . . and [to] make recommendations to the
membership of the Agency or to the Board of Governors or to both
on any such questions or matters." [58] This provision was considered
to be a powerful instrument of pressure on the Board, patterned after
Article 10 of the United Nations Charter enlarging the powers of
the United Nations General Assembly. In fact this increase in the
powers of the General Conference, as the negotiations progressed,
was reminiscent of the genesis of the United Nations. The authority
of the General Assembly was considerably increased at the San Francisco Conference, in contrast to the original Dumbarton Oaks proposals which emphasized the functions of the Security Council.[59]

Again, these concessions proved sufficient to have the new twelve-
power draft endorsed by the Statute Conference. The Soviet Union,
contrary to its position on the issue of Board membership, aligned
itself with the atomic have-nots demanding a more powerful role for
the General Conference. In fact a Polish amendment introduced
during the Conference which proposed that the General Conference
be granted the power "to determine the general policy of the Agency"
was narrowly defeated.[60] The ironic concluding remarks of Mr.
Holloway, delegate from South Africa, expressed the reaction of the
atomic powers to the concessions exacted from them:

> The recipients will bring into the common pool an element of grati-
> tude but no material or technical constituents of fissionable reactors.
> Gratitude has been defined as a lively sense of future favors and I
> may say in passing that judging from the number of requests re-
> ceived from many countries for more representation for the fourth
> group [recipient countries] I can say that there is no lack of gratitude
> in the world.[61]

A similar tug of war broke out during the discussions on the role of
the Director-General as the chief administrative officer of the Agency.

No criticism was leveled at those provisions of the original draft stipulating that the Director-General be appointed for a term of four years by the Board of Governors with the approval of the General Conference. During the twelve-power discussions, however, the U.S.S.R. and India took the position that, once appointed, the Director-General should be equally responsible to the Board and the General Conference. The United Kingdom delegate, Sir Alec Randall, countered with the following argument:

> It is unsound and quite impracticable to make a senior official responsible to two bodies. It is not really fair or wise to ask any man to serve two masters. Once appointed, the Director-General should be responsible to the authority which is ultimately responsible for the conduct of the Agency's operations—the Board of Governors. It seems superfluous and possibly harmful to expect the General Conference to scrutinize the directives issued by the Board to their senior executive. This would suggest that the Director-General and the Board might in some way conspire together against the General Conference. This is an absurd supposition. If the General Conference could not trust the discretion of the Board of Governors even to this extent, there would be something very wrong with the whole organization. It would seem much more sensible for the Board, as the responsible body, to answer to the Conference for the conduct of the Director-General.[62]

At the Statute Conference this view convinced those delegates who felt that sound administrative principles had to overrule mistrust of the atomic powers on the Board. The Soviet Union again associated itself with those Afro-Asian countries which remained unconvinced. At the final vote, however, the Anglo-American position prevailed by a large majority.

The matter of staff recruitment was the only item in the discussions of the Agency's structure which encountered no serious problems. Here United Nations precedent was followed. The eight-power draft worked out three criteria for recruitment which were endorsed without change by both the twelve-power group and the International Conference. It was decided that

> the paramount consideration in the recruitment and employment of the staff and in the determination of the conditions of service [should] be to secure employees of the highest standards of efficiency, technical competence, and integrity. Subject to this consideration, due

regard [should] be paid to the contributions of members of the Agency and to the importance of recruiting the staff on as wide a geographical basis as possible.[63]

In the evolution of the Agency's three major organs the East-West schism sometimes proved less divisive than the schism between the atomic and the non-atomic powers, as illustrated by the ambivalent behavior of the Soviet Union—an atomic power but also the self-appointed champion of the underdeveloped countries. During the dispute over the composition of the Board of Governors the U.S.S.R.'s vested atomic interests forced it to side with the atomic powers, including the United States. On the question of the Board's relationship to the General Conference and the problem of the Director-General's responsibility, however, it chose to subordinate its interests as an atomic producer to its role as chief anticolonial spokesman.

In the case of the United States, its common interest with the Soviet Union as a producer power injected an unusually high degree of harmony into negotiations with the U.S.S.R. once the twelve-power discussions had begun. Disagreements with the Soviet delegation never reached the intensity of the exchanges with India and other representatives from non-atomic countries. Apparently the particular nature of the subject matter elicited a unique negotiating process which compelled many major powers—especially the United States and the Soviet Union—to adopt unusual, at times anomalous, positions at the Statute Conference.

An important consequence of the many compromises made during the negotiating process was the lack of clear demarcation among the three organs of the Agency. The Statute, in its final form, was left vague with respect to numerous aspects of the separation of powers, especially in the area of policy formulation. In fact the Statute does not enumerate a single specific policy function of the Board of Governors and leaves unclear the precise policy powers of the General Conference.

The negotiating powers assumed—probably with some justification —that policies would evolve in a pragmatic fashion once the Agency was launched and that a high degree of flexibility would be an asset. The problems of atomic energy would be in constant flux; the attitudes of governments would change and new methods might become necessary as the work proceeded. The organs of the Agency might become preoccupied with a mass of current business and on some occasions the need for a policy decision might become apparent only when action had already been taken in the field. While many delegates expressed concern over the ambiguities inherent in the Statute's provisions on policy process, others were reassured by the hope that the very flexibility of policy formulation might create an atmosphere of cautious exploration. Many observers thought it wiser to proceed in this tentative way than to make far-reaching decisions on vitally important matters and put them smartly into execution.

THE DETERMINATION OF THE AGENCY'S FUNCTIONS AND POLICIES

1. DEVELOPMENT AND CONTROL:
THE SEARCH FOR THE GOLDEN MEAN

From the day of the Agency's conception its founding fathers were haunted by a formidable dilemma: how was the optimum balance to be struck between the Agency's developmental role as "contributor" to peace, health, and prosperity throughout the world, on the one hand, and its restrictive role as deterrent against atoms-for-war, on the other? It was feared that if safeguard restrictions were too onerous, the Agency might be bypassed in favor of less-demanding bilateral arrangements and hence be stillborn. If, conversely, Agency control and inspection arrangements were not rigorous enough, it would become entirely possible for recipient nations to divert part of the Agency-supplied materials to military programs and convert atoms-for-peace into atoms-for-war.

The search for a solution to this aspect of the atoms-for-peace program occupied the negotiating powers in their attempts to define the Agency's functions and policies. The dilemma was sharpened by the fact that President Eisenhower's 1953 address had had a profound effect on opinion in most of the world's underdeveloped countries. The enthusiastic responses of the Afro-Asian and Latin-American delegations in the United Nations were based on the hope that the United States through the new Agency would be able and eager to make the benefits of atomic energy available to the atomic have-nots of the world's population. Since the President had stated that the capacities of atomic energy were "here, now, today," the realization of this program was seen by many as an immediate reality rather than a distant promise. The eager expectations of the underdeveloped countries compelled the United States to consider rapid implementation of a program which would give priority to the underdeveloped areas of the world.

The early Soviet reluctance to participate in the Agency caused some revisions in the American position. In 1953 the United States hoped that the new Agency might become an international partnership, a sort of world-wide atomic energy authority and TVA combined.[64] With no positive response from the Kremlin, the Agency's role was bound to be very much more modest. This was not the only consideration which took the edge off the early American enthusiasm. The eight-power negotiations almost immediately showed up the difficulties of translating the "Atoms for Peace" address into a workable reality. Concrete technical problems of inspection and control presented great obstacles and induced a sober atmosphere in the committee, a far cry from the dramatic statements of a year before. For instance, it proved impossible during the entire negotiating process to distinguish the "peaceful" from the "military" purposes of atomic energy. Should the definition of "military" be restricted to the testing of nuclear explosions and its concomitant radioactive dangers? What about explosions for "peaceful" purposes? Where would this leave the use of nuclear fuels in the propulsion of a submarine, an airplane, or a missile? But to broaden the definition to include these latter uses might be inadvisable since the menace would not be much greater than that arising from the use of conventional fuels for similar objectives. Should a country with a military program be ineligible for Agency assistance altogether, since Agency-supplied materials might release more of the recipient's own atomic materials for military uses? Under such a restriction, what countries would still be eligible? [65] During the negotiations, then, it became apparent that any attempt at precise definition would create more problems than it would solve.

These and similar difficulties, apparent early in the drafting discussions, made the initiating eight producer powers wary and hesitant. This sense of caution remained when the Soviet Union, Czechoslovakia, India, and Brazil joined the committee in 1956. The Brazilian and Indian delegations minimized restrictive functions and saw the Agency as a benign dispenser to the needy of the blessings of atomic energy. In the words of the representative from Brazil:

> The Agency should not begin by emphasizing limitations and restrictions. Explicit attention should be paid to the needs of the underdeveloped areas, those countries which are hindered by the

lack of conventional power resources. Special attention should be paid to those countries whose economies are in a process of transition from an agrarian to an industrial stage. Atomic energy alone can solve many of these special problems.[66]

Mr. Wadsworth, United State representative, agreed that

the Statute should give the Agency a significant role in furthering the peaceful uses of atomic energy in underdeveloped areas . . .

but added that the drafters should

insist on a prudent degree of safeguards against military use and adequate provisions for health and safety.[67]

The Soviet and Czechoslovak delegations took no position on the Indian and Brazilian views, but reminded the United States that

any inspection and control [must be] carried out with due observance of the sovereign rights of States.[68]

It is significant that early in the twelve-power talks only the two atomic have-nots had a clear-cut conception of the Agency's general function. Obviously these delegations emphasized the developmental aspect. The United States had moved away from its original position of 1953 and now was equally concerned with the Agency's restrictive function. The Soviet delegation, caught between its common interests with the United States as an atomic producer and its role as champion of self-determination, took no well-defined position. The stage was set for a situation in which the underdeveloped countries, by virtue of their unambiguous position on the nature of the Agency's role, were to exercise a preponderant influence.

2. THE DEVELOPMENTAL FUNCTIONS OF THE AGENCY

Throughout the entire negotiations of the Statute, all delegations were in agreement on the principle that the Agency should have broad responsibility for all phases of development of the peaceful uses of atomic energy. In view of the fact that President Eisenhower's address had been very optimistic with respect to the prospects for the peaceful utilization of atomic energy, it was surprising that most delegations relegated the actual production of electric power by atomic fuels to a fairly distant future. In fact, while this aspect of the Agency had aroused great attention in the world's press, the

Statute drafters took a much more modest view of the Agency's early role. The discussions during the drafting process centered around two prerequisites for more ambitious programs: the training of scientists and the exchange of scientific information among Agency members.

In the course of the International Statute Conference numerous specific proposals to expedite the diffusion of scientific knowledge were advanced by delegates from the underdeveloped countries. The representative from Bolivia suggested that the Agency organize a World University of the Atom which would be

> a universal centre where all great professors, all great research men, might come to study the techniques of the field.[69]

The Haitian delegation suggested that the Conference should incorporate in the Statute a provision which would create a fund for the granting of training and research scholarships.[70]

The atomic powers had reservations about the inclusion of specific functions in the Statute. Sir Percy Spender, the Australian delegate, expressed the sentiments of all Western producer powers when he stated:

> If power is already conferred in general terms, what is the use of a special power when the general power already includes the special? Wisdom dictates that authority should be conferred in general or wide terms. To seek to particularize the powers already contained within the general authority is not only unnecessary, but may have the result of restricting the general powers conferred. Since these constitutional powers are being authorized not merely for the immediate and foreseeable future, but for the whole life of the Agency, powers must be conferred to do many things. None of us knows what powers the Agency may need to possess ten years—or less or more—from now.[71]

The Australian view that the Statute's provisions with respect to developmental functions should be brief and flexible made a strong impression at the Conference. However, the underdeveloped countries were interested in spelling out the Agency's functions in greater detail. The Soviet Union agreed with those delegates who stressed the need for scientists, but voiced no opinion on the statutory provisions. The argument of Ambassador Wadsworth, U.S. delegate, to the effect that a broad and general wording would not preclude any specific projects already proposed, placated most of the objecting delegations.[72] It was finally decided to leave specific programs to the Board of Governors and the General Conference and simply to authorize the Agency "to perform any operation or service useful in research." [73]

On the subject of exchange of information among Agency members there was general agreement that the Statute should make a distinction between information arising from assistance rendered by the Agency and other information. In the former case the obligation by a member to submit "all scientific information" would be mandatory.[74] In the case of general information on atomic energy matters it was agreed that members "should make available such information as would in the judgment of the member be helpful to the Agency." [75] Once more, specific projects were to be left to the Agency's operational organs. Foremost among such proposals was a Polish amendment suggesting the publication of an international periodical, *World Atomics*, devoted to the exchange of information on the peaceful uses of atomic energy among the members of the Agency.[76]

With respect to all developmental functions, the delegates at the International Conference outlined areas of collaboration between the Agency and competent organs of the United Nations and specialized agencies.[77]

3. THE CONTROL FUNCTIONS OF THE AGENCY: SAFEGUARDS, INSPECTION, AND SANCTIONS

Establishing safeguards against use of fissionable materials for military purposes was one of the greatest problems raised during the entire negotiating process. The solution of this problem removed the last obstacle to the unanimous approval of the Statute by the International Conference.

The struggle was three-cornered. The Soviet Union during the negotiations made a complete about-face in its attitude toward safeguards, finally identifying itself with the views of the underdeveloped countries. The Western atomic powers opened the negotiations in the eight-power talks with the demand for stringent safeguards, but by 1956 had modified their position substantially toward the view of the atomic have-nots. The underdeveloped countries maintained their position throughout with only minor concessions.

Both the United States and the Soviet Union announced their concern with the problem of military diversion soon after President

Eisenhower's address in the General Assembly, but their solutions differed radically. The possibility of increasing production of atomic weapons with materials granted for peaceful uses was employed by the Soviet Union as an argument against participation in the Agency. They claimed that safeguards would be meaningless in the absence of prohibition of atomic weapons.[78] The Americans advocated rigorous and foolproof safeguards:

> The capacity, existing or potential, to make atomic weapons is a fact. It is a fact for which the Agency is not responsible and which the Agency cannot assume the primary responsibility to correct. But the Agency must assume the responsibility of seeing that its activities do not make the existing situation worse. If the Agency were to make the materials and information for peaceful development of atomic energy available throughout the world *without full assurance that they cannot be used to produce weapons,* it would be adding to a problem which, difficult as it is, is sufficiently confined to keep up the world's hope for a solution.[79]

The deadlock was broken when the U.S.S.R. accepted the eight-power draft as a basis for further negotiations and joined the twelve-power group. In its reversal the Soviet government accepted the principle of safeguards but expressed concern about the infringement of sovereignty through its operation.[80] The most adamant objections, however, were voiced by the Indian delegation. The controversy centered around the American proposal that an international inspection system be established. India insisted that safeguards be imposed only through agreements between the Agency and states which would be beneficiaries of Agency projects. In other words, states would not submit to the system of safeguards merely by ratifying the Statute. The U.S.S.R. supported the Indian position and further emphasized the need for "due observance of the national sovereignty of states." [81] The United States maintained that the very decision whether or not to apply to the Agency for assistance would be an act of sovereignty. Each country could weigh the safeguards before applying for aid, but if it did apply, then safeguards would have to be accepted. In addition, Mr. Wadsworth stated:

> Each project agreement shall specifically provide for the application of safeguards *as relevant.* Hence, there would be no indiscriminate use of safeguards.[82]

This statement invited another attack. The Indian delegation maintained that the American position tended to include all forms of Agency aid in the safeguard system: fissionable material, source material, and technical assistance. The latter two were criticized as irrelevant:

> We agree that all fissionable material supplied by the Agency should be safeguarded. But source materials are on a different footing from special fissionable materials. The former cannot be used directly for military purposes. To control Agency-supplied source material and to leave uncontrolled other source material found in countries would divide the world into two categories of states and place the aid-receiving state at a disadvantage. Since control would be exercised on all fissionable materials resulting from such source material, the division into two categories would become self-perpetuating.
>
> On the matter of technical assistance, we must bear in mind the distinction between *direct* cause and effect and *indirect* cause and effect. The Agency's activities must not contribute directly to any military purpose. But, equally important, the development of the peaceful application of atomic energy must not be hindered because the inspection and control provisions have been made too onerous. For example, information was divulged at Geneva on the extraction of plutonium. This information is useful for both peaceful and military purposes. But it was essential for peaceful uses, hence it was *rightly divulged*.[83]

On the basis of this argument the Indian delegation proposed that a system of "graduated safeguards" be written into the Statute which would virtually exempt source materials and technical assistance supplied by the Agency from accountability. The Soviet and Czechoslovak delegations supported the Indian position on both counts. To the surprise of the Western producer nations, the French representative followed suit and stated:

> Source materials are being found increasingly everywhere. Hence, too rigid controls would reinforce the trend of turning away from the Agency. If technical assistance, too, [were] placed under controls, needy countries [would] bypass the Agency and look for uncontrolled assistance.[84]

The producer powers conceded that controls on technical assistance would create serious problems. However, on the question of source materials the United States held its ground, insisting that source ma-

terial be retained in the accountability system. The decision finally
turned upon the American contention that the processing of source
materials in power reactors yielded weapons-grade by-products:

> Since it is precisely the special fissionable materials recovered or
> produced as a by-product which are the elements most readily sus-
> ceptible of diversion to military use, it is essential to ensure that
> these materials cannot be diverted for military purposes. The Agency
> must guard against the undue amassing or collecting of dangerous
> amounts of special fissionable material. Since a stockpile honestly in-
> tended for future peaceful use is indistinguishable from one intended
> for future military use and, in fact, might be quickly turned to mili-
> tary use, the Agency cannot permit the accumulation of any stock-
> piles of fissionable materials without continuing safeguards.[85]

Mr. Bhabha countered that the Agency might then—for reasons
totally unrelated to safeguards, perhaps for political or economic considerations—dominate recipient countries' economic and technical development:

> Such a policy would segregate the few states not receiving aid from
> those who would need aid. The former would be free to hold their
> own stocks of fissionable material—to use them for peaceful or mili-
> tary purposes without any safeguards—the latter would have the
> stock subject to stringent inspection and control. We would stand
> on the brink of a dangerous era of atomic "haves" and "have-nots" in
> which the "haves" would dominate the "have-nots" through the
> Agency. This would create dangerous tensions. An overzealous
> Agency might feel because the nth step of development might be
> construed to have military significance, such onerous controls would
> be imposed which would place the recipient country in a state of
> continuing bondage to the Agency. Since the atomic "haves" domi-
> nate the Board of Governors, this would produce in the atomic
> age a colonial situation as bad or worse than any that has been
> experienced hitherto.[86]

The Canadian delegate countered by maintaining that

> The Indian position would result in the fact that substantial stock-
> piles of fissionable materials—by-products of reactor operations—
> would accumulate in many parts of the world. As a practical matter,
> under existing technology, very little by-product fissionable material
> can be used for peaceful purposes. Hence, the need to stockpile is
> superfluous.[87]

Finally, an ingenious compromise solution was worked out. The twelve-power draft retained the principle of accountability for source materials but restricted the right of the Agency with respect to the fissionable materials recovered as a by-product. States would be required to return to the Agency idle stockpiles of fissionable materials produced from their reactors but would have the right to retain under continuing Agency safeguards such quantities of the by-product materials as they were able to use "for research or in reactors, existing or under construction." [88] Agency inspectors would decide upon the quantities to be retained. It was assumed that economic and political factors would not deprive states of fissionable by-products produced from their reactors. In fact, even if the Agency believed that the use of fissionable material was economically unsound, such material could be retained if nonmilitary uses could be demonstrated.

The following were specific safeguard powers finally accorded the Agency: First, the Agency would have the right to examine the design of any nuclear reactor before it was built in order to determine whether it complied with Agency regulations. The Agency would withhold approval of a design which would make diversion of materials difficult to detect. Second, the Agency would be empowered to require the maintenance of operating records. Third, the Agency would reserve for itself the right to approve the chemical processing of irradiated material and to specify the disposition of any derived fissionable material not usable for peaceful purposes. Hence stringent controls were to be exercised over those key points in the processing where diversion to weapons could most readily take place. Finally, the Statute established a system of inspection through a staff of international inspectors.[89]

The adoption of the principle of inspection by international civil servants was without precedent. It was consequently surprising that this principle evoked relatively little controversy during the negotiating process. The powers seemed much more concerned with the matters to be inspected than with the principle of inspection *per se*. In the twelve-power discussions only the Soviet Union reminded the delegates that "this function of the Agency was to be carried out with due observance of the sovereign rights of recipient nations." [90] To meet this Soviet reservation, a clause was included in the Statute specifying that inspectors be accompanied by representatives of the state concerned, if the state requested it and the inspectors were not thereby impeded.

In view of the far-reaching powers of the inspectorate, the composition of inspection teams was of some concern to the delegates at the International Conference. The underdeveloped countries wanted to include specific provisions in the Statute, while the atomic powers—this time supported by the Soviet Union—favored leaving the matter in abeyance. Mr. Carpio, delegate from the Philippines, proposed that inspection teams should consist of at least three members:

> One from the region of Western Europe, another one from North or South America, and another from Eastern Europe. This should be done so that there can be no possible collusion on the report as to whether there has been a diversion of atomic energy for military purposes.[91]

The Swedish delegate, Mr. Virgin, expressed the view that the Conference should not attempt to incorporate any detail into the Statute and further stated that

> it [the Philippine proposal] would mean introducing an entirely new principle if staff members from particular countries or a group of countries were to be given the right of being represented in a given function of an international organization.[92]

This argument prevailed and it was decided to leave the precise selection of the inspectorate and the composition of teams to the Board of Governors of the Agency.

The matter of sanctions in the event of noncompliance with safeguard requirements did not evoke significant controversy. It was decided that inspectors would be required to report instances of noncompliance to the Director-General, who would transmit these reports to the Board of Governors. The Board would then exercise pressure upon the recalcitrant member. In case of continued insubordination, the Board would make a report to all members, and to the Security Council and General Assembly of the United Nations. The Board itself would then direct curtailment or suspension of assistance provided by the Agency and call for the return of materials and equipment. It might also suspend the noncompliant state from membership.[93]

During the last days of the International Conference the delegates reached a decision of great potential significance: the Agency was to have the right to extend the "application of these [safeguard] standards, at the request of the parties, to operations under any bilateral or multilateral arrangement, or at the request of a State, to any of that State's activities in the field of atomic energy." [94] Under the same conditions the Statute also authorized the Agency "to establish or adopt . . . standards of safety for protection of health and minimization of danger to life and property (including such standards for labor conditions) . . ." [95]

With the adoption of this provision the ground was prepared for the Agency to contribute to world-wide uniformity in safeguard and health and safety standards.

When the Agency Statute was unanimously adopted by the International Conference in October, 1956, it was hoped that the safeguard and control mechanisms which it provided might delay somewhat the spread of nuclear weapons production. The American position in this respect expressed the sentiments of most delegations to the Statute Conference. Mr. Wadsworth voiced the hope that

> the new International Atomic Energy Agency [would] divert important amounts of fissionable materials from atomic bomb arsenals to the uses of benefit to mankind, and those amounts [would] steadily grow with the maintenance of peace. More tons of these materials [would] be devoted to welfare, fewer tons to weapons and warfare.[96]

Secretary Dulles, however, warned that the Agency had no magic formula to prevent the spread of atomic weapons:

> We must realize that atomic energy materials and know-how will spread, Agency or no Agency. But the new IAEA must not make the existing situation worse.[97]

Although the Statute was adopted unanimously, the apprehensions of the founding fathers outweighed their hopes. First, the delegates realized that the Agency itself would probably be unable to force recovery of materials used in violation of the Statute since the sanctioning process against noncompliant powers depended upon the recipient state. The only exception to this rule would occur if the Security Council—with its five permanent powers in agreement—should choose to use its considerable powers under the Charter to enforce compliance.

Second, it was feared that bilateral arrangements with less-stringent safeguard provisions might force the Agency to relinquish its leadership in the atoms-for-peace program or to lower its own control provisions. Nothing in the Statute prohibited one nation from supplying another with fissionable materials through bilateral channels. While the Agency might extend its safeguard system to any such arrangement, inspection would have to be requested by the negotiating states and not initiated by the Agency. While there would perhaps be some moral obligation to apply bilateral controls as stringent as those of the Agency, there would be no legal commitment to do so.

Third, the Agency control provisions would apply only to Agency-supplied materials. Any national atomic programs unsupported by the Agency would be completely excluded from its inspection system. This was the main objection of the underdeveloped countries when they aptly pointed out that in fact the control provisions would not apply to the atomic powers themselves. It was further feared that for reasons of security and prestige a military nuclear capacity would soon be developed by many countries. As one thoughtful observer analyzed the situation in early 1957:

> The fact is that a large number of countries have now, or will have within ten years, a capability for producing nominal atomic weapons, that is, relatively low-yield bombs of the Hiroshima type. This capability will not result from fissionable materials received through United States bilaterals or through the IAEA, and to make a few such bombs does not call for substantial economic or scientific resources. It must be assumed furthermore . . . that eventually many countries will develop atomic weapons unless substantial and all-round disarmament or arms control becomes a reality, or the nations concerned receive nuclear arms from their allies. If the present "have-nots" are deterred by moral constraints from giving in to such temptations, these constraints will not result from international considerations. For without general nuclear disarmament, any attempts of the "haves" to prevent the appearance of other atomic powers must inevitably lack moral appeal.[98]

Finally, it was conceded that the Statute could not impede the spread of nuclear know-how. It was not even desirable to do so, as the Indian delegation had pointed out, since such a policy would cripple the developmental aspect of the Agency. But it could not be denied that the diffusion of such knowledge throughout the world might eventually enable recipient nations to produce nuclear weapons. Atomic technology, once acquired through the Agency, could be put to use either for peace or for war, and would be totally removed from any form of international supervision.

Some delegations, including the United States, expressed the hope that the Agency safeguard system, if successful, could become a practical working model from which the types of international control considered essential for nuclear disarmament might ultimately be evolved. The fact that the unprecedented principle of international inspection had been incorporated in the Statute gave strength to these hopes. Many delegations, however, felt that this was an overly optimistic expectation. Although it was conceded that an inspection scheme might work, such a scheme might not be permitted to encroach on the highly sensitive area of military preparations. The hopes of "atomic functionalists" that habits of international inspection could be transferred from the peaceful to the military realm—a kind of peace by pieces—were considered unrealistic. Further, it was pointed out that the main problem would be to extend inspection to the United States and the U.S.S.R., but precisely these two powers were, as a practical matter, excluded from the Agency control provisions.

When the International Statute Conference closed three years after the idea of atoms-for-peace had been conceived, most delegations looked with greater hope toward the developmental rather than the restrictive function of the Agency. But coupled with this hope was the realization that, however highly the benefits of peaceful atomic energy were assessed, they paled in comparison with the disaster for mankind which unimpeded nuclear diffusion might bring in its train.

PROBLEMS OF MATERIALS AND FINANCE

The founders of the Agency intended that one of its major jobs would be to supply fissionable and source materials to members for atomic energy projects. During the Statute negotiations numerous offers of such materials were made to the Agency. The problem, therefore, was not the scarcity of atomic materials but the conditions under which they should go to the Agency.

The founders set up different conditions for accepting fissionable materials and source materials.[99] The Agency was to accept any amounts of fissionable materials offered to it subject only to agreement on price and transfer. In the words of the delegate from South Africa:

the Agency should not have the right to refuse these materials since such a right would be incompatible with the disarmament purposes of the Agency.[100]

The Indian delegation felt that the Statute should place the producer powers under a moral obligation to siphon off as much fissionable material as possible from military to peacetime use. Mr. Bhabha proposed that the word "should" be used in place of "may" in Article IX of the twelve-power draft:

Members *may* make available to the Agency such quantities of special fissionable materials as they deem advisable.[101]

The proposal was withdrawn when the United States delegate announced that a generous quantity of fissionable material would be placed at the Agency's disposal:

To enable the International Atomic Energy Agency, upon its establishment by appropriate governmental actions, to start atomic research and power programs without delay, *the United States will make available to the Agency, on terms to be agreed with that body, 5,000 kilograms of a nuclear fuel uranium-235* from the 20,000 kilograms of such material allocated by the United States for peaceful uses by friendly nations. In addition to the above mentioned initial 5,000 kilograms of uranium-235, *the United States will continue to make available to the International Atomic Energy Agency nuclear materials that will match in amount the sum of all quantities of such materials made similarly available by all members of the International Agency, and on comparable terms,* for the period between the establishment of the Agency and July 1, 1960. The United States will deliver these nuclear materials to the International Agency, as they are required for Agency approved projects.[102]

This attempt to translate into concrete terms President Eisenhower's message of December, 1953, was followed by token commitments from the United Kingdom and the Soviet Union. The British delegate announced that his government was prepared to hold available 20 kilograms of fissionable material as an initial contribution to the Agency and the Soviet Union declared itself ready "to deposit into an international fund for atomic materials under an international agency for atomic energy fifty kilograms of fissionable materials." [103] An ample supply—5,140 kilograms of the scarce material—was thus committed to the Agency by the time the Statute Conference was over.

In contrast to the policy on fissionable materials, the Agency would not be bound to accept unlimited quantities of source materials. The twelve-power negotiating group felt that the Agency might be overwhelmed with a surplus supply and therefore decided that the Board of Governors should be empowered to determine limits beyond which the Agency would not accept source materials. [104] Generous offers were made during the negotiations by Canada, Ceylon, India, Portugal, and the Union of South Africa. While Portugal stipulated a contribution of 100 tons of uranium, the other offers did not specify precise quantities but all stated that the quantities available would be sufficient to meet the Agency's likely requirements. [105] Again, scarcity was not a problem.

There was some discussion as to whether the Agency should become an "atomic bank" with physical storage facilities for materials or merely a clearinghouse arranging for the moving of materials from one country to another. While the delegates agreed that the Agency should ultimately serve as a "bank," for the immediate future they saw it as a kind of broker who would bring together suppliers and potential recipients. The Statute Conference therefore decided to authorize the Agency to function in both capacities. [106] The Statute was left flexible on methods of procedure, since the negotiators realized that the Board of Governors would have to work out agreements tailored to different types of projects and different requirements of national legislation. For example, the delegates decided not to specify the legal form transactions should take—whether sale or lease—nor the price at which material would be available to recipient states. [107] Also, supplying members would be permitted to choose between making delivery immediately to the recipient state or concluding an agreement to store the material in the Agency's depots. In this connection the problem of storage facilities came up. Vienna, which was selected by the Statute Conference as the permanent Agency headquarters, did not seem to many delegates a particularly suitable location for storage facilities. [108] The atomic powers made the point that fissionable materials should not be concentrated in any one country. In case of forcible seizure, geographical decentralization would at least ensure a rough balance of materials throughout the world. However, since the Agency's role as "bank" seemed remote, and its "deposits" in any event would include only a fraction of the world's supply of fissionable material, a provisional storage depot in Vienna was reluctantly approved.

The debates about supplying materials to the Agency were intimately linked to the problems of finance. The delegates at first saw an important source of revenue in charges imposed on project agreements between the Agency and recipient states. The producer powers proposed that such charges should include the cost of the fissionable materials plus handling, storage, and safeguard expenses.[109] It was generally agreed that materials would be supplied to the Agency at the lowest possible price. In the words of the United States delegate:

> the prices must be low; even if they are a little higher than the lowest, states will tend to bypass the Agency. Also, this would delay substantially the time when atomic power would be competitive with conventional power.[110]

The underdeveloped countries, however, pointed out that fissionable materials might have to be supplied at less than cost so that their cost to recipient states could include surcharges for safeguards and handling and yet effectively compete with bilateral programs. The representative of India remarked that the net cost of fissionable materials to recipient states was reduced under bilateral programs because the United States bought back the plutonium by-product recovered through chemical reprocessing. The Agency would be in a position to make similar payments only when the technique of utilizing plutonium for peaceful purposes would be sufficiently advanced to make profitable use of the by-products. Until then the only feasible method to cover the cost of safeguards would be an indirect subsidy of the Agency by supplying materials at less than cost.[111] The delegate from Portugal attacked this proposition as irresponsible, since such a policy would induce an artificial lowering of world prices of source materials through Agency initiative.[112] The negotiators did not resolve this dilemma. The Statute was left flexible enough to permit the furnishing of materials at any price. Another problem was that the producer powers, unwilling to bind themselves to long-term costly projects, insisted that materials should be initially available to recipient states for the period of one year only.[113] In view of the fact that a continuous supply of fissionable material would be necessary to sustain any Agency project, this insistence was hardly realistic. Furthermore, agreements under the United States bilateral program generally provided for a continuing supply of materials for at least five years. In order to compete effectively, it seemed that the Board would have to offer comparable terms. This dilemma, too, was not resolved.

An alternate method for financing operational expenditures at first seemed somewhat more promising: the twelve-power group authorized the Board of Governors to accept voluntary contributions from member states, a proposal later endorsed by the Statute Conference.[114] Many delegations commented, however, that voluntary contributions would tend to be limited. This financing technique alone was therefore considered inadequate.

The borrowing powers of the Agency were the subject of lively discussion in the twelve-power group. No delegation approved borrowing for the day-to-day operations of the Agency, but the United States suggested that the Board of Governors, subject to approval by the General Conference, be authorized to borrow funds for the construction of Agency facilities, such as storage buildings for fissionable materials.[115] Loans would be repaid from donations and charges, which would presumably exceed operating costs. The Soviet Union, supported by Czechoslovakia, claimed that Agency borrowing would encourage extravagance.[116] The United Kingdom supported the American position but insisted that this borrowing power should not impose on the individual members of the Agency any liability with respect to the loans.[117] With this proviso, the delegates by a vote of 10–2 decided to grant the borrowing power to the Agency. The decision was endorsed by the Statute Conference, although the language left the precise limits of the borrowing power unclear.[118] Finally, it was decided that the administrative budget of the Agency would be apportioned among the member states in accordance with a scale determined by the General Conference and modeled after the regular administrative budget of the United Nations. Expenses would include the cost of the Agency staff, meetings, and "housekeeping." [119]

By the time the Statute Conference drew to a close it had become clear that the Agency could supply only a fraction of the funds needed for the peaceful development of atomic energy. The problem of

Agency solvency loomed large, since most expenditures would be considerable. However, the vague language in the Statute—especially with regard to the borrowing power—convinced most delegations that the Agency budget could keep pace with the expansion of Agency activities.

THE ADOPTION OF THE STATUTE

Ratification of the Statute implied only one clearly defined legal obligation: the duty to pay the assessed share of the Agency's administrative budget. Therefore, unanimity was fairly easy to attain. The only other automatic obligation incurred was of a moral rather than legal nature: "Each member shall make available such information as would in the judgment of the member be helpful to the Agency." [120] All other obligations, such as safeguards, were to come into being only after a further step—the acceptance by a member of Agency assistance—had been taken. Of all the instruments setting up agencies in the United Nations family, the Agency Statute imposed the fewest obligations upon ratifying members. The very act of joining any of the specialized agencies implies more far-reaching commitments. The International Bank for Reconstruction and Development and the International Monetary Fund, for instance, imposed obligations in the conduct of fiscal policy before a member could receive any benefits whatsoever. The act of ratification of the Agency Statute, therefore, signified little more than a declaration of intention.

The question of amendment procedure to the Statute presented complications. Since the Statute was such a finely balanced compromise that any single change was bound in some way to affect the entire Agency structure, amendments were to go into effect only when approved in the General Conference by a two-thirds majority and by two-thirds of all the member states in accordance with their respective constitutional processes.[121] Members were granted the right to withdraw at any time but had to fulfill their contractual obligations to the Agency.[122] The states at the International Conference insisted upon this right in order to protect themselves against unacceptable amendments which would fundamentally alter the obligations of membership. It in effect gave a veto over proposed amendments to the Statute to states which, like the United States, were indispensable if the Agency was to serve its purpose with success.

This categorical right of withdrawal posed certain problems. What would be the situation if a state supplying fissionable material were to withdraw from the Agency because of an unacceptable amendment? If a state receiving assistance from the Agency over a number of years were to withdraw, what would be the legal status of the reactors in that state's territory? Would the obligations of the recipient state cover the life of the project or terminate with the state's withdrawal? The delegates left it to the Board of Governors, in its project agreements with member states, to incorporate specific provisions covering such contingencies.

The matter of interpretation of the Statute aroused some controversy. The eight-power negotiating group recommended that disputes not settled by negotiation should come under the compulsory jurisdiction of the International Court of Justice. The provision of the original draft read:

> The parties to the present Statute *accept* the jurisdiction of the International Court of Justice with respect to any dispute concerning the interpretation or application of the Statute.[123]

The Soviet Union, after joining the drafting body, strenuously objected to this clause and insisted that any reference to compulsory jurisdiction be deleted. The clause was finally accepted by the International Conference in a somewhat weakened form:

> Any question or dispute concerning the interpretation or application of this Statute which is not settled by negotiation, *shall be referred to the International Court of Justice in conformity with the Statute of the Court* unless the parties concerned agree on another mode of settlement.[124]

The Article was considered flexible enough to cover disputes on Statute interpretation not only among member states but also between the Agency and a member.[125] The Statute also stipulated that any project agreement was to "make appropriate provision regarding settlement of disputes." [126] The United States delegation held that disputes involving project agreements should be referred to the International Court of Justice for an advisory opinion which the parties would agree in advance to accept. This formula was based on the power of both the General Conference and the Board of Governors "subject to authorization from the General Assembly of the United Nations to request the International Court of Justice to give an advisory opinion on any legal question arising within the scope of the Agency's activities." [127] The Soviet delegation, however, rejected this interpretation because, again, it would come close to the principle of compulsory adjudication of disputes. One observer preferred arbitration by a special commission which could develop into an expert judicial body on matters relating to atomic energy.[128] As in the case of amendment procedures, the delegates again decided for flexibility and left specific interpretations to the Board of Governors after the Agency began operations.

The final act of the Statute Conference was the establishment of a Preparatory Commission of the Agency. This eighteen-state Commission included the twelve-power negotiating group plus six countries from the underdeveloped areas of the world.[129] It was to draft the initial program and budget and carry out preparations for the first General Conference. Most important, it was to formulate a relationship agreement between the Agency and the United Nations.

The Commission, under the direction of Dr. Paul Rudolf Jolles of Switzerland as Executive Secretary, began work immediately. The Agency Statute entered into force during the existence of the Preparatory Commission, on July 29, 1957, after twenty-six states had deposited their instruments of ratification.

SUMMARY: THE STATUTE AS INTERNATIONAL LEGISLATION

The legislative process establishing the Agency was unique in United Nations history. What began as a narrowly conceived negotiating process culminated in genuine multilateral diplomacy.[130] The Statute Conference proved that the United Nations General Assembly was able to assert a high degree of initiative in the international lawmaking process.

The problem of universality versus selectivity of membership, common to all international organizations in the United Nations family, emerged with special significance during the debates on the Agency Statute. Exclusion of Communist China and certain other Communist-controlled areas exempted these countries from the safeguard and inspection systems contemplated in the Statute. Hence the decision to restrict the membership of the new Agency was bound to preclude universal application of the Agency's safeguard provisions. At best, however, the safeguard system became effective only in the event of Agency assistance, and such assistance was unlikely in the case of Communist China. This proviso, however, did not discourage those who hoped that the Agency safeguard system would ultimately serve as a model for a more ambitious disarmament scheme. At any rate, despite the unanimous support of eighty-two nations, the Agency Statute could not be considered an unqualified success.

The structure of the new Agency was unique among international organizations. The Board of Governors was clearly meant to be the Agency's most powerful organ. In consequence, the fierce competition among member states to obtain places on the Board resulted in a 23-member governing body not well equipped for efficient administrative and policy decisions. In comparison to the powers of the Board, those of the Director-General and of the General Conference were relatively weak. The Director-General was obligated by the Statute to obtain the approval of the Board on every major administrative decision. The General Conference was granted the right to elect ten rotating Board members and to control the Agency's fiscal policy, both grudging concessions made by the atomic producer powers. The Statute purposely left unclear the lines of demarcation among the three organs of the Agency in the hope that the areas of competence for each organ would evolve more clearly after the Agency began operations. But it seemed to many analysts of the Statute at the Conference that a trend toward enlargement of the powers of the Board might easily gather momentum.

The thinking behind President Eisenhower's atoms-for-peace proposal late in 1953 augured a new approach to the problems of diffusion of atomic energy. As international controls over *all* existing and future fissionable materials seemed impossible, it was the President's hope that the atomic producer countries would agree to siphon off these materials from military stockpiles and store them with an international agency. This agency would in turn make the materials available to its members for peaceful purposes under proper safeguards.

The Agency Statute reflected this thinking. It gave the Agency the *capacity* to play this role but did not give it the *power* to compel its members to let it play this role.[131] The Statute clearly stipulated that safeguard provisions would become applicable only to those members which received Agency assistance, excluding for all practical purposes the three atomic powers: the United States, the United Kingdom, and the Soviet Union. But once a member accepted assistance, the Agency would have truly unprecedented powers of international inspection. These powers were to include the maintenance of health and safety standards against diversion to military purposes. Agency inspectors were to have the right to enter the territory of the beneficiary state and to have access "at all times to all places and data and to any person who by reason of his occupation" dealt with materials to be safeguarded.[132] This principle of international inspection, albeit revolutionary, attracted relatively little attention at the Conference. The debate turned rather on the problem of what types of materials were to be subject to safeguards. The final decision—that all fissionable materials including by-product weapons-grade materials were to be subject to Agency controls—produced an impressive though limited safeguard system.

The sanctioning process outlined in the Statute in the event of noncompliance was equally impressive. The Board would report any infraction to the Security Council and the General Assembly of the United Nations, which presumably would deal with reports from the Board on the basis of their normal jurisdiction under the Charter. The Statute also gave the Board the right to order suspension of Agency assistance and return of all materials by the violator. Here the Statute left an important loophole: the right to "recapture" by the Agency could apparently be exercised only with the cooperation of the delinquent state and as long as the materials remained in its territory. The Statute did not grant Agency inspectors the right to remove or destroy such materials. However, a noncomplying member could be suspended from Agency membership by the Board. Such an order of suspension, in the minds of many delegates at the Conference, might have such far-reaching effects on the economic life of the noncomplying state that the gains from any illegal action would be more than offset by the disabilities of disciplinary action. Moreover, the wide publicity inevitably accompanying such a development would also serve as a deterrent.

As an additional safeguard, the Statute included a provision regarding the settlement of disputes in all project agreements. Two possible formulas for settlement were proposed: to obtain an advisory opinion by the International Court of Justice, accepted in advance by the parties to the dispute, or to create an expert arbitration commission.

Perhaps the most promising aspect of the safeguard features in the

Statute were the two provisions which—if applied—could give the Agency the power of setting universal safeguard standards. The Statute authorized the Agency to apply the safeguard system to any bilateral or multilateral arrangement *at the request of the parties.* Furthermore, the system could be extended—again on *request*—to any activities in the field of atomic energy of a state.[133] In the opinion of one scholar:

> What this means is that Euratom or parties to a bilateral program constituted independently of the Agency could ask the Agency to apply its safeguards system throughout their territory even where they do not receive any assistance from the Agency. The Agency has the authority to accede to this request. And what is perhaps more important: *any state,* including the United States, the United Kingdom, and the Soviet Union, theoretically could ask the Agency to apply controls to their programs, civilian and military, or to any parts thereof.[134]

Any such dramatic extension of the safeguard system would, of course, have to be initiated outside the Agency. But the Statute broke new ground in establishing machinery which had the potential for universality. The Agency was given the power to assume full responsibility for universal safeguards if and when the great powers were ready to avail themselves of the existing machinery.

The questions of finance and facilities presented some problems. The only statutory obligation of a member of the Agency was to pay its assessed share of the administrative budget. Because of the stringent financial policies of most of the delegations, only modest funds were available to the Agency. The low budget augured ill for the creation of ample laboratory and storage facilities. The Statute, while permitting the Agency both a "banking" and a "clearinghouse" function, clearly influenced future development in favor of the latter alternative. The conditions under which fissionable materials would be transferred from the supplying powers to the Agency and the terms of sale or lease under which such materials would go to the beneficiary states were kept flexible. In view of the fact that the Agency would have to adjust itself to different systems of legislation, this flexibility was considered by most observers to be commendable.

Finally, the founding fathers of the Agency were quite aware that IAEA, once established, would tend to live a life of its own—perhaps quite different from that envisaged by its creators. Experience in setting up new international organizations had shown this truth over and over again. The closing statements reflected a carefully guarded optimism about the Agency's prospects. All delegates probably shared the sentiment expressed in the final statement of the representative of Brazil:

> Mankind has discovered the genius to disintegrate the atom. It must now find the genius to reintegrate mankind.[135]

PART II

THE AGENCY IN ACTION: THE FIRST PHASE

POLICY-MAKING PROCESS AND ADMINISTRATION

The Board of Governors was to be the hub of agency activities. Its establishment was an immediate necessity if IAEA was to begin operations. The Preparatory Commission of the Agency, on July 31, 1957, designated the following thirteen states for membership on the first Board of Governors: Australia, Brazil, Canada, Czechoslovakia, France, India, Japan, Portugal, Sweden, the Union of South Africa, the Soviet Union, the United Kingdom, and the United States.[1] The designated members of the first Board comprised all the members of the twelve-power negotiating group of the Statute plus Japan. The membership selected by the Commission was heavily weighted in favor of the atomic powers, since it was expected that the General Conference would restore the balance by electing countries from the underdeveloped regions. The first regular session of the General Conference was held in Vienna October 1 to 23, 1957. The Conference, under its powers granted by the Statute, completed the membership of the Board by electing ten states to the governing body. As expected, most of the new members were from the atomically underdeveloped areas. The following states were elected: Argentina, Egypt, Guatemala, Indonesia, Italy, Republic of Korea, Pakistan, Peru, Romania, and Turkey.[2] With the establishment of the Board, the Preparatory Commission's mandate was discharged and it ceased to exist. The Board held its first meeting on October 4, 1957, and elected Ambassador P. Winkler of Czechoslovakia as Chairman, and Ambassadors M. Wershof of Canada and H. Furuuchi of Japan as Vice-Chairmen. Jointly with the General Conference, the Board approved the initial program and budget of the Agency submitted by the Preparatory Commission, selected Vienna as the permanent seat of the Agency, and appointed an American, Mr. Sterling Cole, as Director-General. The Board and the General Conference also endorsed the Preparatory Commission's draft of an agreement on the Agency's relationship with the United Nations and of a Headquarters Agreement with the Austrian government.

Under the Statute, the Board may meet "at such times as it may determine."[3] During the first year of the Agency's existence it was in almost continuous session. Seven series of meetings amounting to more than one hundred individual sessions took place. The Board has dealt with a large variety of substantive program areas. Initial consideration of technical programs and projects for the Agency has progressed in step with the recruitment of the technical and scientific staff. The Board drew up the outline of the Agency's fellowship program, health and safety activities, technical information program, and plans for technical assistance and safeguards. Questions arising from the offers of fissionable, source, and other materials made by member states under Article IX of the Statute were discussed. Appointments to leading posts in the Secretariat were made following informal consultations between the Director-General and the Board. Negotiations were begun for relationship agreements between the Agency and the specialized agencies, and a resolution was adopted recommending the Agency's participation in the United Nations Expanded Program of Technical Assistance (EPTA).

Any analysis of the Board's policy-making process must be limited by the short period of the Agency's operations. But some interesting trends are already evident. In its early negotiations the Board strenuously attempted to arrive at unanimous decisions, even in highly controversial matters. For example, the nomination of Mr. Sterling Cole, an American, for the post of Director-General, was severely criticized by the U.S.S.R., which wanted a chief executive from one of the neutral powers.[4] Nevertheless, the Soviet delegation chose not to vote against Mr. Cole's appointment. As the subject matter discussed by the Board has become increasingly controversial, the Board has gradually dropped its attempts at unanimity. At least three schisms —at times appearing simultaneously—tend to make the Board a house divided. The Eastern and Western powers frequently adopt rigid positions which are then brought to a vote. The problem of inviting a representative from the European Atomic Energy Community ("Euratom") to the Second General Conference was a case in point. The Soviet delegation maintained that "no argument could cancel the military character of Euratom. Inviting an observer would set a dangerous precedent." [5] The delegate of the United States, supported by the majority of the Board membership, defended Euratom's participation, since "the Community [Euratom] was not only devoted to the peaceful uses of atomic energy, but was destined to become a powerful force in that field." [6] No compromise was possible or even attempted. By a vote of 15-3, with 5 abstentions, the Board decided to issue the invitation.

A second divisive current in the Board has developed between the atomic powers and the underdeveloped countries. As during the Statute negotiations, the Soviet Union is frequently caught between its conflicting roles as atomic producer and self-appointed benefactor of the anticolonial powers. Often the Soviet delegation's solution to this dilemma is to abstain from voting. The problem of planning for the building of reactors was an example. The atomic powers contended that most of the world's underdeveloped regions—for a variety of reasons—were ill-prepared for immediate erection of reactors. The have-nots, on the other hand, reminded the Board of the Statute's injunction to "make provision . . . for materials . . . and facilities . . . including the production of electric power, with due consideration for the needs of the underdeveloped areas of the world." [7] A majority of the Board, the Soviets abstaining, decided to limit the Agency's preliminary activities in this area to the creation of fact-finding teams to determine the needs and absorptive capacities of the underdeveloped countries. Again, unanimity proved impossible to attain.

The third schism is fiscal and is increasingly impeding the Board's work. Since the General Conference approved an administrative budget of only $1.76 million for the first year and $5.23 million for the second, with voluntary contributions carrying the burden of operational expenditures, the Board has been extremely conservative on matters of finance.[8] The American delegation has been the only one defending a generous fiscal policy, but it has been consistently outvoted. The issue of establishing research facilities at Agency Headquarters is a case in point among many. The American delegation felt that laboratory research at Agency Headquarters would lead to "invaluable services to the underdeveloped countries." [9] The Soviet delegate defended the view that such research should be conducted in the underdeveloped countries by visiting experts. Any Agency research laboratory would be premature and "might cost the peoples of member states countless millions of dollars." [10] The Soviet view was supported by a majority of the Board membership, including the United Kingdom and Canada. Only when the United States pledged one half of the proposed voluntary operating budget of $1.5 million for 1959 did the Board reluctantly set aside $450,000 for research facilities at Agency Headquarters.

The underdeveloped countries as a rule tend to support expenditures of immediate benefit to themselves, such as provisions for technical assistance, but refuse to share the financial burden of most other projects. The Board's decision to postpone the appointment of a Director of Safeguards was a striking example of procrastination due to fiscal considerations. The Indian delegation, supported by the U.S.S.R. and the representatives of the underdeveloped countries, held that recruitment for the Division of Safeguards would be premature, since the Agency had not yet received any requests from governments or regional organizations to participate in control arrangements. "Therefore, any expenditure relating to the recruitment of staff for the Division would at present be useless." [11] It was the American view—supported by Canada and the United Kingdom—that it was "essential that the Agency should be prepared at an early date to discharge its statutory responsibilities." [12] Obviously, parties to bilateral agreements would not entrust the application of safeguards to the Agency until it was in a position to assume such a responsibility. The Agency would therefore have to begin its functions in that field as soon as possible. The debate, fundamentally fiscal in nature, continued through twenty-five meetings of the Board. Finally, the recruitment of safeguards personnel could no longer be delayed and on July 2, 1958, the Board, by a vote of 12-1 decided to staff the Division. The Soviet Union cast the only negative vote and nine Governors from the underdeveloped countries abstained.[13] The appointment on July 23, 1958, of Mr. Roger M. Smith, a Canadian nuclear physicist, to the post of Director of Safeguards was somewhat belated. The advantages of possible Agency involvement in bilateral and regional control schemes would have outweighed the financial savings of the recruitment delay. This example suggests that disagreements on fiscal policy within the Board could have far-reaching implications for the Agency's role in international affairs.

Since the Board was to be the controlling organ of the Agency, it is not surprising that most powers wanted to be represented. The Board therefore comprises over one-third of Agency membership.[14] This unwieldy structure, compounded by internal divisions, tends to prevent the Board from exercising its statutory powers efficiently. On the other hand, it should be remembered that the question of Board membership was perhaps the most delicate one during the Statute negotiations and that the compromise finally achieved was the necessary price for the Agency's coming into existence at all.

It has been impossible so far to escape from the dilemma of size versus efficiency. The Board has appointed four committees to which it has delegated fact-finding responsibility, but only on relatively non-controversial matters.[15] The Governors have delegated no responsibility in areas of policy. The establishment of a Steering Committee for the Board was discussed but rejected, since such a body would have to represent the major differences in viewpoint. Since those differences are so complex, most members would insist on seats, and a Steering Committee would probably be no administrative improvement over the *status quo*. Organizational gadgetry cannot obliterate the profound political and economic divisions now plaguing the Board.

It is too early to assess the Board's relationship to the General Conference. Little friction developed during the first two sessions of the General Conference in October, 1957, and September, 1958. However, one area of potential conflict does exist and might manifest itself in the future. It is the joint control of the two organs over the Agency's budget. Under the Statute, the General Conference may

> approve the budget of the Agency recommended by the Board or return it with recommendations as to its entirety or parts to the Board, for resubmission to the General Conference.[16]

Budgetary matters are decided by two-thirds vote by both the Board and the General Conference. The atomic have-nots are more heavily represented in the General Conference—which includes the entire Agency membership—than on the Board. It is quite possible, in view of this, that a disagreement on fiscal policy could arise between the two organs. For example, the General Conference, under pressure from the atomic have-nots, might opt against expenditures for research in favor of technical assistance. The Board, under pressure from the atomic powers, might not be able to muster a two-thirds vote to support the recommendations of the Conference. Hence a deadlock is possible. However, through interpretation of the Statute, a body of constitutional law will no doubt evolve to clarify the currently imprecise areas of competence of the Agency's organs.

The Statute gives the Board wide powers of control over the Director-General. It states that the Director-General "shall be under the authority of and subject to the control of the Board of Governors." [17] However, the Director-General "shall be responsible for the appointment, organization, and functioning of the staff." [18] Major appointments to posts in the Secretariat had to be cleared by the Director-General with the Board. In practice, the Board has insisted on giving its "advice and consent" and has given the Director-General little independent discretionary power on important recruitment matters. The Rules of Procedure adopted by the Board in June, 1958, provide that the Director-General

> shall be guided by the policy of the Agency. He shall report to the Board at least every two months on all major developments in the Agency's work. He shall perform his duties in accordance with regulations adopted by the Board.[19]

This has restricted the Director-General's function as policy maker to a point where he serves mainly as the Board's administrative officer. The office of Director-General—in comparison with the chief executive posts of other agencies in the United Nations family—is probably the weakest in its relationship to the governing body.

One interesting example illustrates this relationship. In January, 1958, the Board requested the Director-General to prepare an analysis of the advantages and disadvantages of establishing a standing Advisory Council, made up of scientists of international repute, to advise the Board on the scientific and technical aspects of the Agency's program. Accordingly, the Secretariat prepared a paper in which it weighed the desirability of such an organ. A scientific council, it submitted, would ensure that the Agency's work would take account of the latest technological developments. Since members of such a council would be in close touch with atomic energy programs in their own countries, their association with the Agency's work might lead to increased contact and support from member states and might increase the Agency's scientific authority and prestige. On the other hand, the paper stated that

> the creation of an independent council might conceivably disrupt the balance and relationships prescribed by the Statute, particularly if the council's functions were to extend beyond those of providing advice, or if it were concerned with other than purely technical and scientific subjects.[20]

On balance, the Director-General felt that the establishment of a scientific council would be desirable but its functions should be limited to providing advice to the Director-General rather than to the Board in order to avoid constitutional and juridical problems.[21] This recommendation was rejected by the Board. The attempt by the Director-General to take the Scientific Advisory Council out of the political arena altogether by making it responsible to himself was interpreted by the majority of Board members as an effort to increase the Director-General's powers vis-à-vis the Board. Finally, in October, 1958, the Board decided to appoint a seven-member Advisory Council, but made the body responsible to itself alone. This action may suggest a trend toward resolving policy disagreements between the Director-General and the Board in favor of the latter if the Board's authority might in any way be affected.

The Agency's Secretariat is developing many characteristics of the specialized agency secretariats in the United Nations family. In making appointments to the Agency's staff, the Director-General was guided by the requirement of the Statute that "the paramount consideration in the recruitment" of the staff be "to secure employees of the highest standards of efficiency, technical competence and integrity." [22] At the same time close attention was paid to the importance of recruitment on as wide a geographical basis as possible, especially in the leading posts of the Secretariat. There are four Deputy Directors-General, each of whom heads a department of the Agency; a fifth department, Safeguards and Inspection, is headed by the Inspector-General. The Department of Training and Technical Information is headed by a Russian; the Department of Technical Operations by a Frenchman; the Department of Research and Isotopes by an Englishman; the Department of Safeguards and Inspection by a Canadian; and the Department of Administration, Liaison, and Secretariat by a Swiss.

Owing to the controversial nature of the Agency's functions, the principle of geographical distribution is more rigorously applied to the Agency than to other secretariats. The nineteen staff members of the Agency at the director level or above represent seventeen different nationalities and each of the major geographical regions. This constitutes the widest geographical staff distribution achieved by an international secretariat.[23] Since two-thirds of the Agency's staff members were to deal with technical and scientific aspects of atomic energy, recruitment of the professional staff on a wide geographical basis presented serious problems. It was only natural that a large proportion of the persons available for appointment to the scientific and technical divisions would be found in states most advanced in the peaceful uses of atomic energy. Nevertheless, the three hundred professional staff members appointed to the Agency by the end of 1958 represented twenty-eight nationalities.[24] The Agency Secretariat will probably be one of the smallest international secretariats, numerically speaking—a total of only about five hundred recruitments is contemplated—but in relation to the rest of the United Nations family it already has the largest operational and directing staff.

A unique problem might face the Agency Secretariat owing to the highly specialized technical nature of the subject matter with which it deals. Areas of friction between the staff, on the one hand, and the Board or the General Conference, on the other, are at times exaggerated by differing conceptions of and perspectives on similar problems since it has become virtually impossible to have a "synoptic view" of atomic energy matters. Thus the Board members, although assisted by scientists, are instructed by governments and at times cannot heed the "scientific" recommendations of the Secretariat. The question of establishing a Scientific Advisory Council was an attempt to solve this problem. Conversely, the staff resents what it at times sees as "political decisions on scientific questions" by the Board and the General Conference. The scientist is often impatient with the statesman and does not recognize the difficulties inherent in finding political answers to the consequences of scientific development. The

Secretariat's pressure on the Board to staff the Division of Safeguards was an example of this. This picture should not, however, convey the impression of the Secretariat as a monolithic apolitical body. But, as one staff member put it, "Arguments in the Secretariat are apt to be more between chemists, physicists and metallurgists than Russians, Indians and Americans."

It thus seems that an important role of the Agency Secretariat might be the functional, though informal, representation of the scientist in the deliberations concerning the peaceful uses of atomic energy. In that sense the United Nations Conferences on the Peaceful Uses of Atomic Energy held in Geneva in 1955 and 1958 serve as useful instruments of coordination. At the Second Conference the Agency Secretariat presented four papers, one on the organizational and the others on the scientific aspects of atomic energy. This may indicate an expanding role for the Agency Secretariat in coordinating the scientific and the sociopolitical dimensions of the peaceful uses of atomic energy and thus help pave the way toward a less compartmentalized approach to the field.

THE OPERATIONS OF THE AGENCY

The objectives of the Agency reflect the dual nature of atomic energy: it is the embodiment of both the highest hopes and the deepest fears of mankind. First, the Agency's developmental responsibility is to accelerate the contribution of atomic energy to peace, health, and prosperity throughout the world. Second, and equally important, is to be the Agency's control function: to create a reliable system of safeguards against diversion of fissionable material to military uses in order that the broadening of the peaceful applications of atomic energy should not increase the danger of strengthening the military potential of nations.[25]

Within this broad framework, the task of the Board and of the Agency's staff is to plan and carry out specific projects and activities. This responsibility is largely a function of the Board and reflects the complicated decision-making process of that body. The initial program hammered out for the Agency is careful to avoid controversial subject matter and stresses the exploratory nature of the Agency's early work. The Secretariat originally submitted an outline of twelve projects, which was considered excessively ambitious by the

Board and was considerably narrowed. The twelve projects comprised the following: nuclear fact-finding teams to underdeveloped areas, isotope research, construction of technical facilities at Agency Headquarters, research contracts with government, waste disposal research, research on the effects of strontium-90, safeguard studies, international radiation monitoring, the creation of radiation hazards emergency teams, fellowship and exchange programs, regional nuclear training centers, and the preparation of conferences on the peaceful uses of atomic energy. One project rejected by the Board was a study on an international scale of the effects of strontium-90 on bone cancer. The Director-General considered such a project as legitimately within the purview of the Agency, but the Board unanimously decided that research in this area would take the Agency outside its statutory responsibilities into controversial territory. Generally, the Secretariat has had a far broader conception of "peaceful uses of atomic energy" than the Board. The Board, when in doubt, has interpreted the Statute narrowly. Consequently, the initial program has been a "safe" one, based on the dubious assumption that—on some projects at least—hard and fast distinctions may be drawn between peaceful and nonpeaceful applications of atomic energy. For example, the Board's rejection of strontium-90 research and its endorsement of an Agency fellowship program for atomic scientists were based on the assumption that the latter was exclusively in the cause of peace while the former was not. As many Secretariat members were quick to note, it would be difficult to prevent an Agency-trained scientist from applying his newly acquired technical skill in the cause of war if he so desired. Similarly, the argument might be raised that strontium-90 research was directly related to the cause of peace because it clarified and increased the knowledge of the dangers of preparations for war. The Board, in its deliberations on programing, rarely admitted that the atomic sword and the atomic plowshare were not always distinguishable.

The General Conference recommended at its first session in October, 1957, that "the Board should give high priority to those activities which will give the maximum possible benefit from the peaceful applications of atomic energy in improving the conditions and raising the standards of living of the peoples in the underdeveloped areas." [26] But political conservatism and considerations of the purse have resulted, initially, in a modest developmental program.

The preparation of atomically underdeveloped member states for the eventual use of nuclear power became the basic aim of the Agency's initial operations. Technical assistance, exchange and training programs, conferences and symposia, the provision of central technical information services, visits of expert missions, research for the wider use of radioisotopes in industry, agriculture, and medicine, comprise the main activities of the first phase of the Agency in action. A survey of current work and plans for further development were published by the Agency in August, 1958.[27] The following is a brief description and analysis of these activities and future projects:

1. TECHNICAL ASSISTANCE

The Board of Governors unanimously approved provisions for technical assistance to the less-developed areas. Consequently, almost all the technical activities of the Agency include such projects. Preliminary work included the organization of expert missions and fact-finding teams composed of specialists in several fields. Upon request by member states, Agency teams surveyed national nuclear energy programs and informed member states of the assistance the Agency could render, thus facilitating the planning of specific projects and the submission of requests to the Agency.

To assist the Agency in meeting requests for surveys, advice, and specific projects, a number of member states have offered the services of experts and consultants. France, Japan, the Soviet Union, the United States, the United Kingdom, India, and South Africa have put at the Agency's service over one hundred specialists in various branches of nuclear science.[28] In almost all cases these services are offered to the Agency free of charge. Most of the Agency's activities up to mid-1959 have concentrated on various countries in Latin America with a view to establishing one or more regional nuclear training centers in that region. It is expected that in 1960 Agency teams will be active in most of the world's underdeveloped areas. In order to facilitate technical assistance the Agency has initiated studies of nuclear economics and of world demand and supply of fissionable materials.

It is very likely that technical assistance will remain one of the Agency's major responsibilities. The Board's unanimous support of the program promises fairly rapid development. It will therefore become increasingly important during the early stages of the Agency's operations that machinery be set up to coordinate Agency activities with the various multilateral and national technical assistance programs already in existence.[29]

2. RESEARCH

It was thought that the Agency could make its most immediate contribution to the welfare of its member states by assisting them in the acquisition of the already substantial body of knowledge about the industrial, agricultural, and medical uses of radioisotopes and radiation. Teams consisting of specialists on the application of isotopes in various fields have already been organized. Like the general technical assistance teams, they give advice to the lesser developed member states. The first teams have already been dispatched to various countries in Latin America. Plans have been laid for various kinds of work to follow the surveys of the isotope teams, such as Agency assistance in procuring and installing laboratories and short-term on-site research using mobile isotope research laboratories donated by the United States.

Isotope research by the Agency itself will, of course, be necessary for these functions. The Board's refusal, for reasons of economy, to establish research facilities at the Agency's headquarters in Vienna has made necessary the placing of a number of research contracts with various national or regional organizations.[30] Whether this alternative in the long run will prove the less expensive one remains to be seen. The Agency-approved research contracts should result in important findings of international significance. Studies on water pollution, the standardization of radioisotopes, and maximum permissible short-term exposure to radiation are among those initiated by the Agency. The work of the isotope teams will undoubtedly be followed by additional research contracts.

The Agency, therefore, has introduced a new field—nuclear research—into the United Nations family. As in the area of general technical assistance, coordination with the United Nations and the specialized agencies will be necessary to determine divisions of labor. The Agency is aware of this need and relationship agreements are being negotiated. In the area of isotope research, however, primary responsibility will probably remain with the Agency.

3. TRAINING AND EXCHANGE OF SCIENTISTS AND EXPERTS

The Agency's only operational activity during the first year was the international training or fellowship program. Both the Board of Governors and the General Conference unanimously endorsed this plan and an amount of $250,000 was appropriated for this purpose from the Agency's General Fund, raised by voluntary contributions. By the end of 1958 Canada, Denmark, Monaco, Sweden, Turkey, South Africa, and the United Kingdom had pledged a total of $62,570 in voluntary contributions to finance the fellowship program.[31] The United States offered to match the contributions of all other member states up to a maximum of $125,000.[32] Fellowships to be financed from the Agency's own funds were classified as Type I. Fifty such Type I fellowships were financed by the Agency in 1958 and double this figure in 1959. The maximum duration of each fellowship is two years. Candidates are first suggested by the governments of member states and are then selected by the Agency on grounds of professional competence and geographical distribution. The majority of Agency fellows are pursuing their studies in the United States, the U.S.S.R., and the United Kingdom.

Member states have offered a second type of fellowship for training or research in their own countries. By the end of 1958 a total of 140 Type II fellowships were offered by Denmark, France, India, Italy, Japan, Poland, Romania, Spain, Switzerland, the U.S.S.R., the United Arab Republic, the United States, and Yugoslavia.[33] The duration of the fellowships varies from six months to six years.

By early 1959 the number of qualified applicants roughly matched the number of fellowships available. However, it is expected that a rapid increase in applications will necessitate a rigorous screening by the Agency Secretariat. It is also expected that Type II offers will be more plentiful than the Type I grants which give the Agency more discretionary powers with respect to placement and amount of stipend. All grants are awarded for training in the use of basic nuclear technology. Neither fellowship attaches "strings" with respect to candidates' commitments after the completion of their studies.

It is quite possible that the Agency's fellowship activities will expand rapidly. In response to a proposal by the governments of Brazil, Argentina, and Guatemala in January, 1958, the Board decided to undertake a study of the feasibility of establishing regional training centers in Latin America.[34] Five months later a group of experts was appointed to carry out a field survey. The group consisted of members of the Secretariat and of experts made available, free of charge, to the Agency by France, the United Kingdom, and the United States. Members from the United Nations Economic Commission for Latin America and the Organization of American States also participated. The initial findings of the group were generally favorable, and on the basis of more specific and detailed information the Board may— if interested member states so request—authorize the Agency to participate in establishing several regional nuclear training centers in Latin America. This project, if successful, may then serve as a model for similar regional or national surveys.

Finally, the Board has authorized the Agency's sponsorship of an exchange program of scientists and visiting professors to give special courses in theoretical and experimental aspects of atomic energy. Concrete implementation of this program will depend largely on the flow of voluntary contributions from member states and on the success of the Agency's fellowship program.

The only major disagreement on scientific training which arose among members of the Board was the issue of establishing laboratory facilities at Agency Headquarters for the training of scientists. Only the United States delegation supported the plan, but it was outvoted by the other Governors, who for fiscal reasons considered the project either impracticable or premature. The American delegate felt that a small but well-equipped training center would lend great prestige to the Agency. The majority contended that it would be far more economical to have scientists trained at existing institutions in member states. It may be that gifts from the United States will enable the Agency to establish some very limited laboratory facilities in Vienna. Two mobile radioisotope laboratories and a research reactor have already been donated to the Agency by the United States. But these facilities will play only a very limited role in the Agency's training program.

The fellowship program—enthusiastically supported by the Board— is a going concern. Clearly within the mandate of the Statute, it is the Agency's first operational experiment. Lasting effects—for a relatively small investment—are anticipated. Yet the rapid dissemination of technical knowledge through the Agency's training program will undoubtedly raise the question of control. In fact, the problem of preventing men from using their newly acquired knowledge in the cause of war might raise even more complex questions than preventing the diversion of fissionable material to military uses. The Agency has shied away from the many dilemmas which such controls would pose. For example, if the Agency required that, after training, its fellows be employed only in activities pursuing peaceful ends, more problems might be raised than solved. What would be the definition of "military"? Who would define it? What about the question of domestic jurisdiction and Agency interference in domestic matters? Where could the line be drawn and by whom? These and other dilemmas have prompted the Agency to concentrate first on the developmental rather than the control aspects of its training program. But the very success of the fellowship program—bringing with it Agency-sponsored diffusion of nuclear technology—will make the necessity of safeguards and controls more urgent. This problem may ultimately confront the Agency with one of its greatest challenges.

4. EXCHANGE OF TECHNICAL INFORMATION AND CONFERENCES

The Agency, by virtue of its broad international character, is in a unique position to assemble and disseminate scientific and technical information on the peaceful uses of atomic energy and to encourage and facilitate exchange of information among its member states. The Board very early recognized the Agency's potential in this domain and has launched a number of programs. The Secretariat has been authorized to assemble, with the help of member states, a comprehensive atoms-for-peace library. Assistance received from thirteen member states by the end of June, 1959, has assured a good beginning. The United States alone has donated 38,000 volumes to the Agency library.[35]

An ambitious scheme is under way for the selection and classification of all documentation received from member states. The collection already includes reports, bibliographies, and translations of abstracts. The goal is a complete reference service on matters pertaining to atomic energy. The Agency will also publish scientific and technical papers produced by its staff and will study the feasibility of developing a standard terminology for atomic energy among its member states. An Agency bulletin, *World Atomics*, reports monthly on the Agency's work.

Finally, the Agency was authorized to participate in planning and organizing the Second United Nations International Conference on the Peaceful Uses of Atomic Energy held in Geneva, in September, 1958. The Agency's role as forum for nuclear scientists of international reputation will probably be an especially hopeful aspect of its work. The 2,300 scientific papers presented at the Second Geneva Conference evidenced the rapid growth of the new nuclear science and the consequent need for continued coordination. The Conference was marked by a refreshing scientific spirit unmarred by extraneous considerations. The fact that disagreements occurred primarily among representatives of differing scientific, rather than political, persuasions gave substance to the hope that the Agency can vitally contribute to a relaxation of international tensions. It is probable that in the future similar conferences will be held under the aegis of the Agency.

5. REACTOR DEVELOPMENT

The Agency's activities in the area of reactor development are still in the preliminary stage. Technical data for the planning and development of reactors must first be collected systematically throughout the underdeveloped regions in order to determine needs and absorptive capacities. Three detailed questionnaires concerning the characteristics of reactors in operation or under construction were sent to member states. On the basis of the information supplied, the Agency is planning to publish an up-to-date international directory of existing power, research, and experimental reactors.

By the end of 1958 seven requests to evaluate new reactor projects—six from Latin-American countries and one from Japan—had reached the Agency. At the present time the Agency's role in these projects is primarily one of giving expert advice and technical assistance. The Agency will probably not be actively engaged in power reactor building for at least five years although a study of research and experimental reactors is presently under way.[36] As requests for evaluations of power reactor projects increase, the Agency will be better enabled to plan several such projects.[37]

The reactor development program confronts the Agency with a serious dilemma. President Eisenhower's speech in 1953 had suggested that nuclear power reactors could become a panacea for the economically destitute regions desperately bent on freeing themselves from the limitations of poverty and on closing ranks with the industrialized countries. This suggestion gave rise to high expectations, which were maintained even in the face of recent far more sober appraisals. The modest and realistic program of the Agency in reactor development has been a bitter disappointment to the underdeveloped countries. Although reluctant to disillusion the atomic have-nots, the Agency now realizes the necessity of warning them against premature requests for aid. This is a delicate task, indeed, and it is further complicated by policy disagreements within the Board of Governors. The Soviet Union, eager to play spokesman for the underdeveloped countries, frequently defends plans for reactor development which are considered premature by survey teams of the Agency Secretariat. The fact is that these countries—according to the survey made—do not yet possess the supporting industrial skill and social structure upon which the development of nuclear energy can rest and that the use of atomic power will be uneconomical for some time to come.

The majority of the Board, therefore, urges rigorous analyses of the economic and social aspects of atomic energy development in the underdeveloped areas. Legitimate requests for aid are encouraged but the utmost caution is exercised in the planning of reactor projects. Unrealistic demands for aid are gently discouraged.

The Agency's usefulness in the reactor field for the next five years "will be largely confined to supplying technical assistance, training, information and project analysis." [38] But the fact remains that in the eyes of most underdeveloped countries the number of Agency-constructed power reactors will be a major criterion for evaluating the Agency's over-all success or failure. Therefore, during the next few years the Agency will face the formidable educational task of counteracting the early unrealistic enthusiasm. This task will be made more difficult by the Soviet attitude and might become virtually impossible if any of the great powers should make a bilateral offer of reactor construction aid which deviates to any extent from the rigorous standards the Agency is now attempting to establish. [39]

6. THE SUPPLY OF FISSIONABLE AND SOURCE MATERIALS

Only one request for the supply of fissionable or source material has been made to the Agency. The government of Japan has applied for three tons of natural uranium to meet its needs for nuclear fuel. Not many applications are likely to be received until the reactor program is further developed.

A considerable number of states have notified the Agency that they are prepared to offer fissionable and source materials. By the end of June, 1959, the total amount of fissionable material offered to the Agency was 5,140 kilograms.[40] Ample offers of source material have been received from Canada, Ceylon, India, Portugal, and South Africa.[41]

As indicated earlier, the problem has been not a dearth of materials but the terms and conditions under which the Agency will take control. Questions of price, terms of transfer, and storage had already presented great difficulties during the Statute negotiations.[42] When Japan applied to the Agency for natural uranium in September, 1958, it became clear that—once handling and safeguard charges were added—materials purchased from the Agency were more expensive than similar materials under bilateral agreements. Only a timely offer by the government of Canada to supply three tons of uranium to the Agency free of charge on a "once only" basis enabled the Agency to meet a legitimate application.

In an effort to obtain information about price and transfer of materials, detailed questionnaires have been sent to the member states which have made offers. The data so far obtained indicates that a standard price schedule is virtually impossible to establish. So far there has been no world market in the supply of uranium and its concentrates although there are indications that such a market may come into being in the not too distant future.

The Board's authority under the Statute is broad enough and the clauses pertaining to the supply of materials sufficiently flexible to permit Agency adjustment to various types of national legislation governing atomic energy. At this stage the Agency is in the process of negotiating an agreement with the United States. In view of the fact that the United States is the largest supplier of fissionable materials, an early Agency agreement with it will be of great importance.

Agency negotiations with the United States government provide an interesting case study of the problem of supplying materials. In this instance the Agency must adjust itself to the United States Atomic Energy Act of 1954. First, to meet the conditions of the Act, the Atomic Energy Commission will have to negotiate with the Agency periodic "agreements for cooperation" specifying the amounts and terms of the United States contribution of fissionable materials for a given period.[43] This seems compatible with the Agency Statute which provides for contributions made available "in conformity with its [the member's] laws" and for periodic agreement with contributors determining the terms of the contributions.[44] However, the Statute does not allow a donor to specify or restrict recipients. Second, the Agency's safeguard provisions seem comparable to those required in the Act. Third, the Statute provides for "ratification or acceptance" in accordance with "respective constitutional processes." [45] While the American constitutional procedure seems cumbersome in this respect, there is no evidence of incompatibility with the Statute. Upon completing the negotiations, the Atomic Energy Commission recommends approval to the President. The President then must make a "determination in writing" that the agreement "will promote and will not constitute an unreasonabe risk to the common defense and security." [46] After presidential approval, the proposed agreement would have to lie before the Joint Committee on Atomic Energy of the Congress for thirty days while Congress is in session. It seems that this procedure might be simplified inasmuch as President Eisenhower has declared his intention to request "appropriate Congressional authority to transfer special nuclear materials to the Agency."[47] But such authority would require an amendment to the Atomic Energy Act. Fourth, the Agency will have to give the United States certain guarantees. No materials supplied by the United States may be transferred beyond the jurisdiction of the Agency except as specificd in thc agrccmcnt itself.[48] The Agency will not be permitted to pass control of the material to a private party as long as private ownership of fissionable materials is not recognized in the United States. The Agency Statute does not preclude these requirements. Finally, neither the Atomic Energy Act nor the Statute specifies the form of the legal transaction through which the material may be made available. A salc or lcase or combination formula may therefore be worked out within the framework of both the act and the Statute. If the discussions during the Statute negotiations are indicative, it will not be easy to find a satisfactory formula in this area. Political and economic, rather than legal, considerations will probably present great difficulties.

In order to ensure that available materials are used, it seems clear that the Agency will have to play a dynamic role in encouraging demand from member states. The first step will be to provide member states with as many details as possible as to quantities, characteristics, prices, and terms of supply of such materials. In supplying member states the Agency will either act as prime contractor and supply materials from those in its possession or at its disposal or it might be a third party to an agreement for the supply of materials directly from one member state to another. In either case the Agency will have to ensure continuity of supply. The extent to which it is able to do so may determine the number of requests for the resources placed at its disposal.

7. HEALTH AND SAFETY AND WASTE DISPOSAL

Next to setting up a safeguard system against diversion of fissionable materials to military uses, the establishment of health and safety standards and the disposal of radioactive waste constitute the Agency's most important control functions. The Statute requires the Agency to

> establish or adopt, in consultation and, where appropriate, in collaboration with the competent organs of the United Nations and with the specialized agencies concerned, standards of safety for protection of health and minimization of danger to life and property (including such standards for labor conditions).[49]

The Agency is to determine and apply such standards to its own operations, and to national, bilateral, or multilateral arrangements at the request of the state or states concerned.

The Board of Governors has encouraged early action by the Agency in this area. The establishment of health and safety standards is a prerequisite for most of the Agency's technical assistance activities. The Statute clearly authorizes the Agency to become the international coordinator of health and safety standards. Many member states and international and regional organizations are in the process of preparing health and safety legislation, for which Agency standards can be used as models. Thus duplication of effort may be avoided and legislation harmonized through the Agency. Such initiative might greatly enhance the Agency's prestige.

The Secretariat has begun an ambitious health and safety standards program. However, a number of recommendations by the staff have been considered premature by the Board and rejected. As has often been the case, the Secretariat proposed a more ambitious scheme than the Board was willing to accept but, on the whole, remarkable progress has been made.

Work has begun on the establishment of safety standards for Agency and Agency-sponsored operations. A field advisory service has been established which is to assist member states in the adoption of health and safety regulations and measures. The Secretariat has also recommended the creation of several radiation hazard emergency teams to act as a kind of fire brigade in case of accidents in Agency projects. The Board rejected the proposal as impractical, reasoning that in most cases such teams would not be able to reach the scene of the accident rapidly enough, and suggested that the Agency would be better served by on-the-spot field services. A survey of international needs and resources in the field of health and safety is currently taking place under the aegis of the Agency. In the formulation of the Agency's exchange and training program the Secretariat is giving special attention to the training of health and safety specialists so that the development of atomic energy programs is not retarded by a shortage of key personnel. The Agency has also concluded a contract with the University of Vienna for research on safety codes.[50]

In view of the Agency's function of coordinating all international efforts to establish health and safety standards, the Secretariat's work has required close collaboration with other organizations. The Secretariat has assembled information from member states on their safety practices and regulations and from numerous international and non-governmental organizations regarding their work in the formulation of codes. The coordinating function of the Agency is particularly important in this field, since it is of paramount importance that no serious divergencies exist among different codes. In order to ensure a high degree of uniformity, the Agency has consulted with ILO, FAO, WHO, UNESCO, ICAO, and WMO. All these specialized agencies deal with aspects of atomic energy. For example, ILO is concerned with the protection of industrial workers and hence is interested in safety code matters. WHO has been most active in public health aspects of radiation. ICAO is involved in the problem of regulating the international transport of radioactive materials, which is also of vital interest to the Agency.[51] The Secretariat is also keeping abreast of the health and safety work done in regional organizations. Pending the conclusion of formal relationship agreements with the Agency, the Secretariat has begun informal coordination with these specialized agencies to determine practical divisions of labor and to ensure that the Agency's view would be represented.

These informal working arrangements are providing useful bases for the negotiation of formal arrangements.

Two projects recommended by the Secretariat requiring coordination with other atomic energy bodies have been rejected by the Board. The Director-General had suggested an Agency study of the effects of strontium-90 on bone cancer. The Board unanimously decided that such a project should not be attempted by the Agency. While the Soviet delegate felt that this study would not be related to the peaceful uses of atomic energy, the United States delegation was concerned that it might overlap the work of the United Nations Scientific Committee on the Effects of Atomic Radiation, which was engaged in similar research. The remaining members of the Board rejected the proposal for fiscal reasons. A similar fate befell a Secretariat proposal that the Agency should set standards in international radiation monitoring. The Director-General maintained that such a project would be highly relevant to the Agency's tasks, since fear of radiation throughout the world would impede the development of atomic energy even for peaceful purposes. The Soviet delegate rejected the project, contending that only a suspension of bomb tests could alleviate that problem. The United States again feared duplication with the Radiation Committee of the United Nations and the rest of the Board censured the project as either premature or irrelevant. As a gesture toward the Secretariat, the Board authorized Agency contact with the United Nations Radiation Committee in order to ensure some measure of coordination of future activities.

An important field in which the Agency has taken initiative is that of the disposal of radioactive waste materials. Studies of the technical aspects of the release of effluents into the atmosphere, into fresh waters, and into the sea are currently in progress. The Agency is planning to send experts to the less-developed countries to study disposal sites. For this purpose the Agency is collecting information from atomically advanced countries which are actually engaged in major waste disposal research. It seems that special attention will be paid by the Agency to ocean studies. Again coordination is a paramount problem here, since many groups have been engaged in various aspects of ocean study, although radioactive waste disposal has only been an adjunct to their major interests. The need for coordination appears greatest in the practical handling of radioactive wastes and in the study of their effect on marine biology. It is significant that the United Nations Conference on the Law of the Sea, held in Geneva in April, 1958, authorized the Agency to serve in an over-all coordinating capacity. The Conference recommended that

> the IAEA, in consultation with existing groups and established organs having acknowledged competence in the field of radiological protection, should pursue whatever studies and take whatever action is necessary to assist states in controlling the discharge or release of radioactive materials to the sea, promulgating standards and in drawing up internationally acceptable regulations to prevent pollution of the sea by radioactive material in amounts which would adversely affect man and his marine resources.[52]

The Agency's work and planning in the fields of health, safety, and waste disposal has had an auspicious beginning. With some exceptions, the Board has taken a positive approach which has permitted the Secretariat, in turn, to employ the broad authority given the Agency by the Statute. The Agency may soon play the international coordinating role in the area of health and safety which many observers hoped it would assume in the areas of safeguards and inspection. A decisive policy by the Board has yielded some remarkable results. The Agency's work is already considered invaluable by national, regional, and international organizations competent in the field.

8. SAFEGUARDS, INSPECTION, AND SANCTIONS

The Agency's operations in both safeguards and inspection are in the preparatory stages. Safeguards and inspection are theoretical and practical aspects of a single problem. The Division of Safeguards is to develop Agency standards, methods, and policies including procedures for accountability, storage, and inspection. It is also to undertake research to further the methodology of safeguards and encourage such research in member states.[53] The Division of Inspection is to implement the safeguard system and to enforce observance of its security, health, and safety standards.[54]

A circular predicament has impeded the Agency's progress in establishing safeguards: reactor plants cannot be set up until the safeguard system is ready to operate. But the safeguard system cannot be developed until reactor building is well along in the planning stage, since the technical details of the safeguard system will depend on the character of the reactors. Progress in the inspection field has been delayed for similar reasons. As a member of the Agency Secretariat put it:

> The Statute authorizes the Agency to inspect plants, if so requested by outside parties. The Agency cannot inspect plants before it has a staff. But if objections are raised to the recruitment of a staff, how can the Agency hope to get requests for inspection? We are perpetuating a vicious circle.[55]

In the matter of staffing the Division of Safeguards, the Secretariat has strongly urged the Board to proceed. The Board's procrastination for reasons of economy has already been described.[56] But even after its reluctant decision to recruit a staff, recruitment has posed problems causing further delay. The Soviet delegate proposed a resolution which would have compelled the Director-General so to staff the Division "as to include at least one representative of each of the eight geographical areas listed in Article VI of the Statute." This proposal, which, if adopted, would have further reduced the discretionary powers of the Director-General, was narrowly defeated by a vote of 13-10.[57] A substitute United Kingdom resolution, less rigid than the Soviet draft, and simply requesting the Director-General "to bear in mind the provisions relating to the recruitment of staff on as wide a geographical basis as possible" was adopted by the Board by a vote of 12-1, with 10 abstentions.[58] Mr. Roger M. Smith of Canada, appointed in July, 1958, as head of the Division of Safeguards, has been the Agency's sole recruit. No appointments have been made in the Inspection Division. The Secretariat has put considerable pressure on the Board to appoint an Inspector-General, and it is probable that in the not too distance future a national from one of the neutral countries will be appointed to the post. For 1959 the Secretariat has proposed a modest staff of twelve to man the Safeguard Division and six, including the Inspector-General, for the Division of Inspection.[59] In view of the broad safeguard and inspection powers under the Statute, this policy of minimum staffing reveals a modest interpretation of the Agency's early functions.

Agency inspectors, once recruited, will probably begin their activities not in Agency plants but in "other arrangements where the Agency is requested by the Parties concerned to apply safeguards." [60] Numerous bilateral agreements negotiated by the United States include an optional clause providing for Agency assumption of safeguard and inspection responsibilities if the parties to the contract so decide.[61] A similar clause was included in the recent treaty negotiated between the United States and Euratom.[62] In the words of the Director of the Division of Safeguards,

> we expect to get business just as soon as we are staffed. We shall then ask member states to ask the Agency for safeguards and inspection. We anticipate a considerable number of such requests.[63]

Only one such request had reached the Agency by the end of 1958: to assume the inspection responsibility for the bilateral agreement between the United States and Japan. Since the Agency's own reactor-building program is in the exploratory stage, the safeguard and inspection pattern may develop in reactor plants erected independently of the Agency.

If the Agency is requested to play an active role in the safeguarding and inspection of nuclear plants in member states, it may soon find itself understaffed. Its responsibilities under the Statute are very heavy. The Agency must ensure "accountability for [all] source and special fissionable materials" involved in Agency projects.[64] It must approve the design of reactors, maintain operating records, submit progress reports, and approve the means to be used for the chemical processing of irradiated materials.[65] It must keep track of all "dangerous by-products" and ensure that they are used only for peaceful purposes. Therefore, the inspectors must determine what quantities of fissionable material a state requires for peaceful activities and allow retention of that quantity and no more. Any excess produced by the state's or the organization's reactors must be handed over to the Agency.[66] This extremely important provision caused greater controversy than any other single issue during the Statute negotiations.

The powers of the Agency Inspectorate are commensurate with its wide responsibilities. The inspectors must have "access at all times to all places and data and to any person who, by reason of his occupation, deals with materials, equipment or facilities which are required by the Statute to be safeguarded." [67] National "assessors" may accompany the inspectors on their missions, "provided that the inspectors shall not thereby be delayed or otherwise impeded" in their work.[68] This means, in effect, that inspectors may remain permanently in any state, take up residence at any plant, exercise continuous supervision of any nuclear process, conduct their own sampling and analysis and call on anybody to explain anything they feel needs explaining. On paper these powers are wide and unprecedented. The Preparatory Commission envisaged even further expansion of inspection powers. It suggested that "it would be convenient in practice to associate Inspection under the safeguards functions with inspection under the health and safety functions of the Agency." [69] The Commission felt that this combination of functions might promote good relations between governments and Agency inspectors, since the inspectors would thus be enabled to render a "positive," constructive service.

In the opinion of one official, a gaseous diffusion plant for the separation of U-235 and U-230 would require twenty to thirty inspectors, of whom one-third would have to be scientists and technicians and two-thirds would be guards. Each high-capacity reactor would need six, or at most eight, inspectors, two or three of whom would be qualified to undertake the work of "accounting" and control. The rest would be guards, who might also assist with health and safety work. Safeguards against diversion during transport would not require many inspectors, since the quantities dispatched from one point must correspond precisely to the quantities received at another. Similarly, the simpler task of controlling source material mines and primary processing mills would not require detailed inspection.[70]

In view of the above estimates, the Agency's plans for itinerant safeguard and inspection personnel can hardly be expected to offset the many problems which are bound to arise through understaffing if the Secretariat's predictions of considerable activity should materialize.

It must be remembered, however, that in the immediate future the Agency's safeguards and inspection activities *will depend on requests* and if such requests are not forthcoming the Agency's inspectors will be temporarily superfluous. Unless the Agency is expressly invited, the safeguards do *not* in practice apply to nations which already have their own nuclear industries; they do *not* apply to nations which may develop their own industries without Agency help; and they do *not* apply to industries established by nations under bilateral or regional agreements with one of the nuclear powers.

These are three great gaps in the Statute which could only be closed
if the nuclear powers applied the Agency safeguard and inspection
system to themselves; if they persuaded all other nations to do the
same; and if they undertook to make no bilateral or regional agreements to supply nuclear fuel, materials, or equipment, except on
condition of Agency control. Such a hope, however, is utopian. The
atomic powers had originally drawn up the Agency's safeguard system as a means of preventing the nonnuclear powers from even
entering the field of atomic armament. They did not intend to apply
the safeguard provisions to themselves. Yet the Western powers have
consistently taken the position in the United Nations that a system
of international inspection is a prerequisite to breaking the deadlock
on the disarmament question. Most states are similarly ambivalent
about Agency inspection. To the NATO countries, inspection by
"friendly" inspectors from allied nations is preferable to international
inspection by the Agency Inspectorate, including representatives of
the Soviet Union and its satellites. But international inspection,
owing to considerations of national pride and sensitivity, may yet
be preferred to United States, British, or any other form of unilateral inspection. Moreover, the rejection altogether by a Western
power of international inspection would expose it to a Soviet charge
of inconsistency with self-proclaimed principles. An underdeveloped
country, if given the choice, might request Agency inspection more
readily than a Western European power. In view of the deep nationalistic orientation of many of these countries and their suspicions
of colonialism, bilateral controls are probably more onerous to them.
Yet many of the atomic have-nots have chosen bilateral arrangements because, as a rule, they cost less. Finally, it is hardly likely
that requests for Agency inspection will be forthcoming in the near
future for Soviet or Eastern European nuclear plants. A careful
weighing by national governments of these conflicting considerations will determine the Agency's role in safeguards and inspection.

The sanctioning procedure against violators has been described
earlier.[71] The entire matter is, of course, still in the theoretical stage.
The Agency Secretariat considers the sanctioning process satisfactory. The Board, on its own authority, may curtail or suspend assistance, call for return of materials, or suspend the offending member. The suspension of assistance might in some circumstances be
a heavy material sanction. The Statute is silent on the nature of

possible Security Council or General Assembly action against a
recalcitrant member. It merely requires reports from the Board to
these two United Nations organs in case of noncompliance. Presumably United Nations action would depend on the gravity of the
offense and the imminence of nuclear aggression. Even though the
Agency Inspectorate could perhaps not "recapture" the fissionable
material, world public opinion would be focused on the crime. It
has been suggested that

> the effectiveness of IAEA action would be increased if the principle
> of the Nuremberg trials were applied to acts which violated a nuclear
> disarmament agreement; that is to say, that the individuals who com-
> mitted the treaty-breaking acts should be personally liable to prose-
> cution and punishment and could not shelter behind the orders
> which they had received from their governments.[72]

While such a policy may raise a number of complicated legal problems, the argument that sanctions would thereby become unduly
onerous, lacks cogency. In the words of de Madariaga:

> Just as prisons are erected not so much to lock people in as to induce
> people to stay out, so sanctions must be devised in order that na-
> tions should not have to undergo them. The most efficient system of
> sanctions is that which will never be applied.[73]

The stronger the sanctions created by the Agency the less grave the
danger that anyone will defy them.

THE AGENCY'S RELATIONS WITH THE UNITED NATIONS AND THE SPECIALIZED AGENCIES

1. THE IAEA AND THE UNITED NATIONS

The task of defining the Agency's relationship to the United
Nations revealed serious disagreements among the Statute negotiators. These differences had not been resolved by the time the
Statute was ready for submission to the General Assembly in October, 1956. The job of concluding a relationship agreement between
the Agency and the United Nations became the most controversial
single task which confronted the Agency's Preparatory Commission.
The eighteen powers comprising the Commission and a special body
representing the United Nations—the United Nations Advisory
Committee on the Peaceful Uses of Atomic Energy—set up by the

General Assembly, finally reached an agreement July 11, 1957.[74] The draft was approved unanimously by the Agency's Board of Governors and the General Conference during its first session. It entered into force upon its unanimous approval by the General Assembly on November 14, 1957.

The eight Western atomic powers comprising the first negotiating group in the summer of 1954 unanimously agreed that the Agency should be kept as removed from the United Nations as possible. These nations feared that the Agency, as a subsidiary organ of the United Nations—a commission or subcommission of the Economic and Social Council or the General Assembly—would, in effect, be controlled by the atomic have-nots making up the majority of United Nations membership. This fear of "creating a bank to be controlled by loan applicants" was further intensified by the Western concern that the Soviet Union would be in a position to exert a measure of control over the Agency through United Nations organs and would use this power to widen the differences between the atomic powers and the underdevelopd countries. In the summer of 1954 it seemed that the Agency would be set up as a specialized agency of the United Nations with a limited membership, its own constitutional processes, and only a loose relationship to the parent organization. The only obligation to be imposed on the Agency by the United Nations was the submission of the administrative budget for consideration by the General Assembly. This provision was to be for coordinating purposes only and would leave the Agency free of any operational control by the United Nations.

Two new factors in the fall of 1954 complicated the picture. First, the Soviet Union decided to join the Agency and to participate in the twelve-power negotiations. Second, as was described earlier, the underdeveloped countries in the Ninth General Assembly refused to regard the General Assembly as a rubber stamp body of the Washington negotiations and insisted that they actively collaborate in negotiating the Agency Statute.[75]

The Soviet delegation in the twelve-power group demanded that the Agency be more closely related to the United Nations than the typical specialized agency:

> The IAEA will have a special responsibility in the area of maintaining international peace and security. This is a United Nations function. Therefore, on the demand of interested governments, the

Agency must submit questions relating to the maintenance of international peace and security to the Security Council. Most important, the Security Council is to establish control over the outlay of fissionable materials.[76]

The Soviet proposal to subordinate the Agency to the Security Council and, therefore, to the veto power of its permanent members was challenged by the United States as superfluous:

To give the Security Council the veto power over the Agency would not be necessary since every nation would have a *de facto* veto in the matter of transferring fissionable materials [to the Agency].[77]

Evidently satisfied, the U.S.S.R. once again proceeded to subordinate its role as atomic producer to that of self-appointed champion of anticolonialism and now supported the Indian view that the Agency be controlled as closely as possible by the General Assembly in order to safeguard the interests of the underdeveloped countries. The United States, eager to remove the Agency from direct control of the Security Council and the danger of Soviet veto, now declared itself ready to integrate the Agency more closely into the United Nations framework than it had originally planned.

By October, 1956, agreement had been reached on the basic framework of the relationship agreement: the Agency was to be tied more closely to the United Nations than was the typical specialized agency, but not so closely as a typical subsidiary organ of the Economic and Social Council or of the General Assembly. The precise details of the compromise formula were worked out by the Agency's Preparatory Commission with the collaboration of the United Nations Advisory Committee on the Peaceful Uses of Atomic Energy.

Disagreements continued during the subsequent negotiations. United Nations Secretariat officials felt that, in view of the Agency's responsibilities in matters vitally affecting military security and economic development, a close relationship to the United Nations would be highly desirable. The Soviet Union and the underdeveloped countries supported a close tie since this would afford them a greater measure of control. Fear of this control prompted the Western atomic powers to support a looser arrangement on the periphery of the United Nations.

The ingenious compromise finally hammered out placed the

Agency in a unique position vis-à-vis the United Nations. The IAEA became neither a specialized agency nor an integral United Nations organ, but an "autonomous international organization." [78] Although the Agency seemed to meet the criteria of a specialized agency as defined in Article 57 of the United Nations Charter—intergovernmental character, international responsibilities, and activity in economic and social development—the negotiators decided to create a special niche for the Agency in the United Nations family.[79] In some matters the Agency was to be similar to a specialized agency, in others it was to depart from the pattern.

The most important departure from the specialized agency norm lay in a sphere closely affecting world peace and security. The Agency was to report directly to the General Assembly at each regular session rather than to the Economic and Social Council, as in the case of the specialized agencies.[80] Moreover, in respect to sanctions, the Agency was obliged to submit reports of noncompliance to the Security Council as well as to the General Assembly.[81] In order to ensure continuous coordination, provisions for reciprocal representation between the Agency and the United Nations were included in the agreement.[82] In these three important ways, the Agency's tie to the parent organization was to be closer than that of the typical specialized agency.

In two other areas, however, the Agency was to enjoy a greater degree of autonomy. The Agency, under its Statute, was to have the power to initiate sanctions against noncompliant member states. Only in case of the Board's failure to discipline a recalcitrant member was United Nations authority to be invoked. Such autonomous disciplinary initiative in the realm of international security had no parallel among the specialized agencies. Second, the IAEA was to be an operational body. This placed the Agency in a special position vis-à-vis the United Nations, comparable to that of the World Bank or the International Monetary Fund: its operational budget was not subject to review by the General Assembly.

In several other areas the position of the Agency is comparable to that of the other members of the United Nations family: exchange of information and documents, reciprocal proposal of agenda items, and review of the Agency's administrative budget.[83] Personnel policy as well as staff privileges and immunities follow the typical pattern.[84] Finally, the General Conference and the Board of Governors of the

Agency are both empowered to "seek an advisory opinion of the International Court of Justice on any legal question arising within the scope of the activities of the Agency." [85]

Since the Agency is neither a specialized agency nor an organ of the United Nations, its legal position is unclear. The General Assembly, on the basis of Article 96 of the United Nations Charter, authorizes the Agency to seek advisory opinions.[86] But Article 96 gives this authority only to specialized agencies and organs of the United Nations. Organs have been defined as integral bodies of the United Nations. It is interesting to speculate whether, under this article, the Agency would be considered a "specialized agency." The problem is typical of the numerous legal ambiguities which the Agency has to clarify in its relations with the United Nations.

In practice IAEA's relationship to the United Nations differs little from that of the specialized agencies. On July 31, 1958, the Economic and Social Council passed a resolution requesting the IAEA to submit annual reports.[87] The Agency has expressed its intention to comply with this request "on matters within the competence of the Economic and Social Council." [88] This provision brings the Agency's reporting procedure more closely into harmony with that of the specialized agencies. The special link to the General Assembly loses some of its significance in the light of the fact that the Economic and Social Council, in terms of powers and membership, resembles a committee of the General Assembly.

The Agency's unique status in the United Nations family is, therefore, more symbolic than real. The only truly distinctive feature is the Agency's independent power to initiate sanctions in an area vitally affecting international security. There seems to be a trend in the direction of narrowing further the differences between the specialized agencies and the IAEA.

The implementation of the Relationship Agreement has, so far, raised no serious problems. To provide for continuity and flexibility, the Secretary-General of the United Nations appointed a permanent representative to the Agency on December 15, 1957, with residence in Vienna. The Agency's Liaison Office at the United Nations was established on March 24, 1958, when the Director-General appointed a representative to the United Nations, with residence in New York.[89] On May 5, 1958, the Agency participated, for the first time, in the meetings of the Administrative Committee on Coordination of the United Nations (ACC) and on May 19 the Director-General attended a special meeting of the Economic Commission for Europe (ECE).[90]

The Board of Governors has had to face only one major problem in the Agency's relations with the United Nations: a decision on Agency participation in the United Nations Expanded Technical Assistance Program (EPTA) and the United Nations Special Fund.

EPTA was organized by the Economic and Social Council and its establishment unanimously approved by the General Assembly in November, 1949. Its primary objective was to help underdeveloped areas

> to strengthen their national economies through the development of their industries and agriculture with a view to promoting their economic and political independence in the spirit of the Charter of the United Nations, and to ensure the attainment of higher levels of economic and social welfare for their entire populations.[91]

The Technical Assistance Board (TAB) was designed under the same resolution to coordinate and supervise the operations of EPTA. TAB consists of the executive heads of the organizations participating in EPTA: the United Nations, ILO, FAO, UNESCO, ICAO, WHO, ITU, and WMO. The International Bank for Reconstruction and Development (IBRD) and the International Monetary Fund (IMF) cooperate with TAB to coordinate their technical assistance activities with those under EPTA, but they receive no funds from EPTA.

The Special Fund was established by the General Assembly at its thirteenth session as an extension of technical assistance and development activities of organizations within the United Nations family.[92] It was set up to concentrate on "relatively large" projects including multinational or regional projects and was to be distinct from, though closely related to, EPTA.

The Board was divided on the question of the Agency's participation in both organizations. The Western atomic powers advocated participation, the underdeveloped countries opposed it. The Soviet Union chose to abstain.

The Western delegates pointed out that participation would hold several advantages for the Agency. First, there would be the obvious possibility of sharing EPTA's and the Fund's resources. Second, the

Agency would have at its disposal the experience and, if needed, the support of the administrative and operational services built up under EPTA and in particular of the TAB field offices in fifty-six countries and territories.[93] There would be, finally, the benefits of closer cooperation, through TAB, among all the organizations participating in EPTA and of more effective coordination of the technical assistance activities of the Agency with those of the United Nations and the specialized agencies. The Western powers felt that through such coordination the legitimate interests and the special position of the Agency would be better safeguarded.

The underdeveloped countries were primarily concerned with the fiscal implications of Agency participation. The Brazilian delegate expressed the fear that Agency projects would lose their identity and, consequently, financial support:

> . . . the flow of voluntary contributions to the Agency would diminish. If the United States were to give one million dollars to EPTA, the American government might consider that it had given the money to the Agency since the Agency would participate in EPTA.[94]

The United States emphasized that its aim in recommending Agency participation was to avoid duplication in technical assistance activities. The United States made it clear that it would not confuse its contribution to EPTA with that to the Agency. The delegate from the United Arab Republic retorted that, should the Agency participate, it would be each Governor's responsibility to make clear to his government that a contribution to EPTA would not take the place of a voluntary contribution to the Agency.[95] American and British assurance to that effect resulted in a vote of 16-0, with 7 abstentions, recommending the Agency's participation in both EPTA and the Special Fund.[96] The Secretariat, in two separate memoranda to the Board, strongly urged participation on the grounds that the Agency would obtain additional resources for technical assistance work.[97] In the light of this recommendation, approval by the General Conference during its 1958 session was assured.

2. THE IAEA AND THE SPECIALIZED AGENCIES

The Agency Statute provides for the conclusion of appropriate relationship agreements with organizations whose work is related to that of the Agency. The Preparatory Commission recommended that the first such agreements should be negotiated with certain of the specialized agencies.[98] It accordingly drew up a series of Guiding Principles for relationship agreements between the Agency and the specialized agencies. At its first session the General Conference authorized the Board of Governors to negotiate agreements with the specialized agencies and requested that they be submitted to the General Conference for approval during the regular session following negotiation.[99]

The relationship agreements are designed to set up workable divisions of labor between IAEA and the specialized agencies. Since the statutory authorizations of many of the specialized agencies are broad, there are a number of fields in which the organizations have a joint mandate to take action. In fact, the need for international action in regard to several of the peaceful applications of atomic energy had become pressing some time before the establishment of the Agency itself. The International Labor Office (ILO) had been active in the development of a workers' security code in industrial establishments and a manual for the protection of workers against the hazards of radiation. The Food and Agriculture Organization (FAO) had been interested in the utilization of radiation techniques in research on conservation and plant growth as well as in botanical and ecological research. The United Nations Educational, Scientific and Cultural Organization (UNESCO) had been active in the field of nuclear research and had been concerned with the social, political, and cultural implications of peacefully applied atomic energy. The World Health Organization (WHO) had been dealing with problems of public health raised by atomic energy, such as the biological effects of radiation. The World Meteorological Organization (WMO) had been studying the possibilities which atomic energy has opened in meteorology. The International Civil Aviation Organization (ICAO) had been interested in the various problems connected with the air transport of radioactive substances, as had the Universal Postal Union (UPU). In the fields of banking and finance, the International Bank for Reconstruction and Development (IBRD) had included atomic energy reactor projects among its numerous development activities.

In view of these prior responsibilities in the atomic energy field shared by the specialized agencies and in the interest of good work-

ing relationships, the Secretary-General of the United Nations urged
that the Agency de-emphasize its primary responsibility in the field.
The term "primarily," in fact, was the object of some difference
between the Agency Preparatory Commission and the Secretary-
General. The Preparatory Commission favored the retention of the
word "primarily" in the phrase

> The United Nations recognizes the International Atomic Energy
> Agency as the agency, under the aegis of the United Nations . . .
> primarily responsible for international activities concerned with the
> peaceful uses of atomic energy in accordance with its Statute.[100]

The Preparatory Commission agreed to delete "primarily" from the
Relationship Agreement with the United Nations.[101] But in a special
exchange of letters between its President and the Secretary-General
it insisted on recording the statement that "the original wording
would have helped to clarify the relationship of the future Agency
with other international organizations which also have an interest
in certain aspects of atomic energy." [102] The Preparatory Commission also informed the Secretary-General that

> with regard to paragraph 1 of Article I of the draft [relationship]
> agreement, it is noted that the Agency, which is established for the
> specific purpose of dealing with the peaceful uses of atomic energy,
> will have the leading position in the field.[103]

The Agency intended to reserve for itself the main coordination
function in the field of the peaceful uses of atomic energy. The
Board, in December, 1957, established a committee to advise the
Director-General on the study of possible overlapping of activities
and to devise arrangements for coordinating programing on a continuing basis.

There was some difference of opinion on the Board as to the
best practicable method of achieving coordination. The French,
South African, and Soviet delegations felt that coordination should
proceed mainly at the governmental level. The secretariats should
do the preparatory work, but policy issues should be settled by
members of the Board.[104] The American, Canadian, and Indian delegations defended the position that greater discretionary power be
given to the Agency Secretariat, and that it be allowed to negotiate
under the supervision of the Board.[105] They suggested that the
Secretariat regularly issue memoranda to the Board listing specialized

agency projects in atomic energy and recommending areas of co-ordination. The Secretariat would then become a forum for an exchange of views and also a stimulant to action by the Board.[106] The Egyptian delegation proposed the creation of a special Atoms for Peace Coordination Committee, but withdrew the draft resolution in the light of the fact that the United Nations Administrative Committee on Coordination (ACC) would, in effect, play this role.[107]

The delegates finally agreed that exploratory consultations should begin at the Secretariat level and should have, as their first objective, the establishment of effective machinery for cooperation at the working level. The text of the eventual relationship agreements would then be adjusted to these practical arrangements for cooperation. It was admitted that, since any substantive discussion of working relations and of delineation of functions must enter the technical field, such discussions could not take place until the Agency was fully equipped with a scientific staff.[108]

Since the beginning of 1958 intersecretariat consultations have been held with ILO, WHO, UNESCO, and FAO.[109] These discussions have enabled the organizations provisionally to delineate spheres of competence at the working level which will probably serve as guides to the final relationship agreements. For example, UNESCO is planning to continue research and training in nuclear science, but will no longer take the initiative in the planning of conferences on isotopes. WHO is determined to continue research on international health standards but is planning to abandon its fellowship program on the disposal of radioactive waste material. FAO is continuing research on the effects of radiation on plant breeding, but will cooperate with the Agency in research on the uses of radiation for the preservation of food.

These emerging divisions of labor follow no definite pattern. They apparently arise from practical considerations of staff availability and working level arrangements as much as from Secretariat blueprints. Many problems of liaison and coordination might be approached through the creation of joint operating units in certain areas, representation by one organization in the executive bodies of the others when questions of common interest are under discussion, and the mutual appointment of liaison officers.

In view of the unique structure of the Agency and the dominant position of its Board of Governors, it seems reasonable to predict that the range of negotiating flexibility accorded the Agency Director-General by the Board will be narrower than that permitted the executive heads of the specialized agencies. Decisions such as the creation of joint operating units might be within the discretionary power of the specialized agency secretariats, but would almost certainly require approval by the Board in the case of IAEA. On the whole, the Agency's negotiations on questions of coordination will mainly take place at the governmental level while similar problems in the specialized agencies may be resolved at the secretariat level.

THE AGENCY'S RELATIONS WITH BILATERAL AND REGIONAL ORGANIZATIONS

1. THE IAEA AND BILATERAL PROGRAMS

The gravest problem in the Agency's relations with bilateral programs concerns the application of safeguards. During the negotiations on the Agency Statute it had become apparent that one of the prime objectives of the Agency—prevention of the diversion of fissionable materials to military uses—could be totally defeated if the United States, the United Kingdom, Canada, or the Soviet Union, in their bilateral agreements, should make fissionable materials available to other countries under less onerous safeguards than those provided in the Agency Statute. No safeguard system can be effective unless universally and uniformly applied.

The Agency Statute makes such uniformity entirely possible. The Statute provides that the Agency safeguard system, including inspection by Agency inspectors, may be extended "at the request of the parties, to operations under any bilateral or multilateral arrangement." [110] It was hoped that this provision would prevent bilateral arrangements from leading to the establishment of competing systems of safeguards based on lower standards than the Agency's own. The Statute negotiators hoped that Agency standards would become an international criterion for safeguard and inspection systems. A further step in the direction of making possible a uniform international system of safeguards was taken at the suggestion of Thailand during the Statute Conference when provision was made to extend the safeguard system "at the request of a state to any of that state's activities in the field." [111]

The United States government has negotiated forty-five bilateral agreements. Of these, thirty-six are for cooperation in the research reactor field and nine are "power bilaterals." [112] A number of other agreements for cooperation are under negotiation. Two important steps in the direction of uniform safeguards have been taken by the United States. First, the United States, in its bilateral agreements after 1955, provided for safeguards substantially the same as those in the Agency Statute. This move was the result of a meeting of experts held in Geneva immediately following the scientific conference in August, 1955. The only difference lies in the method of inspection. In American bilateral arrangements providing for the establishment of nuclear power plants, the recipient countries are inspected by American rather than IAEA personnel. The power bilaterals negotiated with Britain and Canada do not require any inspection, but simply provide for the guarantee by the recipient powers that the materials furnished would be used exclusively for peaceful purposes. The "research bilaterals" include no provisions for inspection. The second step toward uniformity was taken when the United States power bilaterals, after 1955, made explicit reference to the future role of IAEA. States which were parties to these agreements undertook, upon the establishment of IAEA, to consider the transfer of safeguards administration to the Agency. In other words, the parties would be free to avail themselves of the Agency machinery whenever it was established. The salient provisions from a power bilateral negotiated between the United States and the Federal Republic of Germany on July 3, 1957, are a case in point:

The Government of the United States of America and the Government of the Federal Republic of Germany affirm their common interest in the establishment of an international atomic energy agency to foster the peaceful uses of atomic energy. In the event such an international agency is created:

(a) The parties will consult with each other to determine in what respect, if any, they desire to modify the provisions of this Agreement for cooperation. In particular, the Parties will consult with each other to determine in what respect and to what extent they desire to arrange for the administration by the international agency of those conditions, controls, and safeguards including those relating to health and safety standards required by the international agency in connection with similar assistance rendered to a cooperating nation under the aegis of the international agency.

(b) In the event the Parties do not reach a mutually satisfactory agreement following the consultation, either Party may by notification terminate this Agreement. In the event this Agreement is so terminated, the Government of the Federal Republic of Germany shall return to the [Atomic Energy] Commission all source and special nuclear materials received pursuant to this Agreement and in its possession or in the possession of persons under its jurisdiction.[113]

A similar reference to the Agency was included in the most recent bilateral agreement between the United Kingdom and Japan:

Until such time as the relevant safeguards shall be administered by the IAEA . . . the Government of the United Kingdom shall have the right in the event of any breach of the [safeguard provisions] to call upon the Government of Japan to take corrective steps.[114]

Canada, in its two bilateral arrangements with Switzerland and the Federal Republic of Germany, has been most explicit in taking the possible role of the Agency into account:

On or after the time the International Atomic Energy Agency is in a position to carry out the safeguards provided for in its Statute, the contracting parties will consult together to determine whether and to what extent they may wish to modify the safeguard provisions set out in this agreement so that they may conform more closely with those of the said Statute and to have the application of safeguards carried out by the said Agency.[115]

The Soviet Union has concluded bilateral agreements for the provision of "apparatus and equipment" with Romania, Bulgaria, Czechoslovakia, Poland, Hungary, East Germany, Yugoslavia, Communist China, and the United Arab Republic.[116] It is not clear whether provision of fissionable materials has been covered by these agreements. However, the Soviet Union has on a number of occasions stated that it will supply fissionable materials to other countries without any safeguards except for a statement made by the recipient country to the effect that it would devote the materials only to peaceful purposes. Mr. Zarubin, delegate of the U.S.S.R., had stated at the Statute Conference:

The Agency should impose upon no country control that might infringe upon its sovereign rights. It is necessary to note that the agreement on the peaceful utilization of atomic energy concluded between the Soviet Union and other countries does not contain any conditions which might infringe upon the sovereign rights of countries participating therein. The Soviet Union considers that a sufficient guarantee is to provide in the draft statute that countries must be obligated not to make use of the assistance which they receive from the Agency for the production of atomic weapons, and must submit reports with respect to the assistance received.[117]

In view of this statement, it is doubtful that the U.S.S.R. would be willing to permit the Agency's safeguard machinery to supersede Soviet bilateral arrangements. On the other hand, Soviety ratification of the Agency Statute including its safeguard provisions makes Agency inspection possible.

In sum, then, the Agency Statute and the declarations of intention about the Agency safeguard system explicitly contained in some American, British, and Canadian bilateral agreements—and implicitly in those negotiated before the Agency's existence—make it entirely possible to take a first step toward transferring uniform safeguards from the realm of ideas into reality. Such a uniform system would necessitate, first, an agreement among states disposing of fissionable materials through bilateral channels that in each instance the acceptance of the Agency system of safeguards would be required as a condition of turning over the materials. The Statute permits full assumption of this responsibility.

The grave problems in the path of such an agreement are not confined to the political realm. There are fiscal difficulties to be overcome. The problem of financing the safeguard system has not been resolved. All bilateral agreements are silent on this point. In practice, the inspecting country has borne the financial burden. Amounts involved have not been large enough to cause serious controversy. However, should the Agency assume responsibility for safeguarding and inspecting the bilateral agreements, the picture might change. Under the Agency Statute all safeguards and inspection costs are classified under the administrative budget.[118] The Board of Governors is also authorized to establish a scale of charges including safeguard and inspection costs "designed to produce revenues for the Agency adequate to meet the expenses." [119] This means that the recipient states would, in the last analysis, finance the safeguard system. In the words of the Indian delegate:

> If only the recipient state will bear the safeguard charge, no state will request the Agency to apply its safeguards to bilateral arrangements.[120]

On the other hand, the Soviet delegate pointed out:

> If the costs [of safeguards] were to be borne by all member states, there might be a tendency to turn away from the Agency. The project might get too costly. Therefore, the Indian argument cuts both ways.[121]

This vexing issue has not been settled. It is hoped that the amounts involved will be small enough to permit practical solutions to situations as they arise. But it is clear that, from a fiscal point of view, it would not now be advantageous for the recipient partners to bilateral agreements to request Agency safeguards and inspection.

Fiscal considerations may, however, be counterbalanced by other factors. As indicated earlier, in the case of atomically underdeveloped partners to bilateral agreements, Agency inspection may be preferable to any form of inspection by the donor country. National pride and sensitivity may be more important than economy. In the case of the more highly industrialized Western partners to bilateral agreements, inspection by "friendly" allies as before may well seem preferable to the possible intrusion of Soviet inspectors via the Agency system. As the number of bilateral agreements grows, however, and the diffusion of nuclear technology further progresses, recipient partners to bilateral agreements may find it impossible to obtain all the assistance they want from one donor country. They might, therefore, conclude several bilateral agreements with differing safeguard and inspection provisions, making application extremely difficult. Such a development can be prevented if the Agency is permitted to play its coordinating role as early as possible.

The government of the United States has intimated that, in American assistance programs, it will prefer the bilateral to the Agency channel.[122] The United Kingdom and Canada have followed the American example and the outlook for Agency application to Soviet bilaterals is equally unpromising. It seems that bilateral arrangements will continue to develop side by side with the Agency safeguard and inspection system, observing virtually identical standards but avoiding a fusion of their control machineries.

The greatest obstacle to a uniform system of safeguards has, of course, been the constant refusal by the atomic powers to apply the Agency system to their own establishments. The paradox of this position, in view of the Western stand on inspection taken in the United Nations, has already been discussed.[123] Recent bilateral agreements negotiated by the United States have, however, made a small beginning in the direction of reciprocity. For example, the agreement with Switzerland provides that all fissionable by-product materials repurchased by the United States be used only for peaceful purposes.[124] This proviso is stated in the form of an American guarantee, but entails no inspection rights by Switzerland. It appears doubtful that this example will serve as a meaningful precedent for future agreements.

It is clear that the greatest obstacle to the coordination of bilateral agreements with the Agency is presented by safeguards and inspection. But the future role of the Agency will also depend upon an effective development program. The United States, Canada, the United Kingdom, and the Soviet Union have made available not only fissionable materials but various other types of technical assistance through bilateral channels. If the terms offered via bilateral agreements are more favorable than those offered by the Agency, or if the machinery is less cumbersome, incentive to request assistance from the Agency will diminish accordingly. It has already been pointed out, for instance, that coordinating the price of materials will present numerous complications.[125] Moreover, effective coordinations of bilateral and Agency research fellowship programs, reactor development, and general technical assistance will be a prerequisite for the success of the Agency.

2. THE IAEA AND REGIONAL PROGRAMS

The Agency's relations to regional arrangements for peaceful uses of atomic energy have an important bearing on the fate of the Agency itself. First, to what extent do the parties to the regional arrangements utilize the Agency system of controls against diversions for military uses? Second, to what extent may the Agency replace regional with international development in the atomic energy field?

(a) *IAEA and the European Atomic Energy Community (Euratom)*. Euratom is the most ambitious of the regional atomic projects. It is an enlargement of the "supranational" experiment known as the European Coal and Steel Community (ECSC), consisting of France, Italy, West Germany, the Netherlands, Belgium, and Luxembourg. While it is a flexible instrument for the rapid and orderly development of atomic energy available to all European nations, it is in fact made up of the "little Europe" of the six. The agreement among the six European powers went into force on January 1, 1958. Euratom's executive organ is a commission whose members, within their mandate, wield authority as international civil servants rather than as representatives of national interests. The Commission is responsible to the Council of Ministers and to the enlarged Common Assembly of the Coal and Steel Community. The Assembly is elected by the national parliaments of the six and has control over Euratom's budget. There is also a provision for a Court of Justice and a number of consultative committees.

The aims of the Community have been stated in A *Target for Euratom,* prepared in May, 1957, by official representatives of the six countries:

> The purpose of the common organization is to contribute to the formation and the rapid growth of a nuclear industry as well as to the application of nuclear development in industry and the economy as a whole:
> 1. By developing research and ensuring the broadest dissemination of knowledge and techniques;
> 2. By establishing and seeing to the enforcement of uniform safety norms for the protection of the labor force and of the general population;
> 3. By facilitating its investments and creating the fundamental installations which cannot be undertaken by isolated industries or by individual countries;
> 4. By providing it with security and equal treatment in its conditions for supply of nuclear ores and fuels; and
> 5. By assuring it wide outlets and the best technical means by the merger of markets as regards materials, supplies and specialized equipment, and by the unrestricted migration of specialists.[126]

The system of security control envisaged by the Community entails standards of inspection and safeguards as high as those provided for in the IAEA Statute. Each Euratom plant is subject to Commission supervision of fissionable materials, their use and processing. Any infringement of security standards or any diversion of materials from stated and legitimate purposes would involve withdrawal of such materials by the Commission. All fissionable materials not actually in use at plants are to be deposited at special depots controlled by the Commission. At the end of the processing cycle all fissionable materials are to be returned to the Commission for reprocessing or disposal.[127]

As in the case of bilateral arrangements, nothing in the Agency Statute precludes a transfer of safeguard and inspection responsibility to the IAEA, provided such a transfer is requested by Euratom. The Agency's role as safeguard and inspection coordinator was the subject of a protracted debate between the United States and Euratom during the recent negotiation of a bilateral agreement between the Community and the United States. A 25-year agreement for cooperation established the broad principle that "the parties [would] cooperate in programs for the advancement of the peaceful application of atomic energy." [128] For this purpose the United States will assist in the construction in the Euratom countries by 1963 of one million kilowatts of nuclear power capacity, using "nuclear reactors of proven types on which research and development have been carried to an advanced stage in the United States." [129] The United States and Euratom will also undertake a joint ten-year research and development program aimed primarily at lowering fuel costs and improving the performance of the types of reactors to be constructed under the joint program. In order that Euratom may be adequately supplied with fissionable materials, the United States has agreed to sell to the Community up to 30,000 kilograms of U-235 for use in the reactors constructed under the joint program.[130] The over-all purpose of the program is to bolster the economic strength of Western Europe and to encourage European unification.

The control issue was raised when Euratom officials resisted the United States demand for unilateral inspection rights. The Euratom negotiators took the position that United States insistence on inspection challenged the international sovereignty of the Community and impugned the effectiveness of the Euratom inspection system. The European officials also felt that the Community should not be treated less favorably than Britain and Canada, with whom the United States had bilateral agreements waiving inspection.[131] The controversy seemed solved when the United States retreated from its position on unilateral inspection rights and Euratom, in turn, guaranteed that inspection standards would meet those set by the United States in its other bilateral agreements. The actual inspection of plants, however, would be carried out by Euratom personnel.[132] At this point a lack of coordination between the United States Department of State and the Atomic Energy Commission became apparent. The AEC, on two grounds, objected to the State Department's approval of Euratom's right to self-inspection. First, such self-inspection would undermine the principle of international inspection represented by the IAEA. Second, self-inspection by Euratom would create a dangerous precedent. The Soviet bloc, for example, could set up an organization corresponding to Euratom and insist that its own self-inspection was as adequate a safeguard as Euratom's. For both these reasons, the AEC maintained, the IAEA should be brought into the picture.[133] Because of the AEC objections, Mr. Cole, the Agency's Director-General, flew to Washington in order to present the Agency's view. The final compromise on the inspection issue provides that Euratom itself will run its control system, but will establish it in a manner satisfactory to the United States:

> The government of the United States will provide assistance in establishing the Community's safeguards and control system, and will provide continuing assistance in the operation of the system.
> The parties agree that there will be frequent consultations and visits between the parties to give assurance to both parties that the Community's Safeguard and Control System effectively meets [agreed upon principles] and that the standards of the materials accountability system of the governments of the United States and the Community are kept reasonably comparable.[134]

The problem of the Agency's rights was resolved in a manner similar to that in other American bilateral arrangements:

> In establishing and implementing its safeguards and control system, the Community is prepared to consult with the International Atomic Energy Agency with the objective of establishing a system reasonably compatible with that of the Agency.
> In recognition of the importance of the International Atomic Energy Agency, the government of the United States of America and the Community will consult with each other from time to time to determine whether there are any areas of responsibility

with regard to safeguards and control and matters relating to health and safety in which the Agency might be asked to assist.[135]

The control provisions of the U.S.-Euratom agreement are, with one exception, comparable to Agency standards. The exception concerns the disposition of fissionable by-product materials. The Agreement for Cooperation provides that Euratom may keep, subject to the proviso that they be used only for peaceful purposes, any of the materials, including U-235 and plutonium, extracted from the fuel initially purchased from the United States. However, with respect to such materials which are in excess of Euratom's needs:

> The International Atomic Energy Agency is granted the right of first option to purchase [them] at the announced fuel value price in effect in the United States at the time of purchase.[136]

The Agreement then goes on to say:

> In the event this option is not exercised by the International Atomic Energy Agency, the U.S. government is prepared to purchase such material at the U.S. announced fuel value price in effect at the time of purchase.[137]

The significant difference between the Agency Statute and the Agreement for Cooperation is that in the Agency's case the recipient country must return by-product materials in excess of its needs while in the latter case the return is optional.[138] The clause covering this subject was bitterly debated during the Statute negotiations, and attempts to coordinate Agency and Euratom control provisions may be seriously impeded by this disparity.

The argument advanced by the AEC—that regional self-inspection may create a dangerous precedent—is unanswerable. Since Euratom will practice self-inspection, any Eastern regional scheme can do the same on the basis of Western precedent, and thereby endanger, if not destroy, the principle and practice of international inspection through the IAEA. Thus, while inspection standards may be comparable, the actual participation of the Agency seems necessary to assure eventual uniformity of safeguards. And as long as such participation must depend upon initiative taken outside the Agency, progress in this direction cannot be assured.

The hostility toward Euratom of the Soviet and Eastern members of the Agency's Board of Governors was discussed earlier. The Board's reluctance to invite Euratom observers to the Second General Conference of the Agency may be attributed to the Soviet assertion that Euratom was a paramilitary organization.[139] A Euratom request for Agency assumption of inspection responsibilities might somewhat assuage this Soviet hostility. Agency inspectors would then be given an opportunity to test the Soviet charges by determining the purposes for which the U.S.-supplied fissionable materials are put to use. It appears, however, that an early assumption of such responsibilities by the Agency is unlikely.

(b) *The IAEA and the OEEC European Nuclear Energy Agency.* On December 20, 1957, the seventeen countries of the Organization for European Economic Cooperation (OEEC) set up a European Nuclear Energy Agency within the framework of the organization.[140] The OEEC Nuclear Agency is a specialized institution of the OEEC responsible for furthering atomic cooperation for peaceful purposes among its members. At the same time the first European joint stock company, the European Company for the Chemical Processing of Irradiated Fuels ("Eurochemic"), was launched under OEEC auspices. Eurochemic has a membership of twelve countries and is the first fruit of the efforts of the OEEC to achieve effective technical cooperation in experimental atomic and industrial installations built or operated jointly.[141]

Euratom and the OEEC Nuclear Agency cover largely the same technical fields, but their objectives differ. One of the goals of Euratom is to bring about a closer association among the "six" who are already linked in the European Coal and Steel Community and in the Common Market. The OEEC Nuclear Agency is to promote liaison and technical cooperation between the Six and the other countries of Western Europe. Eurochemic is to be a pilot project which may serve as an example of cooperation in nuclear technology among a large number of European countries.

The OEEC Nuclear Agency, unlike Euratom, provides for a pooling of effort on an intergovernmental, rather than a "supranational" level. Eurochemic, on the other hand, in its character as a joint stock company, mainfests certain "supranational" characteristics. The OEEC Nuclear Agency has three main organs. Its executive organ is a Steering Committee whose members are the chairmen of the atomic energy commissions in the seventeen member countries. Representatives of the United States and Canada take part in its work as associate members. Second, there are technical commissions, set up by the Steering Committee, to help in its work. Finally, an international secretariat prepares and helps to carry out the work of the Steering Committee and its technical commissions. The OEEC Nuclear Agency as a whole is under the authority of the Council of the OEEC, composed of plenipotentiaries from the seventeen member states.

Broadly speaking, the OEEC Nuclear Agency emphasizes coordination and research while Euratom is primarily of an operational character. The major functions of the OEEC Nuclear Agency will be the establishment of joint undertakings like Eurochemic, the coordination of such programs, the training of specialists, and the furtherance of economic, legal, and social conditions favorable to the rapid development of nuclear energy.[142]

The Convention establishing the OEEC Nuclear Agency included an Agreement on Security Control which applies to all undertakings organized under the auspices of the OEEC Nuclear Agency. The Eurochemic Convention also includes this Security Control.

On paper the control provisions are rigorous. A Special Control Bureau, consisting of one representative from each member state, is responsible for the elaboration of inspection procedures and safeguards and will be assisted by an international inspectorate.

One additional feature of the OEEC control system is a Tribunal of seven independent judges appointed for five years by the Council of the OEEC.[143] Appeals may be made on control provisions and will be decided by the Tribunal by majority vote. The standards of inspection are largely modeled on those of the IAEA but differ in one important respect. Article 11 of the "Convention on the Establishment of a Security Control" states that inspection is only to be "periodic" and that "in each case the government concerned must be notified in advance that the inspection is to be carried out." The IAEA Statute grants continuous and unannounced inspection rights. As in the case of Euratom, the less stringent regional control provisions may cause difficulties should the IAEA assume control responsibilities.

In sum, then, Euratom is superimposed upon the OEEC Nuclear Agency, which in turn is superimposed upon the IAEA. Of the three, IAEA has the most stringent control provisions. Coordination has begun between Euratom and the OEEC Nuclear Agency. The Convention of December 20, 1957, provides that the Euratom authorities will be entrusted with the responsibility of control in the territory of the Six on conditions to be agreed upon between the two organizations.[144] With regard to IAEA the Convention includes a statement to the effect that

> An agreement may also be entered into between the European Nuclear Energy Agency and IAEA in order to define the cooperation to be established between the two institutions.[145]

While the IAEA Statute again would authorize IAEA control if requested by the OEEC, prospects for such a transfer are unpromising. As in the case of Euratom, the luxury of OEEC's less-stringent control provisions is the result of an intra-Western European accord. The powers to this agreement would be mose reluctant—even on the basis of reciprocity in the case of Eastern regional schemes—to accept the more demanding standards and possibly unwelcome composition of an IAEA Inspectorate.

3. AREAS OF CONFLICT AND COOPERATION

The dual nature of the IAEA is reflected in the Agency's relations with bilateral and regional atomic development schemes. It is not only possible but desirable that the developmental aspects of atomic energy for peaceful purposes be shared among organizations at the regional and the universal levels. In fact, it would be difficult to present a case in favor of total IAEA absorption of atomic development activities presently carried out through bilateral and regional arrangements. However, the control responsibility cannot be successfully met and yet shared by a number of organizations, each maintaining different safeguard criteria and enforcing different standards of inspection. The Agency's positive task permits diffusion, but its negative responsibility demands cohesion.

To the donor the bilateral or regional approach to atomic development may often seem preferable to the Agency channel. The donor's freedom to choose the recipient and to define precisely the conditions for cooperation may result in more extensive assistance. In the case of Agency assistance, however, the donor's influence on the recipient must go through the machinery of the Board of Governors and the General Conference. Thus Agency assistance cannot be identified with any one country and tends to assume a more apolitical character than its bilateral or regional counterpart. This explains why Agency assistance is at times preferred by the underdeveloped countries and why bilateral arrangements are frequently preferred by donors. Finally, recipients like to point out, a universal organization like IAEA may be better suited for atomic development by virtue of the fact that its membership includes both the advanced and the underdeveloped areas. Hence it can fulfill the function of an intermediary more satisfactorily than a regional organization.

For certain types of atomic development and research, regional arrangements may often be better adapted to common enterprises than IAEA. The Euratom countries and the Latin-American countries form regions reasonably homogeneous geographically and technologically. These factors are favorable to a regional approach although regional autarky may be their result. Regionalism may also be better suited to furthering atomic research. The European Organization for Nuclear Research (CERN), founded in 1956, comprises twelve Western European countries at comparable stages of atomic research development.[146] Its Eastern counterpart, the Joint Institute for Nuclear Research, also founded in 1956, consists of eleven countries from the Soviet bloc.[147] Both these organizations are based on the common experience and goals of the countries comprising their respective regions.

Agencies engaged in nuclear development will probably continue to proliferate. It is not possible to make a case for exclusively regional or exclusively universal nuclear development. In the absence of a general principle, the IAEA will have to adapt itself to constantly changing patterns of development.

In the area of control, however, uniform safeguards must be imposed if the Agency is to be successful. The IAEA is in a logical position to play the coordinating role and is empowered by the Statute to assume this responsibility provided it is asked to do so. If the Agency should assume safeguard coordination responsibilities, its task will be made more difficult by regional organizations than by bilateral agreements. American, Canadian, and British control standards incorporated into bilaterals are virtually identical to those of the Agency Statute, and coordination would present no difficulties. Soviet bilaterals, on the other hand, seem to exclude inspection requirements entirely. Regional controls are less stringent than those of the Agency: neither Euratom nor the OEEC Nuclear Agency requires certain controls that are incorporated in the IAEA Statute. In view of the fact, however, that the member states of both Euratom and OEEC are also signatories to the Agency Statute, the obstacles to coordination, once given to the Agency, would probably not be insurmountable. The basic problem lies in neither the legal authority nor the professional competence of the Agency to establish uniform safeguards. It is to be found in the fact that political decisions taken outside IAEA will determine the Agency's future role in the safeguard and inspection fields.

There are three possible ways in which bilateral and regional development and control functions might be shifted to the Agency. First, the nuclear powers might gradually arrange for the Agency to take over bilateral and unilateral programs in their entirety. This is the hope of the Agency Director-General, but it is shared neither by the Board as a whole nor by the nuclear powers. Second, the bilateral and regional arrangements might continue with the parties requesting the Agency to assume responsibility for the administration of safeguards. While the Statute contemplates this possibility, political considerations render it unlikely. Third, the bilateral and regional arrangements might cover the same broad fields of development and control covered by the Agency. This is the most likely development. The Agency will therefore have a piecemeal coordination job, dealing with limited and specific situations as they arise from day to day. The size of reactors, division of labor in isotope research, concrete inspection provisions, might pose some of the typical problems of coordination which the Agency will face. The reconciliation of regionalism with universality in atomic energy will become primarily a process to be managed, not a problem to be solved.

SUMMARY: THE AGENCY IN ACTION

The structure of the Agency is marked by the powerful role of the Board of Governors. Precisely because of the executive organ's great power, most states demanded representation on it, thus making the Board an unwieldy body. The twenty-three states comprising the Board are rarely able to achieve unanimity. Three schisms—at times appearing concurrently—hinder efficient decision making. First, the East-West split frequently manifests itself. The issue of the Agency's relationship with Euratom was one example among many. Second, the split between the atomic powers and the underdeveloped areas often cuts across East-West lines. The problem of reactor programing was a case in point. On such issues the Soviet Union usually subordinates its interests as an atomic producer to its role as self-appointed champion of anticolonialism. Finally, fiiscal disagreements have consistently plagued the Board. The Western powers, as a rule, have adopted a somewhat more generous attitude than the rest of the Board. The problem of establishing research facilities for the Agency and the issue of staffiing the Division of Safeguards were cases in point. In fact the Board's procrastination in appointing a director of the Division of Safeguards may be in some measure responsible for the reluctance of bilateral and regional organizations to involve the Agency in developing a uniform control system.

The Board's relationship to the General Conference is strained because of the different composition of the two bodies. While the Board is weighted slightly in favor of the atomic producer powers, the General Conference has a majority of underdeveloped countries. This suggests the possibility of conflict in areas of common statutory authority. Disagreements are most likely to occur in the area of fiscal policy.

Owing to the Board's extensive power over the Director-General, the office of the Agency's chief executive is primarily that of administrator rather than policy maker. It is probably the weakest administrative office in the United Nations family. All major appointments to the staff, for instance, must be approved by the Board. The Agency Secretariat departs from the United Nations pattern in two important ways. First, it is primarily an operational rather than a "housekeeping" staff. Second, the fact that its professional contingent consists largely of scientists has introduced areas of friction between the staff and the Board. The "political" perspective of the Board at times has differed from the "scientific" perspective of the Secretariat. Disagreements within the Secretariat itself are more apt to take place among representatives of different branches of science rather than different nationalities despite the fact that the Agency staff has a wider geographical distribution than any other international secretariat.

The main structural problem confronting the Agency is to improve the executive efficiency of the Board without impairing its broadly representative character, which was the *sine qua non* of the Agency's establishment.

In its operations the Board has consistently refused to view the developmental and control aspects of atomic energy as two sides of a single coin. The initial program has been based on the dubious assumption that "peaceful" and "nonpeaceful" activities in atomic energy may be neatly separated. An element of artificiality has consequently entered the programing discussions. The Board has often tended to accept a "safe" interpretation of the Statute. When, for example, the Secretariat suggested that the Agency concern itself with research on the effects of strontium-90 and international radiation monitoring, the Board rejected the proposal, but enthusiastically supported as unambiguously "peaceful" a broad fellowship program for the training of nuclear scientists. This ingenuous and somewhat misguided search for politically unequivocal programing has led the Board to move ahead with assistance to the underdeveloped areas but to procrastinate on control and safeguard activities. However, even the Agency's developmental functions have been circumscribed by the Board's political conservatism and mood of economy.

Preparation for various types of technical assistance has therefore become the main concern of the Agency's programing. Thus far the most advanced program is the fellowship scheme under which two hundred stipends are offered. Agency survey teams are investigating the capacity of underdeveloped regions for the building of reactors and the industrial absorption of atomic energy programs. In this area the Agency has had to deflate some of the high hopes raised by President Eisenhower's "Atoms for Peace" address. A great deal of research will have to precede the establishment of Agency reactors in most underdeveloped areas. Exchange of information and the organization of conferences have been included in the Agency's program. The Secretariat's participation in the Second General Conference in September, 1958, has been a valuable coordination device.

In atomic development the Agency faces a dilemma. Since it deemphasizes control activities, its success or failure is being evaluated in terms of developmental criteria. But, because of the large amount of preparatory work to be done, only one request for fissionable materials has so far been made to the Agency. Vexing problems of price, storage facilities, and methods of transfer will have to be solved before the fissionable materials pledged by the nuclear powers are actually used. This lag between the early assertion that the blessings of peaceful atomic energy were "here, now, today" and the far more modest proportions of actual programing, poses a serious educational problem. If early expectations of the Agency tended to be too high, they now frequently err in the opposite direction.

Agency activity in the area of control has just begun. Health and safety standard coordination has been placed high on the list of control functions. The Board has had the felicitous idea of combining health and safety with safeguard functions in order to add a "constructive" role to the inspectors' police responsibilities. Progress in safeguards and inspection, however, has been impeded by a kind of circular thinking: the Board has refused to staff the Safeguard and Inspection Division on the grounds that no Agency projects existed that needed controls. But reactor plants cannot get far beyond the planning stage until the safeguard system is ready to operate. The appointment of a Director of Safeguards in July, 1958, was a somewhat belated attempt to break the circle.

It seems that the Agency's first inspection "business" may originate from bilateral and multilateral arrangements. Under the Statute outside parties may request the Agency to assume control responsibilities. Only one such request had reached the Agency by the end of 1958: to assume inspection responsibility for the bilateral agreement between the United States and Japan. If many other requests should follow, the Agency might well find itself understaffed.

The Agency's control system, including sanctions against violators, is still in the theoretical stage. Three great gaps in the Statute must be closed if the Agency is to establish a uniform safeguard system. The control provisions do not apply to the nuclear powers; they do not apply to bilateral and regional arrangements unless the Agency is expressly invited; and they do not apply to countries developing their own industries without Agency help. The sanctioning process seems sound but is applicable only to Agency-supported projects. Even then "recapture" of materials would have to depend more on an incensed public opinion than on the Agency Inspectorate.

The necessity of coordination with bilateral and regional organizations has increased in importance with the recognition that the Agency's control provisions can be totally defeated by the availability of materials under less onerous controls. Recent American, British, and Canadian bilateral agreements envisage possible future transfer of control activities to the Agency. In these cases coordination with Agency standards could be easily achieved because of virtually identical control provisions. However, the Western powers have given little indication of permitting inspection by the Agency. This reluctance is inconsistent with the Western powers' consistent defense of the principle of international inspection in the United Nations disarmament discussions. The Soviet Union, in its bilateral agreements, seems to rely on guarantees rather than inspection and has indicated no willingness to coordinate its control system with the Agency's.

Unresolved fiscal questions further complicate coordination. In the case of bilateral agreements, the inspecting country has been paying inspection costs. But the Agency's inspection plans require that the recipient country reimburse the Agency for inspection and safeguard expenditures. This added financial burden to the recipient state, however, should not be regarded as an open-and-shut case against the success of the Agency's assistance program. It is entirely possible that, although an underdeveloped country might prefer bilateral inspection because it is cheaper, it might nevertheless decide in favor of Agency inspection because of national pride and sensitivity to colonialism.

Agency coordination with regional organizations presents even greater obstacles since the regional control standards are somewhat lower than the Agency's. Under Euratom's Agreement for Cooperation with the United States, the return of idle fissionable by-product materials to the supplier is not made mandatory as in the Agency Statute. Moreover, the Euratom agreement has established a precedent of regional self-inspection which may lead to similar self-inspection by an Eastern regional bloc. While a possible future role for the Agency is provided for in the U.S.-Euratom agreement, it is unlikely that Agency inspectors will be invited in the near future.

In the case of the OEEC Nuclear Agency, control standards are again below those of the Agency. While they provide elaborate control machinery, including a Tribunal, they incorporate the principle of "periodic" and "announced" inspection which the Agency has expressly rejected. Again, early coordination seems improbable.

Although geographic contiguity and comparable technological advancement provide objective grounds for the continued existence of bilateral and regional arrangements, it is nevertheless desirable that uniformity be encouraged between these and Agency development programs. The Agency could be seriously undermined if assistance were offered on more attractive terms via bilateral channels. But in the area of safeguards and inspection uniformity is mandatory if the Agency is to be successful. The developmental aspects of the peaceful uses of atomic energy permit diffusion but effective control demands progress toward cohesion.

Another problem of coordination, the Agency's relationship to the United Nations, was the subject of extended controversy among four groups. The Western atomic powers wanted a specialized agency aloof from the parent organization in order to prevent control of the Agency by the underdeveloped countries through the General Assembly. The Soviet Union wanted an Agency directly responsible to the Security Council in order to safeguard the veto power. The atomic have-nots desired an integral United Nations organ responsible to the General Assembly. The United Nations Secretariat supported this position with minor variations. The ingenious compromise finally reached created a special niche for the Agency in the United Nations family. IAEA became an "autonomous international organization," to be tied more closely to the United Nations than the typical specialized agency but not so closely as an integral United Nations organ.

In three ways the Agency's relationship is closer to the United Nations than is that of the specialized agencies. IAEA is to report directly to the General Assembly rather than to the Economic and Social Council; its sanctioning process may involve the Security Council; and continuous reciprocal representation exists between the two organizations. In two areas, however, the Agency enjoys a greater degree of autonomy than most specialized agencies. First, IAEA's operational budget is not subject to review by the General Assembly. Second, the Statute gives the Agency the power of autonomous disciplinary initiative against violators of project agreements. This control function in an area vitally affecting international security is the Agency's most distinctive feature. Otherwise its unique status in the United Nations system is more an accidental result of the initial compromise agreement than a planned departure from the typical specialized agency pattern.

Within the framework of the Relationship Agreement the Agency has had to deal with two major problems. The first was the question of Agency participation in the Expanded Technical Assistance Program and the Special Fund. After protracted debate the Board of

Governors recommended Agency participation in both programs. The second problem has been the Agency's relationship with the specialized agencies. Since many of them had been engaged in various aspects of atomic energy work before the Agency was created, the issue of coordinating overlapping activities has loomed large. The Agency's claim to have "primary" coordination responsibility has been dropped in the interest of good working relations. Intersecretariat negotiations have been proceeding at the working level with several of the specialized agencies. They will provide the basis for later formal relationship agreements. In view of the powerful position of the Agency's Board of Governors, the Director-General has less flexibility in negotiating these agreements than the executive officers of the specialized agencies. On this, as on other matters, the Board of Governors will speak for the Agency in the United Nations family.

PART III

CONCLUSIONS: RETROSPECT AND PROSPECT

The dual nature of its mission has made the International Atomic Energy Agency a major testing ground of United Nations effectiveness. First, the developmental activities of the Agency have begun to test the proposition that, through the peaceful application of atomic energy, economic and social welfare may be brought, for the first time in history, within the reach of all. As a minimal goal in this area, the Agency hopes to *stimulate* the development of atomic power in the world's underdeveloped regions; as a maximum goal, it hopes to *achieve* it. Second, the Agency's control function may test the proposition that the diffusion of atomic power does not necessarily increase the danger of nuclear war. The Agency's limited aim is to ensure that its assistance will not make the dangers of nuclear war even greater than they are. Its long-range objective is to provide a major stimulus to progress in the field of disarmament.

This dual character of the Agency has given rise to a dilemma: The Agency will be judged by both its development and its control achievements; but its performance in both these areas will depend less upon its own initiative and resources than upon the policies

of national governments. There is less to prevent the Agency from
attaining its goals in atomic development than in control; it may
provide both knowledge and materials from its own resources to
attain them. But in the field of armaments control even minimal
goals are not certain to be attained, since the Agency must play a
passive role *until* it is asked to take action.

While the Agency is more self-sufficient in atomic development
than in control, development too will be vitally affected by national
policies. There have been indications that the United States' preference for bilateral and regional arrangements is threatening to
undermine the Agency. The sale of 30,000 kilograms of fissionable
material by the United States to Euratom is a case in point. Another
is the fact that, because of the addition of handling and safeguard
surcharges, fissionable materials bought from the Agency are generally
more expensive than similar materials purchased from the United
States directly. Mr. Sterling Cole, the Agency's Director-General,
in a speech before the Atomic Industrial Forum, was particularly
critical of the United States among the nuclear powers for continuing to extend atomic assistance to nations on a bilateral basis,
thus bypassing the international agency:

> The bilateral agreements are the Achilles heel of the Agency. If the
> demands of nations for atomic assistance are to be met by bilateral
> assistance, IAEA cannot achieve its objectives. If IAEA is to con-
> tinue, there must be a change in policy by the United States and
> other nuclear powers to give more preferential treatment to the
> Agency.[1]

President Eisenhower's "Atoms for Peace" address in 1953 had
clearly implied that bilateral programs were temporary arrangements
and would be terminated when the Agency came into being. In the
light of this early internationalism the current American penchant
toward bilateral and regional arrangements is puzzling. Actually the
trend away from internationalism was already in the making in 1953.
While the Executive Branch favored an international approach, the
Congress was reluctant to transfer large amounts of fissionable material to an international organization which would include the
Soviet Union and its satellites. Congressional leaders preferred direct
bilateral negotiations between the United States and the recipient
countries, safeguarding American inspection rights. The State De-

partment, during the period of "thaw" in the cold war following the death of Stalin, still continued to support the Agency. The nomination of Sterling Cole—a former U.S. congressman—for the post of Director-General, may in part have been an attempt to make the Agency more attractive in the eyes of the Congress. However, the increasing intensity of the cold war and the Soviet Union's powerful influence on the Agency's governing body changed the Administration's attitude toward the IAEA. By the time the Agency had completed its first year of operations the State Department had decided to give preferential treatment to bilateral and regional arrangements.

The erosion of American support has therefore relegated the Agency to a secondary role. The other nuclear powers have followed the American example. By the end of 1958 sixty-eight of the world's nations were accommodated by bilateral agreements: forty-five by the United States, twelve by the United Kingdom, nine by the Soviet Union, and two by Canada.[2] It seems that only a radical change in national policies can restore the Agency's leading position in the atomic development process.

There are some signs that the trend away from the Agency may be reversed. A recent Canadian offer has encouraged Agency officials. In response to the first request made to the IAEA for nuclear materials the government of Canada offered three tons of natural uranium free of charge. The Agency thus for the first time was in a position to sell materials on more favorable terms than the applicant—in this case Japan—could obtain via bilateral channels. IAEA sold the material to Japan at $35.50 per kilogram, including safeguard and handling charges. The best offer to the Agency by an American firm was $54.34 per kilogram.[3] To be in a position to offer preferential terms to the Agency the United States might have to amend its Atomic Energy Act. Such action would encounter much resistance but is becoming increasingly mandatory if the Agency once more is to become a major instrument of American foreign policy.

The United States government has shown greater initiative in another phase of the Agency's development work. It has contributed a major portion of the initial cost of establishing a research and service laboratory for the Agency in Vienna. The United States delegation is also planning to recommend to the Agency's Board of

Governors a study of the power needs of underdeveloped countries and of the technology of small and medium-sized reactors. Plans for pilot projects are being considered.[4] The Soviet Union, too, has been showing increasing interest in the nuclear programs of the underdeveloped countries and has made its first voluntary contribution of $125,000 to the Agency's General Fund.[5] In sum, it seems that the Agency role in the atomic development process will become increasingly important.

In the case of its own assistance project in Japan, IAEA's safeguard system will apply automatically. More important, the governments of the United States and Japan have announced their intention to request the application of the IAEA safeguard system to their bilateral agreement.[6] This may set an important precedent. But, on the whole, the Agency's role in the control process is still a minimal one. The Agency differs little from other international organizations dealing with disarmament: its role in the control aspect of the development process is largely determined *for* it. International gadgetry can never be a substitute for policy in military and security questions; and policy, although it may be *proposed* by international organizations, is *disposed* by national governments.

One might conclude that the Agency may become one of the many United Nations agencies in the field of technical assistance, without great responsibility in the field of armaments control. This may well happen if the Agency's development and control functions are rigidly separated. But it can be avoided. *It is possible to build control machinery into the development process itself.* The following are a number of specific recommendations for action to this end:

First, the Agency's major developmental responsibility, under the Statute, is the building of reactors in the underdeveloped areas. The Preparatory Commission endorsed this aim, "taking into account the need for balanced development of the various regions." [7] This proviso may be interpreted to imply a "strategic distribution" of atomic facilities throughout the world, an accomplishment the United Nations Atomic Energy Commission had regarded as vital to the long-term preservation of peace. The plants can be built where power is needed but can be so distributed that, in the event of forcible seizure of some plants, a "strategic balance" will prevent any one country or group of countries from dominating the rest. The governments of the major creditor nations and the International Bank for

Reconstruction and Development could—together with the IAEA—plan such a "balanced development" of nuclear projects.

Second, the Agency should encourage close cooperation between its own research staff and national and private research establishments. The more nuclear research is internationalized the better are the chances that abuses will be detected at an early stage. In the words of the United Nations Atomic Energy Commission:

> Cooperative development [of atomic energy] and complete dissemination of information alone promise to remove fears and suspicion that nations are conducting secret activities.[8]

The Second United Nations Conference on the Peaceful Uses of Atomic Energy has made remarkable progress in the declassification of secret materials.

> The United States and Britain took the secrecy chains off the scientists working to control the hydrogen bomb reaction. From now on the nuclear burning of hydrogen will be born unclassified. V. S. Emelyanov, chief of Russia's atomic program [also Governor of the U.S.S.R. on the IAEA Board of Governors], said his country would disclose all its scientists know about their attempts to control the hydrogen process. In effect, all the doors are now open. The Russian said it might even be possible in the near future to have American scientists . . . visit Russian thermonuclear laboratories. A United States-British announcement also laid the way for the same kind of visit of Russians to the west.[9]

IAEA's professional staff of scientists, too, might be admitted to national laboratories if the intentions announced at the Geneva Conference are carried out. The Agency's scientists are in an ideal position to further the internationalization of research and freedom of communication among the world's scientists. In addition to making valuable contributions to research and reactor development, Agency scientists can also call attention to violations and thus minimize the police function of the Agency's Inspectorate.

The third recommendation is a corollary to the second. The Agency's scientific authority and prestige should be enhanced through the establishment of its own research centers and facilities. A beginning in this direction has been made. The Agency budget for 1959 is $5.23 million compared with $1.76 million for the first year;

$450,000 has been earmarked for laboratory and research facilities in Vienna. But the Board of Governors still considers research a luxury to be subordinated to technical assistance. An ample research budget would increase the Agency's scientific and managerial influence upon national governments. States might then decide to appoint Agency consultants to their own atomic plants and research installations. While these Agency consultants would be unable to determine national policy, they could nevertheless influence plant management. The objectives of the Agency Inspectorate in many ways are the same as those of efficient management: good accounting procedures, proper inventories, detection of the cause of unaccountable losses, and general control responsibilities. This Agency consulting scheme might contribute to a system of "constructive inspection" and help to reduce the Inspectorate's police duties.

As a fourth step, the Agency should further emphasize the constructive aspect of the Inspectorate by combining the safeguard functions with those of health and safety. Such a policy might promote good relations with governments, since the Inspectors would thus be rendering a "positive" service. The Agency could become the source of an important body of administrative law designed to protect the public against radiation hazards and other dangers arising from the operation of nuclear power plants. The lessons of this experience might ultimately be translated into terms applicable to the development of an international control system over the military uses of atomic energy.

Finally, the Agency may have to come to grips with a very difficult problem: how can it prevent the scientists in its training program from diverting their newly acquired knowledge to military uses? Since the fellowship program is expected to expand rapidly, this problem might well become more pressing than that of preventing the diversion of fissionable materials. Is it politically feasible for the Agency to require that, after completion of their training, its fellows be employed only in "peaceful" enterprises? And who would define "peaceful"? Would Agency action in this regard not be considered an infringement on the sovereignty of states?

Any attempt at this time to approach the question raises more problems than it solves. Yet, as indicated earlier, the very success of the fellowship program—bringing with it Agency-sponsored diffusion of nuclear technology—will make the necessity of safeguards and controls increasingly apparent. Some form of "constructive control" will have to be found.

These suggestions, if adopted by the IAEA, could lead the Agency to greater activity in the disarmament field via its development program. But the fact still remains that they are devious routes to the final goal. A frontal attack is made difficult, if not impossible, because of the three shortcomings in the Agency Statute: Agency controls do *not* in practice apply to the nuclear countries; they do *not* apply to countries developing national atomic programs without Agency help; and they do *not* apply to bilateral and regional arrangements estalished outside the Agency. In all these cases the Agency controls can be introduced only at the request of a sovereign state or group of states. But if no requests are made, new reactor plants, like those of the present nuclear powers, will escape Agency control.

Bilateral and regional self-inspection schemes have created dangerous precedents. The presence of Agency inspectors is necessary to achieve uniformity of safeguards. The purpose of the Agency is in large part defeated if safeguards are made obligatory for nations which need its help and left optional or made less rigorous for those who do not. There are indications that the nuclear powers may invite the Agency to take over the safeguard function of some of their bilateral arrangements, but it is highly unlikely that the Agency will be requested to extend its control system to the national programs of the nuclear powers. These have established a double standard, according to which only recipients of Agency assistance are subject to Agency controls while donors remain exempt. The fear of intrusion by "hostile" inspectors via the Agency system makes it improbable that the great powers will soon abandon this posture. Yet it is clear that this double standard must be abandoned if an effective control system is to be established.

A possibility for such a breakthrough existed in the agreement reached in July, 1958, in Geneva among technical experts from eight nations on the feasibility of detecting nuclear test explosions. The agreement was the result of seven weeks of technical discussions among scientists from the United States, the Soviet Union, Britain, France, Canada, Poland, Czechoslovakia, and Romania. The scientists' report called for the three steps which would be necessary to implement a detection system:

1. A network of control posts around the globe. About 170 would be land-based. Of these ten would be in the United States, fourteen in the U.S.S.R., and eight in Communist China. The remaining land-based posts would be distributed on the continents and on large and small oceanic islands. Ten additional posts would be on ships.
2. Creation of an "international control organ," which would run the global system, pick the staff, select the detection devices, study reports and generally see to it that no nation violated the test suspension agreement.
3. Use of weather reconnaissance aircraft to sample the air for radioactivity. They would rush to a suspicious area to see if a bomb had been set off or whether the tremor was due to other causes.[10]

The talks were conducted on purely technical grounds and steered clear of political problems.

It seemed that, for several reasons, the IAEA was the logical "international control organ" to assume the inspection function. It was the only global atomic authority in existence and therefore probably best suited for a global inspection responsibility. The states to be inspected, with the exception of Communist China, were all signatories to the Agency Statute, which endorsed the principle of international inspection. The Agency had safeguard personnel on its staff ready to go into action. The underdeveloped countries, comprising a majority of the Agency's membership, welcomed an opportunity to subject the nuclear powers to a form of reciprocal control, thus correcting one of the inequities of the Agency control system. Finally, the cost of setting up an entirely new organ would involve a great deal of wasteful duplication.

The Agency, however, was not permitted to assume this responsibility. The assertion that inspection—when extended to test suspension control—would no longer be a "peaceful activity," prevented the nuclear powers from authorizing the Agency to act for them. Besides, the Board's conservative programing had tended to exclude all "unsafe" projects. Moreover, the Agency's machinery would not easily lend itself to vital negotiations, such as the number of nonnative employees to be allowed on the territory of each country, the freedom of the Agency's representatives in pursuance of their duties, and obtaining the consent of countries for the establishment of control posts. These problems might be attacked more successfully by a less cumbersome body than the Agency's Board of Governors.

Since October, 1958, negotiations on the matter of bomb test controls have proceeded outside the Agency and the United Nations framework. It is possible that a new "international control organ," if agreed upon by the nuclear powers, may come to grips somewhat more easily than the Agency with the problem of Communist China, since the Chinese Communist government would hardly permit the establishment of Agency control stations without Agency membership. But with or without the Agency, a safeguard system excluding Communist China would be ineffective, especially in the light of the fact that the Chinese government has been equipped with atomic bombs.[11] It is to be hoped that the Agency will be permitted to collaborate with the United Nations Disarmament Commission or any international control organ set up to govern the restriction or prohibition of the testing and production of nuclear weapons.

Atomic energy poses three distinct challenges to international statemanship: the development of peaceful uses, the control of such development to prevent diversion to war uses, and disarmament. The first two functions are clearly within the Agency's bailiwick. Its role in the third is less clear. Despite the difficulty of separating the peaceful from the war uses of atomic energy, the nuclear powers have always insisted on this artificial distinction. A major role for the Agency in the field of disarmament is therefore unlikely while that irrational attitude persists.

Yet a crucial measure of the Agency's success will be its contribution to a global system of safeguards. Some observers feel that uniformity is evolving regardless of Agency initiative. It is pointed out that the American and British governments include in their bilateral agreements safeguard standards virtually identical to those of the Agency Statute. The view has also been advanced that, regardless of Agency action, a rule of customary international law has already been established to the effect that a state which makes available fissionable materials to another state without effective safeguards against diversion to military purposes acts in violation of international law.[12] In support of this view, the following statement by Sir Frederick Pollock has been cited:

> There is no doubt that, when all or most of the Great Powers have deliberately agreed to certain rules of general application, the rules approved by them have very great weight in practice *even among states which have never expressly consented to them.* It is hardly

too much to say that declarations of this kind may be expected, in the absence of prompt and effective dissent by some Power of the first rank, to become part of the universally received law of nations within a moderate time.[13]

It appears unrealistic, however, to speak of a crystallization of customary international law. While the great powers are signatories to the Agency Statute, only the Western powers uphold inspection standards comparable to those of the IAEA in their bilateral agreements. The Soviet Union relies upon written guarantees, and the Western regional arrangements—Euratom and the OEEC—are less stringent than the Agency in their control provisions. The maintenance of Agency standards, enforced by Agency personnel, is therefore indispensable for the evolution of an effective system of global safeguards.

The Agency represents the grasping of an opportunity, rare in the history of mankind, to impose a pattern of international purpose and policy upon a process of fundamental change at the very beginning of its operation.[14] This brave response to the challenge of atomic power gave rise to the early hope that IAEA could consecrate the atom to the cause of peace. Much disillusionment with the Agency stems from this early romanticism. Some observers now tend to set their sights too low. It is necessary to strike a balance. The Agency has not fallen as low as many fear; nor has it been allowed to rise as high as many had hoped. Realism and vision are needed in equal measure to help the International Atomic Energy Agency fulfill its promise for peace.

FOOTNOTES

Part I

[1] Official Records of the 1956 Conference on the Statute of the International Atomic Energy Agency, IAEA/CS/OR.39.

[2] "Atomic Power for Peace" address delivered by President Eisenhower before the General Assembly of the United Nations, Dec. 8, 1953.

[3] *Ibid.*

[4] The definition of "fissionable material" incorporated into the Statute of the Agency in Art. XX was identical with the definition of "special nuclear material" found in the United States Atomic Energy Act of 1954. (P.L. No. 703, 83rd Congress, 2nd sess., August, 1954).

[5] The definition of "source material" incorporated into the Statute of the Agency in Art. XX was identical with the definition of "source material" in the U.S. Atomic Energy Act of 1954.

[6] Interview with Ambassador James J. Wadsworth, U.S. representative in the twelve-power negotiations on the Agency Statute in 1956, New York, Feb. 4, 1958.

[7] Bernard G. Bechhoefer and Eric Stein, "Atoms for Peace: The New International Atomic Energy Agency," *Michigan Law Review*, Vol. 55, No. 6, April, 1957, p. 785.

[8] For the text of these documents see *Atoms for Peace Manual*, S. Doc. No. 55, 84th Congress, 1st sess., 1954, p. 274.

[9] *Ibid.*, p. 269, 271–272.

[10] *Ibid.*, p. 278.

[11] Memorandum by Assistant Secretary of State Merchant on July 9, 1954, to Ambassador Zarubin; see *Atoms for Peace Manual*, No. 55, p. 276.

[12] Inis L. Claude, Jr., *Swords Into Plowshares* (New York: Random House, 1956), pp. 316–317.

[13] *Atoms for Peace Manual*, p. 278.

[14] Soviet Union Aide Memoire of Sept. 22, 1954, *ibid.*, p. 278.

[15] Interview with Mr. Albert Watson, Executive Director, United States Mission to the United Nations, New York, May 30, 1958.

[16] Ninth General Assembly, First Committee, A/C.1/SR.723, Nov. 19, 1954.

[17] *Ibid.*

[18] *Ibid.*

[19] *Ibid.*

[20] Resolution 912 (X), Doc. A/3116, in UN General Assembly Official Records, 10th Sess., Supp. 19, pp. 4–5.

[21] Report of the Working Level Meeting on the Draft Statute of the International Atomic Energy Agency, Doc. 31 (Washington, D. C., July 2, 1956), pp. 1–2.

[22] For a list of amendments and their authors see IAEA/CS/INF/4/Rev. 1, Oct. 3, 1956.

[23] See IAEA Statute, Art. IV.

[24] Doc. 5, IAEA Working Level Meeting on the Draft Statute of the IAEA, March 2, 1956.

[25] *Ibid.*

[26] *Ibid.*

[27] Conference on the Statute of the International Atomic Energy Agency, IAEA/CS/OR.17, Oct. 5, 1956, pp. 56–57.

[28] *Ibid.*, p. 58.

[29] For a discussion of safeguard and inspection problems see pp. 140–148 and pp. 181–186.

[30] For a discussion of relationships between the Agency and bilateral arrangements see pp. 196–210.

[31] For additional comments supporting the Indian view on the problem of Communist Chinese membership see IAEA/CS/OR.17 and 18, Oct. 5, 1956.

[32] See IAEA Statute, Art. II.

[33] *Ibid.*

[34] Report of Ambassador Morehead Patterson, 34 Dept. of State Bulletin, No. 5 (1956).

[35] *Ibid.*

[36] *Ibid.*

[37] Working Level Meeting on the Draft Statute of the IAEA, Doc. 5, March 2, 1956.

[38] *Ibid.*

[39] *Ibid.*

[40] *Ibid.*

[41] *Ibid.*

[42] *Ibid.*

[43] *Ibid.*

[44] The eight major regions of the world were defined as North America, Latin America, Western Europe, Eastern Europe, Africa and the Middle East, South Asia, South East Asia and the Pacific, and the Far East.

[45] Report of the Working Level Meeting on the Draft Statute of the International Atomic Energy Agency, Doc. 31 (Washington, D.C., July 2, 1956).

[46] Amendments to that effect were proposed by Egypt, Ethiopia, Indonesia, Philippines, Syria, and Japan. IAEA/CS/OR.6, Sept. 26, 1956.

[47] IAEA/CS/OR.20, Oct. 3, 1956.

[48] *Ibid.*

[49] *Ibid.*

[50] Bechhoefer and Stein, *op. cit.*, p. 755, fn. 40.

[51] Six members with the largest interest in the international seaborne trade and six with the largest interest in providing international shipping services are represented in the IMCO Council. Four members are elected by the IMCO Assembly.

[52] Both the Bank and the Fund have a system of weighted voting based on actual contributions.

[53] Report on the eight-power negotiations by Ambassador Morehead Patterson, 34 Dept. of State Bulletin (1956).

[54] Working Level Meeting on the Draft Statute of the IAEA, Doc. 5, March 2, 1956.

[55] *Ibid.*

[56] *Ibid.*

[57] See IAEA Statute, Art. V, para. F.

[58] *Ibid.*, Art. V, para. D.

[59] Bechhoefer and Stein, *op. cit.*, p. 753.

[60] The vote was 37 to 24, with 18 abstentions. IAEA/CS/OR.22, p. 42.

[61] IAEA/CS/OR.5, Sept. 25, 1956.

[62] Report of the Working Level Meeting on the Draft Statute of the International Atomic Energy Agency, Doc. 31 (Washington, D.C., July 2, 1956).

[63] See IAEA Statute, Art. VII, para. D.

[64] Klaus E. Knorr, "American Foreign Policy and the Peaceful Uses of Atomic Energy," *Atoms for Power: United States Policy in Atomic Energy Development* (New York: The American Assembly, Columbia University), p. 111.

[65] IAEA/CS/OR.28, pp. 66–67.

[66] Working Level Meeting on the Draft Statute of the IAEA, Doc. 5, March 2, 1956.

[67] *Ibid.*

[68] *Ibid.*

[69] IAEA/CS/OR.14, Oct. 3, 1956, p. 36.

[70] IAEA/CS/Art. III/Amend. 1.

[71] IAEA/CS/OR.15, Oct. 4, 1956, pp. 31–32.

[72] IAEA/CS/OR.16, Oct. 4, 1956, p. 17.

[73] See IAEA Statute, Art. III, para. A.

[74] *Ibid.*, Art. VIII, para. B.

[75] *Ibid.*, Art. VIII, para. A.

[76] IAEA/CS/Art. III/Amend. 2/Rev. 1.

[77] See pp. 186–196.

[78] Soviet Aide Memoire of Sept. 22, 1954, in *Atoms for Peace Manual*, U.S. Doc. No. 55, 84th Congress, 1st sess., pp. 278–281.

[79] Working Level Meeting on the Draft Statute of the IAEA; Statement by Ambassador James J. Wadsworth, March 2, 1956. (Emphasis added.)

[80] *Ibid.*

[81] *Ibid.*

[82] *Ibid.* (emphasis added).

[83] *Ibid.*, Statement by Mr. H. J. Bhabha, March 2, 1956. (Emphasis added.)

[84] *Ibid.*, Statement by Mr. S. J. Goldschmidt.

[85] *Ibid.*, Statement by Ambassador James J. Wadsworth.

[86] *Ibid.*, Statement by Mr. H. J. Bhabha.

[87] *Ibid.*, Statement by Mr. J. Wershof.

[88] See IAEA Statute, Art. XII, para. A.

[89] *Ibid.*

[90] Working Level Meeting, *op. cit.*, Statement by Ambassador Zarubin.

[91] IAEA/CS/OR.27, Oct. 12, 1956, p. 36.

[92] *Ibid.*, p. 68.

[93] See IAEA Statute, Art. XII, para. C.

[94] *Ibid.*, Art. III, para. A.

[95] For a discussion of this see pp. 178–181.

[96] IAEA/CS/OR.38, Oct. 22, 1956, p. 14.

[97] Quoted by Knorr, *op. cit.*, p. 107.

[98] *Ibid.*, p. 109.

[99] IAEA Statute, Art. XX.

[100] IAEA/CS/OR.20, p. 28.

[101] Working Level Meeting, *op. cit.*, Doc. 5, March 2, 1956. (Emphasis added.)

[102] IAEA/CS/OR.40, p. 7. (Emphasis added.)

[103] Working Level Meeting, *op. cit.*; see also Note of the Soviet Ministry of Foreign Affairs to the American Embassy, in U.S. Department of State Press Release No. 527, Oct. 6, 1956, p. 11.

[104] IAEA Statute, Art. IX.

[105] First Annual Report of the Board of Governors of the IAEA to the General Conference. GC (II)/39, July, 1958, p. 39.

[106] IAEA Statute, Art. IX.

[107] The loose term "reimbursement" is used in Art. XIII.

[108] IAEA/CS/OR.39, p. 62.

[109] IAEA Statute, Art. XIV.

[110] Working Level Meeting, *op. cit.*, March 2, 1956.

[111] *Ibid.*

[112] *Ibid.*

[113] *Ibid.*

[114] IAEA Statute, Art. XIV.

[115] IAEA/CS/OR.31, p. 42.

[116] IAEA/CS/OR.36, p. 22.

[117] IAEA/CS/OR.31, p. 42.

[118] IAEA Statute, Art. XIV.

[119] *Ibid.*

[120] *Ibid.*, Art. VIII.

[121] *Ibid.*, Art. XVIII.

[122] *Ibid.*

[123] Eight-power draft of the Statute, Art. XIX. (Emphasis added.)

[124] IAEA Statute, Art. XVII. (Emphasis added.)

[125] Bechhoefer and Stein, *op. cit.*, p. 777.

[126] IAEA Statute, Art. XI.

[127] *Ibid.*, Art. XVII.

[128] Eric Stein, "The New International Atomic Energy Agency," *Proceedings of the American Society of International Law*, 1957, p. 161.

[129] The members of the Preparatory Commission were: Argentina, Australia, Belgium, Brazil, Canada, Czechoslovakia, Egypt, France, India, Indonesia, Japan, Pakistan, Peru, Portugal, Union of South Africa, U.S.S.R., United States, and United Kingdom.

[130] For a discussion of multilateral diplomacy see Inis L. Claude, Jr., "Multilateralism—Diplomatic and Otherwise," *International Organization*, Winter, 1958.

[131] Eric Stein, *op. cit.*, p. 159.

[132] IAEA Statute, Art. XII.

[133] *Ibid.*

[134] Eric Stein, *op. cit.*, p. 162.

[135] IAEA/CS/OR.38, Oct. 22, 1956, p. 44. (Emphasis added.)

Part II

[1] First Annual Report of the Board of Governors to the General Conference, Vienna, July, 1958, GC(II)/39, p. 9.

[2] *Ibid.* By a letter dated March 6, 1958, the Director-General of the Agency was informed that Egypt and Syria had formed one state—the United Arab Republic. Consequently, the United Arab Republic henceforth succeeded Egypt as a member of the first Board of Governors.

[3] IAEA Statute, Art. VI.

[4] IAEA/GOV/OR.1, Oct. 21, 1957.

[5] IAEA/GOV/OR.74, June 19, 1958.

[6] *Ibid.*

[7] IAEA Statute, Art. III.

[8] GC(II)/39, p. 21.

[9] IAEA/GOV/OR.67, June 12, 1958.

[10] *Ibid.*

[11] IAEA/GOV/OR.83, July 2, 1958.

[12] *Ibid.*

[13] *Ibid.*

[14] On June 30, 1959, seventy states had ratified the Agency Statute in accordance with their respective constitutional processes.

[15] The committees established by the Board up to June 30, 1959, were the following: Committee to Advise the Director-General on Negotiations with Specialized Agencies; Committee to Advise the Director-General on Permanent Headquarters; Committee on the 1959 Programme and Budget; Committee on the Agency's Second Report to the United Nations General Assembly.

[16] IAEA Statute, Art. V.

[17] *Ibid.*, Art. VII.

[18] *Ibid.*

[19] GOV/INF/5, Vienna, June, 1958, Rule 8.

[20] IAEA/GOV/105, Feb. 27, 1958.

[21] *Ibid.*

[22] IAEA Statute, Art. VII.

[23] GC(II)/29, Vienna, July, 1958, p. 19.

[24] Ibid.

[25] IAEA Statute, Art. II.

[26] GC.1 (S)/RES/5, Oct. 10, 1957.

[27] IAEA/GC (II)/36 and 39.

[28] IAEA/GC (II)/29, Vienna, July, 1958, p. 28.

[29] For a discussion of these problems see pp. 196–210.

[30] For example, a research contract has been awarded to the Pharmacological Institute of the University of Vienna for investigating the factors involved in the neurological responses of animals to short-term irradiation with medium X-ray doses.

[31] GC (II)/29, July, 1958, p. 24.

[32] Ibid.

[33] Ibid., p. 30.

[34] Ibid., p. 40.

[35] Ibid., p. 32.

[36] GC (II)/36, August, 1958, p. 29.

[37] GC (II)/29, July, 1958, p. 39.

[38] "American Foreign Policy and the Peaceful Uses of Atomic Energy," Atoms for Power (New York: The American Assembly, Columbia University, 1957), p. 122.

[39] For a discussion of the Agency's relationship to bilateral and regional reactor programs see pp. 196–210.

[40] Offers of fissionable material were made by the United States (5,000 kgs.), U.S.S.R. (50 kgs.), and the United Kingdom (20 kgs.). The United States, in addition to its regular offer, has matched the other two contributions, bringing the total amount to 5,140 kgs.

[41] GC (II)/29, July, 1958, p. 39.

[42] For a discussion of these problems see pp. 148–153.

[43] Sec. 2154 (P.L. 703, para. 124) of the Atomic Energy Act of 1954, 42 U.S.C. (Supp. III, 1956).

[44] IAEA Statute, Art. IX.

[45] Ibid., Art. XXI.

[46] Sec. 2153 (P.L. 703, para. 123) of the Atomic Energy Act of 1954, 42 U.S.C. (Supp. III, 1956).

[47] President Eisenhower's message read by the Chairman of the Atomic Energy Commission to the International Statute Conference on Oct. 26, 1956. IAEA/CS/OR.40, p. 6.

[48] P.L. 703, para. 123, of the Atomic Energy Act of 1954.

[49] IAEA Statute, Art. III.

[50] GC (II)/29, July, 1958, p. 35.

[51] For an analysis of the Agency's relationship with the United Nations and the specialized agencies, see pp. 205–231.

[52] GC (II)/36, August, 1958, p. 33.

[53] GC (II)/36, August, 1958, p. 41.

[54] Ibid., p. 43.

[55] Statement made by Mr. G. Randers, Scientific Consultant to the Agency, to the Board of Governors, March 14, 1958.

[56] See p. 162.

[57] IAEA/GOV/OR.83, July 2, 1958.

[58] Ibid.

[59] Ibid.

60 IAEA Statute, Art. XII.
61 For a discussion of this see pp. 196–210.
62 For a discussion of this see pp. 196–210.
63 Interview with Mr. Roger M. Smith, Director of the Division of Safeguards, Vienna, August 20, 1958.
64 IAEA Statute, Art. XII.
65 *Ibid.*
66 *Ibid.*
67 *Ibid.*
68 *Ibid.*
69 Report of the Preparatory Commission of the IAEA (New York, 1957), GC(I)/1, p. 22.
70 Testimony of Mr. J. Moch, Commissioner of the French Atomic Energy Commission, before the Sub-Committee on Atomic Energy, July 5, 1957, p. 11. Quoted by Philip Noel-Baker, *The Arms Race* (New York: Oceana Publications, 1958), p. 273.
71 See p. 145.
72 Noel-Baker, *op. cit.*, p. 300.
73 S. de Madariaga, *Disarmament* (London: Allen and Unwin, 1929), p. 229.
74 IAEA/GOV/4, July 11, 1957; Recommendation by the Preparatory Commission for the Relationship between the United Nations and the International Atomic Energy Agency.
75 For a discussion of the legislative process see pp. 119–124.
76 Working Level Meeting on the Draft Statute of the IAEA, Doc. 6, March 6, 1956.
77 *Ibid.*
78 IAEA/GOV/4, July 11, 1957, Art. I.
79 *Ibid.*, Art. III.
80 *Ibid.*
81 *Ibid.*, Art. VII.
82 For a description of the sanctioning process see pp. 181–186.
83 IAEA/GOV/4, July 11, 1957, Arts. VI, VII, XIII, and XVI.
84 *Ibid.*, Arts. XVIII, XIX, and XXIII.
85 *Ibid.*, Art. X.
86 General Assembly, 12th Sess., Dec. 14, 1957 (A/3805), p. 58.
87 ECOSOC Resolution 694 (XXVI), July 31, 1958.
88 IAEA/GOV/4, July 11, 1957, Art. III.
89 GC (II)/29, July, 1958, p. 12.
90 *Ibid.*
91 ECOSOC Resolution 222A (IX), Appendix I, Annex I, "General Principles," para. 1.
92 United Nations General Assembly Resolution 1240 (XIII), Oct. 14, 1958.
93 IAEA/GOV/111, March 3, 1958.
94 GOV/OR.70, May 5, 1958.
95 *Ibid.*
96 *Ibid.*
97 GOV/111, March 3, 1958, and GOV/115, March 10, 1958.
98 GC (I)/4, July 11, 1957.
99 GC.1 (S)/RES/11, Oct. 10, 1957.
100 GOV/4/Add.1, Aug. 21, 1957.
101 GOV/4, July 11, 1957, Art. I.
102 GOV/4/Add.1, Aug. 21, 1957.

232   Organizing Peace in the Nuclear Age

103 *Ibid.*

104 PC/OR.12, Feb. 25, 1957.

105 *Ibid.*

106 *Ibid.*

107 PC/OR.14, March 28, 1957.

108 GOV/84, Jan. 14, 1958.

109 GC (II)/29, July, 1958, p. 15.

110 IAEA Statute, Art. III.

111 *Ibid.*

112 For a list of these countries see "Records of Agreements for Cooperation," Division of International Affairs of the Atomic Energy Commission, October, 1957.

113 Agreement Between the United States of America and the Federal Republic of Germany, Washington, D.C., July 3, 1957, Art. XII, Department of State Treaties and Other International Acts Series 3877, U.S. Government Printing Office.

114 Agreement Between the United Kingdom and Japan, June, 1958, Art. VIII.

115 Agreement Between Canada and Switzerland, March, 1958, Art. IV.

116 Statement by Mr. Emelyanov, Governor from the U.S.S.R., Summary Records, Board of Governors, 1958.

117 IAEA/CS/OR.3, pp. 31–35.

118 IAEA Statute, Art. XIV.

119 *Ibid.*

120 Statement by Dr. Rajan, Governor from India, Summary Records, Board of Governors, 1958.

121 Statement by Mr. Emelyanov, Governor from the U.S.S.R., Summary Records, Board of Governors, 1958.

122 Knorr, *op. cit.*, p. 126.

123 See pp. 185–186.

124 Agreement Between the United States and Switzerland, Washington, D.C., July 18, 1955.

125 See pp. 148–153.

126 Report of the Intergovernmental Committee on European Integration, Brussels, 1956, reprinted in University of Michigan Law School Summer Institute, *Workshops on Legal Problems of Atomic Energy*, 1956, p. 203.

127 Klaus E. Knorr, *Nuclear Energy in Western Europe and United States Policy*, Center of International Studies, Princeton University, Sept. 10, 1956, p. 4.

128 Agreement for Cooperation Between the United States and the European Atomic Energy Community, quoted in "A Package for EURATOM," *Forum Memo*, July, 1958, p. 10.

129 *Ibid.*

130 *Ibid.*

131 *New York Times*, April 13, 1958.

132 *Ibid.*, May 8, 1958.

133 *Ibid.*, June 9, 1958.

134 *Forum Memo*, p. 18.

135 *Ibid.*

136 *Ibid.*, p. 14.

137 *Ibid.*

138 IAEA Statute, Art. XII.

139 See p. 160.

140 The seventeen members of the OEEC are: Austria, Belgium, Denmark, France, Germany, Greece, Iceland, Ireland, Italy, Luxembourg, the Netherlands, Norway, Portugal, Sweden, Switzerland, Turkey, and the United Kingdom.

141 The member states of the Eurochemic are: Austria, Belgium, Denmark, France, Germany, Italy, the Netherlands, Norway, Portugal, Sweden, Switzerland, and Turkey.

142 Convention on the Establishment of the OEEC Nuclear Agency, Paris, Dec. 20, 1957.

143 *Ibid.*, p. 30.

144 *Ibid.*, p. 33.

145 *Ibid.*

146 The member states are: Belgium, Denmark, France, Germany, Greece, Italy, the Netherlands, Norway, Sweden, Switzerland, the United Kingdom, and Yugoslavia.

147 The member states are: Albania, Bulgaria, Communist China, Czchoslovakia, East Germany, Hungary, North Korea, Outer Mongolia, Poland, Romania, and the U.S.S.R.

Part III

1 *New York Times*, Nov. 13, 1958.

2 *Ibid.*

3 Press Release IAEA/128, Dec. 12, 1958.

4 *Bulletin of the Atomic Scientists*, January, 1959, p. 47.

5 *New York Times*, May 25, 1959.

6 Press Release IAEA/137, Jan. 22, 1959.

7 Report of the Preparatory Commission of the IAEA, p. 13.

8 Third Report of the United Nations Atomic Energy Commission, May 17, 1948, p. 4.

9 New York *Herald Tribune*, European Edition, Sept. 1, 1958.

10 *Ibid.*

11 *Ibid.*, Aug. 11, 1958.

12 Eric Stein, "The New International Atomic Energy Agency," *Proceedings of the American Society of International Law*, 1957, pp. 162–163.

13 Sir Frederick Pollock, "The Sources of International Law," *Columbia Law Review*, Vol. 2 (1902), pp. 511–512. (Emphasis added.)

14 Eleventh Report of the Commission to Study the Organization of Peace (this volume), pp. 3–24.

APPENDIX

APPENDIX

APPENDIX

A Political Classification of UN Member States

	CONTRIBUTIONS %	SERVICE IN SECURITY COUNCIL (YEARS)	POPULATION *
I. The American group			
A. American members of NATO			
1. U.S.A.	32.51	14	172.3
2. Canada	3.11	4	16.7
B. European members of NATO			
1. United Kingdom	7.78	14	51.2
2. France	6.40	14	44.0
3. Italy	2.25	1	48.3
4. Belgium	1.30	4	8.9
5. Netherlands	1.01	3	11.0
6. Denmark	.60	2	4.4
7. Turkey	.59	4	24.7
8. Norway	.49	2	3.4
9. Greece	.23	2	8.0
10. Portugal	.20		8.9
11. Luxembourg	.06		0.3
12. Iceland	.04		0.1
C. SEATO and other Asian Allies			
1. China	5.01	14	Mainland 621.2
			Formosa 9.8
2. Japan	2.19	2	90.0
3. Australia	1.79	4	9.5
4. Philippines	.43	1	22.6
5. New Zealand	.42	2	2.2
6. Pakistan	.40	2	84.7
7. Thailand	.16		21.0

* Estimates for 1956 (in millions). See UN Demographic Yearbook 1957, Table I.

	CONTRIBUTIONS %	SERVICE IN SECURITY COUNCIL (YEARS)	POPULATION
D. Latin-American members of OAS			
1. Argentina	1.11	3	19.8
2. Brazil	1.02	6	61.9
3. Mexico	.71	1	31.4
4. Venezuela	.50		6.2
5. Colombia	.31	6	13.2
6. Chile	.30	2	7.0
7. Cuba	.25	4	6.4
8. Uruguay	.12		2.6
9. Peru	.11	2	9.9
10. Ecuador	.06	2	3.8
11. Dominican Republic	.05		2.6
12. El Salvador	.05		2.3
13. Guatemala	.05		3.4
14. Bolivia	.04		3.2
15. Costa Rica	.04		1.0
16. Haiti	.04		3.3
17. Honduras	.04		1.7
18. Nicaragua	.04		1.3
19. Panama	.04	2	0.9
20. Paraguay	.04		1.6
II. The Russian group (Warsaw Pact)			
1. U.S.S.R.	13.62	14	200.2
2. Ukraine	1.80	2	40.6
3. Byelorussia	.47		8.0
4. Poland	1.37	2	28.1
5. Czechoslovakia	.87		13.3
6. Hungary	.42		9.8
7. Romania	.34		17.7
8. Bulgaria	.16		7.6
9. Albania	.04		1.4
III. The Bandung Neutrals			
1. India	2.46	2	392.4
2. Indonesia	.47		85.5
3. United Arab Republic	.32	Egypt 3	23.8
		Syria 2	4.0
4. Iran	.21	2	18.9
5. Malaya	.17		6.2
6. Morocco	.14		9.8
7. Ceylon	.10		8.9
8. Iraq	.09	2	6.5
9. Burma	.08		20.0
10. Ghana	.07		4.7
11. Afghanistan	.06		12.0
12. Ethiopia	.06		20.0

	CONTRIBUTIONS %	SERVICE IN SECURITY COUNCIL (YEARS)	POPULATION
13. Saudi Arabia	.06		6.0
14. Sudan	.06		10.2
15. Lebanon	.05	2	1.5
16. Tunisia	.05	1	3.8
17. Cambodia	.04		4.3
18. Jordan	.04		1.5
19. Laos	.04		1.4
20. Liberia	.04		1.2
21. Libya	.04		1.1
22. Nepal	.04		8.4
23. Yemen	.04		4.5
24. Guinea	(.04)		2.5

IV. The Independent Neutrals

1. Sweden	1.39	2	7.3
2. Spain	.93		29.4
3. Union of South Africa	.56		14.1
4. Austria	.43		6.9
5. Finland	.36		4.3
6. Yugoslavia	.35	3	18.0
7. Ireland	.16		2.8
8. Israel	.14		1.9

V. Nonmembers of the United Nations *

1. Germany	5.33 †		West 52.9
			East 17.6
2. Switzerland	.97		5.0
3. Korea	.21 §		31.4
4. Vietnam	.20 ‡		26.6
5. Mongolia			1.0

* Contributions to Specialized Agencies and International Court of Justice.
† West Germany.
§ South Korea.
‡ South Vietnam.

Other Reports of the
COMMISSION TO STUDY THE
ORGANIZATION OF PEACE

Preliminary Report and Monographs, International Conciliation, April 1941.

Second Report—The Transitional Period and Papers Presented to the Commission, International Conciliation, April 1942.

Third Report—The United Nations and the Organization of Peace and Papers Presented to the Commission, International Conciliation, April 1943.

Fourth Report
Fundamentals of the International Organization, General Statement, Commission to Study the Organization of Peace, November 1943.
Part I. *Security and World Organization,* November 1943
Part II. *The Economic Organization of Welfare,* November 1943
Part III. *International Safeguard of Human Rights,* May 1944

Fifth Report—Security and Disarmament Under the United Nations, June 1947.

Sixth Report—Collective Self-Defense Under the United Nations, Memorandum and Draft Treaty for Implementation of Article 51, May 1948.

Seventh Report—Collective Security Under the United Nations, July 1951.

Eighth Report—Regional Arrangements for Security and the United Nations and Papers Presented to the Commission, June 1953.

Ninth Report—Charter Review Conference, and Papers Presented to the Commission, August 1955.

Tenth Report—Strengthening the United Nations, October 1957.

240

INDEX

Acheson-Lilienthal-Baruch plan, 17
Administrative Committee on Coordination, 190, 191, 195
Advisory Committee on the Peaceful Uses of Atomic Energy, 186, 188
Afghanistan, 71, 72
Aggression, 43, 44, 45, 49, 56
Algerian question, 38, 51, 74, 75
Antarctica, 93, 94
Arab States, 70, 74. *See also* individual countries
Arbitral awards, 41
Argentina, 38, 159, 171
Aristotle, 101
Asian-African states, 34, 35, 40, 65, 131, 136. *See also* individual countries
Atomic Energy Commission (UN), 220
Austin, Warren R., 66
Australia, 70, 119, 121, 130, 139, 159
Austria, 65, 68, 71, 160

Baghdad Pact, 52, 65, 66, 68, 69, 71. *See also* individual countries
Bahrein Island, 38
Bandung Conference, 65. *See also* Neutrals
Barrington, James, 122
Baxter, John Philip, 129
Bechhoefer, Bernard G., 226, 227, 229
Belgium, 119, 121, 130, 202
Belize, 38
Bhabha, Homi J., 129, 131, 143, 149, 228
Brazil, 71, 116, 119, 123, 130, 137, 159,171
Bricker Amendment, 12

Britain. *See* United Kingdom
Bulgaria, 198
Burma, 72
Byelorussian S. S. R., 98

Calhoun, John C., 77
Cambodia, 70, 75
Canada, 116, 119, 121, 128, 130, 143, 150, 159, 162, 171, 176, 196, 197, 218, 222; and atomic bilateral agreements, 198, 200, 201
Carman, Harry J., 24
Carpio, Victorio, 145
Ceylon, 71, 72, 176
Chamberlin, Waldo, 24
Charter of the UN, 5, 8, 11, 21, 27, 31, 36, 38, 41, 44, 45, 47, 48, 49, 51, 55, 58, 67, 77, 79, 80, 83, 84, 85, 86, 90, 91, 93, 94, 95, 96, 108, 109, 110, 112, 115, 116, 133, 189; amending process of, 90, 91, 104, 114
Charter Review Conference, 3, 15
China, 6, 38, 65, 71; Communist China, 5, 6, 20, 68, 73, 86, 95, 125, 126, 127, 198, 221
Churchill, Sir Winston, 90
Clausewitz, Karl von, 58, 59, 82
Clay, Henry, 77
Cole, W. Sterling, 160, 204, 217, 218. *See also* IAEA, Director-General
Colombia, 116
Commission to Study the Organization of Peace: *Ninth Report*, 3; *Tenth Report*, 3, 9, 9n, 11n, 14, 14n, 93, 104
Committee to study peaceful uses of outer space, 74, 75
Conference of experts on detection and suspension of nuclear tests, 222